SELLING IN OUR ECONOMY

*An Economic and Social Analysis of Selling
and Advertising*

SELLING IN

OUR ECONOMY

AN ECONOMIC AND SOCIAL ANALYSIS OF
SELLING AND ADVERTISING

BY HARRY R. TOSDAL, Ph.D., LL.D.

Professor of Business Administration, Emeritus
Graduate School of Business Administration
Harvard University

1957

RICHARD D. IRWIN, INC.

HOMEWOOD, ILLINOIS

To

T. H. T.

PREFACE

Selling in our Economy is so titled because it essays to examine selling and advertising not only or even primarily from a business point of view, but from the standpoint of the economic and social welfare of our society. As with any important human activity to which access is wide open, there are competent and incompetent, honorable as well as dishonorable, persons who engage in it. Consequently, many and diverse judgments have been passed upon it.

This study presents an analysis of selling taking as a basis only the persuasive, influential aspects of advertising, personal selling, and other activities of sellers in their efforts to bring about buying action. Since the cost of this activity has been conservatively estimated as considerably in excess of 5 per cent of our gross national product, possibly running as much as 10 per cent, its magnitude alone warrants study and examination; but there are many social and economic implications whose importance cannot be measured in quantitative terms.

Selling in its manifold forms of leadership-to-buying-action has not been carefully studied from an over-all point of view. The reasons therefore are not wholly clear, although a few come quickly to mind. Satisfaction with existing explanations, neglect on the part of economists and other social scientists, the focusing of attention primarily on abuses and broad social attitudes, have each played a part.

Recognition of the over-all function of selling and of its relation to social welfare has been extremely slow in developing. In view of the growing necessity of increased and improved selling leadership, this cannot be a matter of indifference. It is for this reason that the analysis was attempted; also in the hope that better understanding of the selling function would lead to greater respect for its work and accomplishments on the part of the public and of business in general, as well as on the part of those engaged in the work of selling and those contemplating selling as a career.

In my opinion, selling furnishes a challenge to able men. It enables them to serve society. Selling gives many men those satisfactions which right-thinking men want beyond making a living. It should give many more those satisfactions. It should entitle all who practice it decently and honorably the public regard which makes for high and rising standards of social responsibility. My intention, in the present volume, has not extended beyond that of outlining in preliminary fashion an analysis of selling which better fits the observed facts of human behavior.

Since selling deals with important aspects of human behavior, the task of investigation can be expanded to a point where a lifetime would be too brief for completion. Studies of consumption and of the forces and factors influencing consumption during various periods of history and in various parts of the world would be only parts of such a comprehensive study. Thus, economic theory and economic history, sociology and anthropology, as well as psychology, all have contributions to make. All of these fields have been touched upon in this study, because business practice and theory cannot arbitrarily assume models or patterns of human behavior and base policy and action thereon. Motivation of consumers, of sellers, and of buyers goes much beyond any simplified assumptions.

In the development of the present study my sincere thanks are due to many businessmen and to many of my academic colleagues who have graciously taken the time to discuss basic ideas with me. Special acknowledgment is due both to Dean-Emeritus Donald K. David of the Harvard Graduate School of Business Administration and to Dean Stanley F. Teele, whose encouragement has taken both the form of active interest and provision of relief from teaching duties to permit more rapid progress. Professor Bertrand Fox, Director of Research, has likewise been helpful. Finally, only with the able assistance of my secretary, Mrs. Charles Snow, has it been possible to bring this volume to a conclusion at this time.

HARRY R. TOSDAL

HARVARD UNIVERSITY
February 1, 1957

TABLE OF CONTENTS

xi

Chapter I

SELLING IN THE AMERICAN ECONOMY

SOCIALLY AND ECONOMICALLY, selling—the persuasive leadership that influences people to buy goods and services—has become essential to the development, maintenance, and improvement of the high standards of living that have been achieved in the United States. The desirability of raising standards of living is not seriously questioned in any responsible quarter. It is the declared objective of peoples and their governments, principal political parties, economists, and social reformers. Achievement of high material standards of living to most people represents progress in the attainment of human welfare.

The provable facts of the American accomplishment have set off many searches for causes and explanations. Articles, books, and speeches dealing with basic causes and conditions of prosperity have appeared in many quarters. On the whole, they have tended to overlook or underrate one of the most pervasive, dynamic influences toward improvement in material standards of living, particularly the economic leadership activity that we call selling.

Our economy is essentially an economy of machine and large-scale production, of buying and selling. We produce, exchange, and consume goods at a rate which is not only the envy of the world but the unique accomplishment of the American way of life. We have brought together in the United States

1

a combination of favoring elements, most of which have been noticed and remarked upon; so that today, our people are the best-fed, the best-clothed, the best-housed people on the globe. These standards of living have not been obtained by a minority at the expense of the masses. In the United States, the masses enjoy these high standards of living to a degree unheard of before the American republic was founded and unknown elsewhere today. High living standards are enjoyed in an atmoshpere of freedom of consumer choice, freedom of enterprise, and freedom for the individual to improve his lot in life.[1]

Selling activity is much broader in scope than is commonly observed by the layman. With few exceptions it is a necessary part of the work of every retailer, every wholesaler, every manufacturer—in fact, of every producer and every middleman. The work to be done in order to sell may be only the simplest of displays at a roadside stand or statements to other persons orally that goods are for sale. But it may comprise elaborate world-wide advertising and the personal selling efforts of widespread organizations. Selling ranges from the simplest urging of the small retailer to the protracted and intricate negotiations of a president or vice-president of a large corporation for the sale of a power plant to a public utility company. It is as wide in scope and influence as the range, for instance, in political leadership, from the lay worker in a city ward to a national committeeman or elected chief of state.

With much of this, the public never comes into contact. The specialized sales engineer, the pharmaceutical representative calling upon physicians, the tens of thousands who sell to retailers, to hospitals, and to manufacturers, in bringing about buying actions are important leaders the existence of whom is un-

---

[1] The statistical supports for the assertions concerning the levels of living in the United States are to be found in many places, e.g., in governmental documents such as Federal Reserve Board *Surveys of Consumer Finances* and various other articles in the *Federal Reserve Bulletin, Bulletins of the U.S. Department of Labor.* Also see *Economic Report of the President* (annual issues) and "National Income, 1955 Edition," *Supplement to Survey of Current Business,* U.S. Department of Commerce. Professor William E. Rappard in his recent *The Secret of American Prosperity* (New York: Greenberg, 1955), devotes the first part of his book to "The Fact of Economic Superiority of the United States Today."

known to many and dimly appreciated by others. Some of these men are highly trained in law, others have engineering degrees; some have training in medicine, others in business administration. Each works with specific but influential groups to obtain the buying actions essential to high standards of living. Some of these deal with products which consumers eventually buy. Others deal with products which are used to produce those consumer goods and services. Some are concerned with simple products sold in mass quantities through multiple outlets. Others are concerned with special designing of products to serve highly complex technical needs—for instance, in the application of electronic devices to proposed automation of a production plant. Included in this selling activity also is advertising in its manifold forms, simple and complex. There is the plain handbill, the newspaper or magazine advertisement; there are radio programs and television spectaculars. Selling effort appears in the many fairs, expositions, and displays designed solely or in part to accomplish a portion of the task of furthering buying action.

Finally, the wide range of ancillary and auxiliary functions, packaging, market research, and record keeping, constitutes an integral part of total selling activity. So also do the sales, marketing, advertising, supervisory, and other staff activities become essential to the effective performance of this selling function.

The importance of selling in broad economic and social terms is difficult to measure; but there are certain evidences of magnitude from which one may secure impressions of this importance. For instance: It appears that expenditures for this activity, in terms of gross national production, are at least 5 per cent and may be as high as 10 per cent. The probabilities are that a conservative figure would range in annual costs from $30 billion to $35 billion.[2] This is not the only evidence. The number of persons involved, the nature of the service performed also must be examined in order to form any judgment as to the place of selling in our economy. But an understanding of the full im-

---

[2] See note on expenditures for selling, Chapter II, page 30.

the public pays for. There is much more selling of types that the average citizen never encounters. Advertising, radio, magazines, newspapers, and television, demand attention from so many people and at so many different times that the fact that personal selling, in terms of costs and employment, is vastly more important than advertising as a form of selling is overlooked.

However, even more serious is the realization that many businessmen, such as engineers, technical men, production men and others, are themselves not really convinced of the social and economic necessity of selling effort. Many appear to be concerned as to the wastefulness of the process. Among nonselling executives, it has been observed that the most common opinion is that selling is extraordinarily wasteful, that much more selling is done than is needed. Only after they are compelled to study the problems and difficulties and realities of selling do they come to have respect for the function and the work done by selling executives.

The results of such opinions and attitudes are serious. In the first place, the men and women now in the selling field derive less satisfaction from their work than they would otherwise, even though they like the work itself and are successful in it. Secondly, both older and younger men frequently exhibit a reluctance to go into the work because they feel it is not as useful socially or economically as alternative occupations or professions. The inevitable result of such ideas is an impending shortage of men to do selling work, a shortage which affects both the numbers and quality of men who will have to assume selling responsibility within the next few years. If selling is essential, if these persuasive activities are required, as I believe they are, we must face boldly the problem of examining selling to see whether the attitudes that have brought about such adverse points of view are sound, or whether they have failed to take into account certain vital factors.

Lastly, unless our efforts to induce buying action in the future are sufficiently resultful, we are in for a bad time. One of the inherent instabilities of our economic system, which has yielded so high a standard of living, is its vulnerability to shock and fear that may come from the failure to consume the increasing production of industry rapidly enough to maintain employment. Failure to sell goods in amounts necessary to maintain employment compels unemployment. The fear of such unemployment tends to decrease further purchases in a society whose purchases go much beyond the necessities of life and much beyond even the simple comforts. The downward spiral of decreasing consumption can be disastrous to our social and economic welfare.

Need for Economic and Social Analyses of Selling

The average businessman, when called upon to justify expenditures for selling and advertising, usually falls back upon the assertion that his business could not survive without selling. But the economist, looking at the broad economic picture, might reply that the businessman might be correct so far as his own firm is concerned but that if his firm goes out of business, people will simply buy elsewhere; the failure of one or several business enterprises in competition merely indicates failure to offer products or prices satisfactory to consumers.

It might and has been argued that if a business enterprise does not sell, it saves that cost, could therefore sell for less, and people would buy from it at lower prices. This common attitude among Europeans is illustrated by the remark made by a member of a ECA Productivity Team when he learned that a firm that the team visited spent $1,000,000 annually for advertising. "Why not save the money and reduce your costs," he queried, not realizing that volume might decrease and costs would rise. Higher prices might further decrease volume to a disastrous point. Actually, such attitudes assume that buyer initiative will adequately energize production and productivity, rather than seller initiative. This is a naïve and unrealistic assumption, as subsequent examination will disclose.

The opinion of many technical and research men who have had little contact with selling in their careers is similar: namely, that buying and selling will take place *without persuasion* in a competitive market. Sales transactions would not take place unless mutually beneficial, each party to the transaction securing therefrom an increase of satisfaction. Therefore, since buyers seek satisfaction and sellers want to dispose of their products, selling is unnecessary. Usually, some statement is made or implied that a sufficiently good product will sell itself. As subsequent analysis also will bring out, this view assumes characteristics of demand that are contrary to the facts. It assumes that people desire a high standard of living beyond living necessities so much that they will take the necessary steps to obtain it. It assumes the existence of intense desire to buy and to acquire the means to buy.

The need for a positive explanation of selling, of why we spend so many billions of dollars each year to be persuaded to buy goods and services, grows out of the fact that present explanations are inadequate.[6] Whether the viewpoints held by various groups question the necessity of some or of all selling activity; whether the opinions relate to costs, abuses, and weaknesses, the need for an objective over-all explanation of the function of selling and its relationship to our society is essential to full understanding of our American way of life.

The persons engaged in selling activity need to understand their function in our society if they are to improve performance and are to acquire that dependability and responsibility that comes from the performance of essential tasks in the public interest. If selling is essential in a society marked by free enterprise and free consumer choice, then we should know it and understand it before it is too late.

A better understanding in order to meet the coming challenge of operating a peacetime economy on a high-production and full-employment basis, will demand new thinking and action.

1) In the first place, we must through our research facilities and improved technology have better goods and services to sell, goods and services that will more nearly meet the consumers' needs than those on the market. We need goods and services that represent, not unattainable perfection, but more acceptable compromises between ideals and current possibilities.

---

[6] Some economists have asserted, and many others have implied by their attitudes of neglect and indifference toward selling, that production really creates its own demand; thus selling is unnecessary. This theory, originally enunciated by Jean Baptiste Say in 1825 in his *Law of Markets*, is discussed in Chapter XII. Such assumptions are likely to be the starting point for the general disregard of selling in economic theory.

2) We need an intellectual and practical understanding of selling on the part of our major business executives and an understanding of its relationships not only to the individual firm but to our entire economy. Out of it should grow full and intelligent support of the sales activities of the business and a respect which will aid in bringing more men to assume coming burdens.

3) Again, we need a practical understanding and a "feel" for the essentials of selling on the part of operating marketing and sales executives, a sensing of the present needs for preparation, both quantitatively and qualitatively, for the tougher selling tasks ahead. Administrators must prepare themselves and their organizations for more and better selling direction. They must be prepared and take definite action because of the time requirements for preparation.

4) We need a genuine change in the attitudes and understanding of many nonselling executives, both in their attitudes toward sales executives and the selling function itself, and in their attitudes toward the general public and those who look to selling as a career.

5) We need further a deeper and broader understanding on the part of our economists and other leaders of youth as to the place of selling in our economy. They must test and recognize that selling furnishes honorable and remunerative careers to many young men now dissuaded from pursuing them because of careless and adverse ideas that have been expressed to them. We cannot expect that such leaders of thought will appraise selling objectives as an essential economic function in view of the present economic literature and its general neglect of the selling function. Present economic literature and its neglect of selling have led to invalid assumptions and fallacious generalizations based on easily obtained surface facts, while the main body of data and fact has remained hidden primarily because businessmen and social scientists did not seek it.

6) Finally, through these and other developments, we need and hope to secure a better understanding by the public of selling, so that its full benefits may be realized, its inefficiencies corrected, and its abuses eliminated.

Selling, a Form of Economic Leadership

The starting point for developing an adequate explanation of selling is obviously an analysis of what selling is, its nature and essential characteristics. Selling is persuasive leadership to bring about buying action. The seller influences both individuals and groups; but whether a particular effort is intended to bring immediate purchase or to lay the foundation for future sales, the ultimate goal is buying action by those toward whom selling influence is directed.

Selling is a form of leadership. The seller, whether salesman or sales executive, seeks to influence other persons to take action. But selling is only one form of leadership essential to economic and social welfare in a democratic society. It is a form of leadership, directed ultimately toward high and rising standards of living.[7] Other forms of leadership have their implied or expressed objectives, however faultily they may pursue them. Political leadership in its best form offers leadership toward better government, toward betterment of the people. Intelligent, intellectual leadership is aimed at the extension of knowledge and its better application. And finally, religious leadership strives toward the enhancement of spiritual life and spiritual development.

We have in all these groups—church, school, state, and business—various forms of leadership, inevitably overlapping, but having many things in common. In any of these many fields, leadership on a broad scale is necessary. In the political field, there are tens of thousands of leaders, some part time, some full time. At all levels, leadership may strive to achieve greater welfare and better government; but occasionally there will emerge leadership that aims at goals far removed from the welfare of the people. In the religious sphere, leadership consists not only of the clergy but of organized and paid laity and the millions of more or less unorganized and unpaid lay workers. In the intellectual and educational field, the leadership goes all the way from lay members of school boards and teachers in small ele-

---

[7] The objectives of selling in relation to high and rising standards of living are examined in Chapter IV, p. 79.

mentary schools to the outstanding individuals in administration and in the teaching and research in universities, schools, and in business.

It is thus the conclusion of this study that selling is that leadership to buying action essential to provide high and rising standards of living. It is persuasive leadership to buy what we need and want. It is leadership to maintain our position as the nation with the highest standard of living in the present-day world. It is leadership that permits new products to be proposed and launched and that brings rewards to the innovator so that he may continue to serve the public. It is the leadership that enables new enterprises to start and to live.

These are broad, unproved statements at this stage of our discussion. If they are true, businessmen should have a deep respect for the selling function. The public should have a more fundamental appreciation of the services of selling, together with a more balanced view of its abuses. If they are true, economists can no longer ignore selling in discussions of economic topics and no longer blithely assume that consumers alone develop and maintain a high level of living or that levels rise automatically with incomes. Income also depends upon demand; and demand depends in part upon existing needs and wants but also, in part, upon persuasion to expand to new wants or satisfy newly felt needs.

Requirements of an Adequate Theory of Selling

Starting from the premise that selling is a form of economic leadership, an adequate explanation of selling in the American economy must deal with several definite sets of problems. Specifically these are:

1. The objectives of selling; the economic and social desirability of these objectives; and the relationship of private gain to the objectives of selling.
2. The demand characteristics which must be considered in relation to productivity, production, and selling.
3. The economic and social climate in which selling must be carried on to make its greatest contribution.
4. The production and productivity requirements for attainment of the objectives, and selling's relation to them.

5. The place of selling as an energizer of our economic system and as a contribution to social welfare. The criticisms and abuses.

6. The alternatives to selling leadership.

Furthermore, developing the explanation of selling, which constitutes the purpose and content of this volume, cannot be simple because the influencing of human behavior within a complex society such as ours cannot be simple. It is based upon several important propositions.

First, material welfare is one desirable goal of human thought and effort, but not the only goal. The goal of material welfare encompasses all the people, not just a privileged class.

Second, in the economic sphere as in other aspects of life, widespread effective leadership is essential to progress.

Third, selling is a form of leadership generally directed in its final analysis to buying actions that result in higher material welfare.

Fourth, people must be led to want goods and services that make up higher and rising standards of living. But since the goals are to be reached for all the people, these same people must produce the goods and services going into living standards. Therefore, the desire for material welfare must be strong enough to induce people to undertake this production.

These propositions need elaboration and proof, just as do various other elements in this explanation. One more premise needs to be kept in mind in subsequent discussions, namely, the existence of a free-enterprise system in a country enjoying democratic liberty. The close relation between economic freedom and political freedom is discussed in Chapter V, but for earlier discussions, it is taken for granted.

SUMMARY OF THEORY OF SELLING

The Objectives

The objectives of selling are economically and socially desirable. The objective of the individual sale is either to complete the transfer of title and goods to consumers or transfer to those who will, with or without charge, carry the goods forward in their journey to consumers. The ultimate objective of purchase is consumption, either intermediate or ultimate. Insofar as goods are sold to all the people, the net result is that more goods and services are consumed; and this means, by and large, higher standards of living for all the people, not just for a few buyers.

In the study of the objectives of selling, we need to distinguish between the objectives of the selling process as a whole, both immediately and ultimately, and the objectives of individuals. The immediate objective of selling activity is that of obtaining buying action which results in the purchase of goods and services, to increase goods and services in the hands of buyers and in consumption. It is clear that the production and distribution of these goods and services determine the standards of living in our economy. Great quantities of goods and services distributed widely spell higher standards of living for a wide group.

The goods and services may be good, bad, or indifferent from the standpoint of welfare of individuals and society; but there are both implicit and explicit checks upon the bad and indifferent. Strong incentives operate upon businessmen to sell good goods and services. The objectives of the individual engaged in selling are obviously to secure specific buying actions on the part of individuals or group buyers. But the attainment of that objective is a means of satisfying several types of desires on the part of the selling individuals. First, the common desire to make a living necessarily characterizes a very large proportion of salesmen, as it does every other occupational group. But as in most other groups, other motivation may be important. Many salesmen who possess the qualifications for successful selling get much satisfaction out of their work, out of contributing by selling to the satisfaction and accomplishment of others. These men probably do not get as much satisfaction as they should from it; but all who have had contact with selling work know that out of the building of customers and the making of sales that are mutually beneficial, the salesman gets real satisfaction.

The salesman may, of course, be motivated by a desire to secure money as a means of extra satisfactions or power; but in this respect again, he does not differ from those engaged in other occupations and professions. The real problem is to determine how, in proportion, the various types of motives seem to be operative in the sales field as compared to other fields.

The motives of individuals are varied and often mixed; but undoubtedly the motive in a large proportion of cases of selling activity is selfish: the salesman is thinking of his own and his family's welfare and sometimes of the power and influence money promises him. But having said this, we must recognize one of the great merits of our free-enterprise system. What may appear to be individual selfishness does not preclude a socially desirable result. To a very large extent, the money and profit motive is what may give the individual operator his incentive to do things consistent with public welfare; but it would be naïve to assert or believe that the interests of the individual seller and his conduct on occasion would never be contrary to public interest.

Demand and Selling

The need for selling leadership grows out of the characteristics of human behavior, specifically the characteristics of the demand for economic goods and services. Consumers in our society must generally secure goods and services by purchase, that is, by buying action. This is inevitable in view of specialization, large-scale production, division of labor, and other characteristics in our economy. In order to purchase, the consumer must have income. To have income he must work and work productively. He must secure an increasing share of what is produced, and a full share of what technology and management development have been able to add to productivity.

The consumer buys: (*a*) necessities, but even in his necessities he wants higher than minimum qualities; (*b*) comforts, although initially he may have to be persuaded to buy comforts; and (*c*) luxuries which go beyond comforts. Initially and even ultimately, he must be persuaded to buy them.

The consumer buys because he is influenced by:

1. Necessity and habits.
2. Education.
3. Example and environment.
4. Selling and advertising influence.

But high and rising standards of living cannot be built upon necessity, education, or example and environment alone, for a variety of reasons. Rapid progress in any field of human behavior is not brought about by necessity or education alone, or by example and environment. Leadership must add its contribution. In the economic field, if people are to produce and consume more goods, selling influence is necessary. Here, as elsewhere, some men must lead.

Leadership is necessary because without it not enough people want a high standard of living with sufficient intensity to cause them to produce and distribute goods. Active and energetic leadership is needed in order to cause them to want these goods enough to produce them, just as it is needed in the processes of planning, producing, and distributing them. Our technology requires a timing of demand and purchase, demand for great quantities of goods and services, and a uniformity of demand, which for most products will not develop spontaneously or without selling leadership within sufficiently short time periods to enable business enterprise to exist.

Selling leadership performs a necessary economic and social function in maintaining desire, so that there is no spiralling deterioration of living standards. Without such leadership, some people would maintain their efforts and continue their desire and willingness to produce the high standards of living if they could. There would be, however, enough whose desires would turn in other directions through laziness or harmful types of consumption so that living standards would deteriorate for all. In this area as in so many others, sound leadership and its influence resembles that of leadership in other fields. In the field of politics in a democratic society, the absence of continuous persuasive and effective leadership is followed by deterioration of government.

Political, Social, and Economic Climate

These objectives of high and rising standards of living for people generally can be reached to a maximum degree under supporting economic and social conditions of favoring natural resources, a vigorous population, sustaining political conditions, a fluid society, free enterprise, optimism, and absence of stratified social or consumption patterns.

The desirability of natural resources to support substantial production will readily be granted; but it is easy to find countries where low standards of living prevail but which possess large and sufficient natural resources. Natural resources are not in themselves assurance of high standards. Similarly, the desirability of a vigorous and potentially productive population will be conceded, but instances can likewise be cited of such populations with low living standards.

Not quite so obvious is the need for a political climate that does not discourage enterprise and a social and political climate that does not destroy or discourage ambition. The lower productivity and lower standards in parts of western Europe where tax and other political barriers to consumption exist furnish a case in point.

A social climate that does not deter individuals from wanting higher standards of living and striving to attain them is essential to fullest realization of economic welfare. Political and social conditions are favorable if the government tends to look to the interest of the individual and the dignity of mankind, if there is social fluidity so that men can pass from lower economic groups to higher economic and social groups, and finally if there is an absence of rigid social patterns of consumption.

Any peaceful society that desires a high standard of living for all the people must itself produce what goes into that higher standard of living. If people want high and rising standards of living, they must produce a high and rising flow of goods and services. The people who produce will do so only if they are motivated and energized by desire for those goods and services. Thus the greatest volume of goods and services, and therefore the highest standard of living, will result if a people works regularly and skillfully to produce them, using the most efficient equipment that technological progress affords and the greatest skills which wise management can develop.

High Production

High and rising standards of living require both increasing quantities of known desired goods, new goods, and services at low prices. The labor required to produce the goods must be limited, with time to enjoy their consumption on the part of those who buy them.

In order to produce the greatest quantity of goods and services, the full utilization of mass production and of a highly developed technology are required. Only by the application of such scientific and technical developments can the highest productivity for workers be achieved.

Productivity

The highest productivity per worker also requires skill and regular effort, teamwork, and skilled management, plus adequate incentive for the worker and management. Increasing and maintaining the standard of living with respect to known products already on the market comes about through incentive to maintain and improve the production of workers, as well as through incentive to management to improve methods of production by applying new technology. In a society which aims at high and rising standards of living, consumers and producers are largely identical. If society produces, it must consume. If it is to consume, it must produce.

Alternatives to Selling

The only alternatives to selling leadership in its influence upon high and rising standards of living are the predominant leadership by buyers or government allotment. A careful analysis of the predominant leadership by buyers shows that it is on the whole impracticable. Government allotment requires regimentation, removes freedom of choice, and tends to result in totalitarian government, which is anathema to lovers of freedom and democracy. Careful analysis of human experience indicates that neither predominant buyer initiative nor government allotment promises improvement or success in reaching the levels of welfare attained by the socially responsible capitalism of which selling is a part.

Selling Abuses and Weaknesses

The abuses of selling or advertising are often adverted to by economists, social reformers, and members of consumer groups.

Some of these abuses are real. Some criticisms represent the effort of certain groups to impose their own tastes and ideas for other groups for whom these tastes and ideas may not be appropriate. That real abuses and practices contrary to public welfare should be eliminated wherever possible or reduced to the lowest proportions needs no argument. However, the total of such abuses appears to be relatively small when considered in light of the billions of transactions and huge quantities of goods purchased to make up the high standards of living that people enjoy in the United States.

Plan of Study. Conclusion

The plan of this study of selling is a simple one. Because many people have little opportunity to observe the varied facets of selling in business, the second chapter describes briefly some of the types of selling organizations and the way they operate. The need for selling is a logical outgrowth of certain characteristics of consumer and producer demands for goods and services (Chapter III). A detailed examination of the individual and aggregate objectives follows (Chapter IV).

Selling leadership has developed most rapidly and performed its greatest services under conditions of free enterprise and under conditions of political, social, and economic freedom. This prompted an examination of the social and economic conditions under which selling has developed and best performed its functions (Chapter V).

The fact that if all our people want high levels of living they must themselves produce the necessary goods and services led to analyses of production and productivity and innovation (Chapters VI and VII) in relation to selling.

Three chapters are devoted to an economic and social evaluation of selling, the first (Chapter VIII) dealing with the contributions and costs of selling, the second (Chapter IX) with criticism of selling, and the third (Chapter X) with abuses and correctives.

Since it has been argued that the consumer and the public might be better served by some alternative to sellers' efforts to dispose of goods, two principal alternatives to predominant buyer control and initiative and government allotment are discussed in Chapter XI.

The three final chapters include one dealing somewhat more technically with selling and economic theory, another with selling careers, and a third presenting final conclusions.

The many explanations of American prosperity which issue from the pens of economists, both domestic and foreign, point out rightly that no one factor is responsible. An able and distinguished Swiss economist and statesman, who has spent much time in the United States, attributes our prosperity to mass production, the application of science to production, the passion for productivity, and the spirit of competition.[8]

One may well accept these as important and characteristic of the American economy. But mass production depends on markets that must be opened up and maintained and expanded by selling. The application of science to production becomes possible and is undertaken on the assumption that selling will bring markets and yield sales income to cover outlays and profit. Furthermore, those responsible for the development and applications of science to production, and for the making of equipment and new material have long since discovered that selling leadership is needed for rapid progress.

The passion for productivity can be attributed to the desires for the higher incomes and shorter hours that higher productivity affords. Only the strong desire for the elements of material welfare causes workers to work productively—and to fight for and get a full share of that increased production.

The spirit of competition develops in its most intense form in the efforts of competing firms to sell their products. The spirit of rivalry is present in all phases of human activity; but in the functioning of our economic society, it is at the point where effort is made to sell that the success or failure of the firm is usually decided.

Thus the relationship of selling to this, as well as other, explanations of American prosperity is definite and clear. Selling is directed toward fundamental human desires. By creating and

---

[8] Rappard, *op. cit.*, Part 3.

intensifying these desires, selling becomes an energizer of the economic system, a factor of such influence that it is to be hoped that future analyses of our economy will take full account of it.

Several millions of our people are engaged in selling activities and are engaged, therefore, directly or indirectly in persuading other people to buy goods and services. On the whole, they are neither better nor worse than other citizens in other fields of endeavor. Their work is necessary, and they are entitled to feel that it is an essential part of free enterprise in a democratic society where human welfare is to be advanced materially as well as in other ways. That the effort of these people to increase material welfare has been successful admits of no doubt. That material welfare furnishes by itself alone the basis of a balanced life is a proposition which no right-thinking person would accept. What is needed is leadership in other aspects of our living comparable in effectiveness to the leadership in the selling field.

Thus we have in selling one form of social and economic leadership which has desirable objectives,

whose methods are consistent with normal human behavior,

whose abuses are lessening,

whose contributions to its objective of material betterment and to human welfare are impressive,

whose leadership is essential to economic and social progress in our society.

The challenge which confronts business, sellers, and buyers is to improve the contributions which selling can make, to reduce the abuses, and finally and hopefully, to find the limits of this contribution in terms of a balanced life.

Chapter II

SELLING IN BUSINESS

THE TASKS of persuading people to buy goods and services which must be performed by business are prodigious in size, extraordinarily varied in type, frequently very complex, and usually dispersed in time and place. Because most people are not in position to observe more than partial and often unrepresentative aspects of selling, a brief survey of selling activities of business may be useful as a background for subsequent analysis.

Most of us come into contact with retail sales clerks or proprietors who do selling. Some of them are inefficient and some do little to persuade us to buy; but the fact that the goods have been purchased and displayed has required in itself effort on the part of retailers and others who are endeavoring to bring about retail purchases and retail sales. Many of us come in contact with door-to-door salesmen. Some of these contacts are pleasant, others unpleasant. All of us read, hear, and see advertising. Our impressions are varied; our mental reactions and our buying actions may be consistent or, as often observed, quite inconsistent. Our general judgments of selling are likely to be based on such contacts or upon the statements or opinions of those whose experiences are essentially of similar limited scope.

There are many types of selling effort, however, with which the general public never comes in contact: selling by producers to wholesalers and retailers; negotiation of manufacturers with purchasers who themselves are businessmen, merchants, or manufacturers; skilled, highly technical work of so-called detail

21

or specialist salesmen with physicians, men who are representatives of pharmaceutical manufacturers; engineering specialist salesmen for electrical equipment manufacturers—these all deal with business or governmental buyers and not with the general public. Beyond this, there is the advertising of manufacturers, merchants, and other producers in thousands of informational trade papers and magazines, all of which go to specialized groups with which most of us have little or nothing to do. There is throughout the country a succession of fairs, exhibits, and expositions, intended primarily and often exclusively for prospective buyers of specialized products.

Even persons employed in business and industrial enterprise may only to a limited extent come into contact with those engaged in selling work. Men whose jobs may be in production, technical research, personnel management, or accounting, may or may not get to know much about the selling activities of the enterprise of which they are a part. Certainly there is evidence that they do not secure that understanding of selling which enables them to accord to the function the respect which it deserves and to accord to the men engaged in it the status which is their due. Nonselling executives all too often grant in a vague way the necessity for sales effort but believe that salesmen and sales executives do not perform as useful a service as men engaged in production or in other branches of the enterprise.

The fact that intelligent persons have developed such ideas is understandable only if one considers the social and educational influences to which they have been subjected and the assumptions which they are led to make as to the characteristics of demand and the need for selling effort. Coupled with these is the general inability of sales executives themselves to give a convincing explanation of selling in terms which controvert the express or implied appraisals of economists and the adverse criticism of various other groups.

The need for selling arises from the characteristics of demand, the concentration of production, and the dispersion of consumption in time and place, out of which emerges the necessity of influencing both producers and consumers to buy in their own best interests. More specifically:

In our economy large quantities of goods and services are produced by large-scale methods utilizing advanced technology at a limited number of producing points.

Every man, woman, and child in our country participates in consumption. Every governmental and private institution must purchase and consume or resell. Every business enterprise must purchase and consume or resell. Purchase and consumption take place at widely scattered locations.

The range of products produced in our country is extremely wide, whether one considers products for ultimate consumption or products for business, institutional, or industrial use. Hundreds of thousands of different products in millions of variations, sizes, colors, and materials, have to be distributed, sold, and bought. The pages of huge catalogues of mail-order houses, the multivolumed catalogues of electrical equipment manufacturers, the lists of wholesale hardware or wholesale drug stocks, give only a limited impression of the enormous variety.

Furthermore, in a free-enterprise society, the objectives of consumer freedom of choice and high standards of living impose the general requirement that production of consumer goods take place in advance of purchase or order. When such goods are produced, buyers must take buying action if consumption and production are to be maintained or increased. The businessman knows that except in very unusual situations, active efforts must be made to get people to buy products beyond vital necessities and minimum comforts.

Finally, this buying action must take place within more or less limited time periods. Most manufacturers, large and small, produce only because they are convinced that they will be able to dispose of their products within a short period so that the returns will enable them to continue operations. No concern can persist indefinitely in the accumulation of stocks and depend upon buyers' initiative to come to the seller to purchase them. There are, of course, some special circumstances under which this might happen; but as a general statement, producers cannot build up stock for five-year, ten-year, or twenty-year periods and continue to exist. Firms would be unable to continue; they would be forced into bankruptcy. The wholesaler who buys goods to provide retailers in his territory would go out of business very quickly if he could not undertake selling effort, although again he might reduce this selling effort to a relatively small amount in some types of operation, as in cash-and-carry wholesaling. This type of wholesaler must confine his selling effort to goods which move rapidly, frequently goods which have already been partially sold by advertising; and to customers who have been induced by such selling effort as is required to inform retailers of the existence and advantages of purchases from cash-and-carry wholesalers.

Similarly, the retailer must move the goods he buys within limited periods if he is to be successful. Depending upon the type of store and the method of operation, the retailer may turn his stock from little more than once a year to almost once a week. Average department store sales in 1955 were 4.3 times the average stock.[1] Grocery chains average 15.63 stock turns per year. Discarding extremes and using middle range figures, department stores stock turn ranged from 2.77 times per year to 4.85 times per year;[2] grocery chains from 12.12 to 21.79.[3] In a competitive market, failure to achieve sufficient volume of sales and adequate stock turn for any extended period threatens survival of the enterprise.

Thus, selling is essential for every kind of business or commercial or industrial enterprise, because only through the consummation of buyer and seller transactions can business and industry perform completely its functions. Even those businesses which are classed as completely integrated must sell, for no business enterprise is completely self-sufficient. The manufacturing enterprise must buy the equipment or supplies or materials sold by previous owners and, in turn, must sell its products to others.

The manufacturer or wholesaler or retailer, whether selling

---

[1] Figures supplied by Harvard University Bureau of Business Research. Average department store stock turn in 1955 was 4.3 times, based on average monthly inventories. Grocery chains averaged 15.63 as a median figure, based on beginning and ending inventories.

[2] Malcolm P. McNair and David Carson, *Operating Results of Department and Specialty Stores in 1955* (Boston: Division of Research, Harvard Graduate School of Business Administration, 1956).

[3] Figures supplied by Harvard University Bureau of Business Research.

new or old products, cannot expect under ordinary circumstances that the buyer generally will take the initiative and come
to buy the services and goods. Such demand will not be or become sufficiently large or uniform *within the needed time limits*
to enable him to carry on. In order to meet payrolls and to re-
coup his costs, in order to secure a return for his services and
for the use of his capital as well as for the risks he will assume,
he must sell in amounts that have a profitable relationship to
his capital, to his purchases, and to his working force. He has
to sell at prices which cover buying and manufacturing costs
if he can. But he knows, or soon finds out, that prices are not
determined ordinarily by him but by market conditions not under his own control. He must finally do his selling at costs
which are competitively comparable. He must keep those selling
costs within proper limits in a competitive market, for consumers will not generally pay high prices that will cover costs
if they can secure satisfactory goods elsewhere at lower prices
as conveniently.

Otherwise expressed, in large-scale production a producer
turns out quantities of goods for markets that are usually in advance of the expected demand of the ultimate buyers or sellers. Today our factories, large and small, turn out products for
consumers, most of whom the producers do not know or have
never seen. The producers do not sell to them directly but often to middlemen who resell, or to other producers who use
the product in manufacturing and processing to turn out additional things for sale.

The large-scale producer may sell direct to users under certain circumstances. For instance, the large-scale producer of
electrical products may sell turbines directly to an electric
power company for its own use in a central station; but he will
sell small electrical supplies to a wholesaler, who in turn sells
to a retailer for resale to the consumer. A food processor sells
goods ordinarily to wholesalers who supply retailers, but he
may sell direct to retailers, such as chain-store organizations.
Thus today, in the disposition of the products of large-scale
production, every business enterprise finds that it is compelled
to buy and sell goods or services. It must buy and sell in order

to survive, whether its main function is that of extracting wealth from natural resources or processing or manufacturing products that it buys.

Since selling is influencing people to buy either immediately or at a later time, tentative choices must be made by businessmen and sellers as to the emphasis to be placed on securing immediate buying action compared with the effort required to prepare the way for future purchases by communicating information and ideas favorable to future purchase. The most desirable objective for many firms is to secure immediate buying action, and at the same time to develop a predisposition to repeat purchases. The seller can initiate such a development, but he can maintain goodwill at reasonable cost only if the buyer's experience with the vendor, with the products, and with the sales representative proves satisfactory.

The amount of selling work varies widely between firms, buyers, and products. The amount of effort that must go into selling or into buying will vary from the simplest form of limited exchange of words or display to protracted persuasive efforts and negotiations; but even minimum selling effort is required at least, whether the initiative is taken by private or by government buyers. While governmental officials have at times taken pride in assertions or implications that the government "buys" and is not "sold," it is nevertheless true that selling effort of various types and in various guises is necessary if purchases are to be made effectively by government and desirable firms are to participate in the supply of governmental needs.

It is the purpose of the remainder of this chapter to describe the widespread application of selling effort in business, some of the forms it takes, and the business problems to which it gives rise.

Selling, as we shall be using it in these chapters, needs to be clearly described, because it is used in the broad, although not the figurative, sense of the term. From the sellers' point of view, it is the effort to consummate selling transactions, to make sales in which a buyer purchases what a seller offers. It is the effort to influence prospective buyers to take buying action. It is intended to bring about economic exchanges that are mutually advantageous and is therefore a part of the economic functioning of our society. Since it is intended to secure buyers' decisions to take action, it involves psychological processes and subjects the student of selling to the necessity of dealing realistically with the pertinent aspects of human behavior.

FORMS OF SELLING EFFORT

The selling work with which we are concerned assumes many forms, although it is only a part of the total process of getting goods from producers to consumers. The seller takes the initiative, but the energizing and economic force which causes transportation of goods from producer to consumer is buying action. The portion of the seller's marketing work to which this study is devoted is his effort to secure that buying action. The seller must influence the buyer to buy, whether the buyer's action is brought about by simple recital of fact, by persuasive reasoned or emotional portrayal of benefits to be derived. Thus the seller deals primarily with aspects of human behavior, with his competitors' selling behavior in free enterprise, and with the behavior of prospective buyers, whether present customers or not.

While the effort expended to influence buyers to make pruchases appears in many forms and in innumerable variations of those forms, two principal types predominate. These are personal selling, person-to-person contact, in which the seller informs and persuades the buyer to buy; and advertising of many types such as seen in newspapers and magazines, on radio or television, in publicity, in direct mail, and many others.

Personal salesmanship represents the largest portion of selling effort, both in terms of man power involved and in expenditure of national income. It is employed at every level of business activity, by producers, by wholesalers, by retailers, and by other middlemen. However, an accurate estimate of the number of persons engaged in personal selling is difficult if not impossible to obtain. We can nevertheless find some facts which may provide a basis for an impression of magnitude.

The number of salesmen that manufacturing and trading enterprises employ varies from none at all in small companies in which proprietors may do the selling, to sales forces which number thousands of men. In a questionnaire study undertaken several years ago, sales forces ranged from one or two men to a top figure of 18,000. Even some of those whose replies indicated that they employed no salesmen, however, found it necessary to perform the functions of sales representatives. Under some circumstances, the selling may be done by persons whose titles and responsibilities are broader than the sales task itself. Selling may be done to large buyers by men who are not called salesmen but who nevertheless are performing the functions of salesmen. In larger companies, personal selling likewise may be done by many different persons in the organization. Not infrequently, in the conduct of large negotiations, the amounts involved are such that buyers' representatives are principals of the buying enterprise and the situation demands that the sellers' representatives be correspondingly placed with adequate authority to represent the seller. Many a company vice-president may be a salesman so far as his principal functions are concerned.[4]

Commonly, the size of wholesalers' or manufacturers' traveling sales forces is less than fifty men. Over 90 per cent of the sales forces about which current data were collected comprised less than 100 men. The opinions of various consultants and various sales managers with wide experience in large as well as many of the medium- and smaller-size companies, all confirm the ob-

---

[4] Distribution of companies by size of sales force:

Number of Salesmen	Companies
Over 5,000	1
2,000–2,999	5
1,000–1,999	9
500– 999	16
300– 499	22
200– 299	18
100– 199	71
60– 99	66
40– 59	61
30– 39	66
20– 29	116
10– 19	217
7– 9	122
4– 6	157
1– 3	72
No answer	3
Total	1,022

Source: Salesmen's Compensation, H. R. Tosdal and W. W. Carson, Boston, Division of Research, Harvard Graduate School of Business Administration, 1953; p. 451, vol. I.

servation that while large sales forces exist, the total number is not great, and such sales forces are not typical.

Brief reflection will suggest why sales forces do not follow any of the usual measures of size, such as the total number of employees, dollar sales of firms, and the like. The number of salesmen is basically determined by the number of prospective buyers and customers to be solicited, the frequency of that solicitation, the amount of time required for such calls, by transport, and other external factors. In a situation in which there are few buyers making large purchases and annual contracts, only a few or perhaps even no men with the title of salesman would be required for a multimillion dollar business. Selling a product in small lots to retailers at frequent intervals might require a salesman to spend full time to dispose of a volume that represented only a very small fraction of the sales of the first type of sales representative. But firms selling the same products to the same types of customers and having similar selling programs are likely to have sales forces that in comparative size vary closely with the volume of sales.

Although many loose and unsupported statements have been made concerning the total number of outside salesmen, no really reliable figures are obtainable. The number of traveling or outside salesmen as stated in the United States census publications is not adequate, since its classifications do not correspond precisely with the groups with which this study is concerned. Beyond the obvious difficulty presented by those persons who classify themselves as executives, although their duties are primarily those of traveling representatives, there is the difficulty of determining the proportion of the general classification of sales workers (1955: 3,740,000) who properly fall within the classification of outside salesmen. A compilation of the subgroups of sales workers who pretty clearly are engaged in outside sales activities, taken from the 1950 census, gives a very conservative total of approximately 1,500,000 persons. In 1954, more than 7,500,000 people were employed in retailing in 1,748,000 stores of all sizes and types.[5] The proportion of those engaged in selling is not clearly shown in census figures. An ap-

[5] Delbert J. Duncan and Charles F. Phillips, *Retailing: Principles and Methods* (4th ed.; Homewood, Illinois: Richard D. Irwin, Inc., 1955), p. 33.

proach to determining the number of selling employees can be made by referring to the information furnished by the Harvard University Bureau of Business Research in its studies of the operating expenses of retail department stores. In its 1955 report, the proportion of selling employees averaged 50 per cent of total employees, ranging from 54 per cent in stores selling $2 million to $5 million a year, to 45 per cent in large department stores selling over $50 million per year.[6] Similar data are not available for chain stores, but since self-service stores are increasing in number, the proportion of selling employees of the usual type tends to decrease. It must be recalled, however, that the effort which goes into making attractive displays, signs, and demonstrations is effort to sell—not simply to store or stock goods. The large number of independent stores of medium and smaller sizes are believed to show a relatively larger percentage of selling employees, since in smaller establishments proprietors often join clerks in selling. Therefore, an estimate that 50 per cent of total employees in retailing, or 3,750,000 persons, are engaged in selling activities would appear reasonable. Thus we have a total of over 5,000,000 persons engaged in personal selling. Furthermore, in terms of cost, there appears to be basis for regarding as conservative an annual estimate of $10 billion for sales-force salaries, commissions, and other payments; $3 billion for travel and other expense; and $2.7 billion for supervision of selling; or a total for personal selling of $16 billion a year.[7]

Personal selling is the most effective selling method when

---

[6] McNair and Carson, *op. cit.*

[7] Accurate figures on the total cost of selling persuasion are impossible to obtain. For the purpose of forming an opinion as to the importance of selling, several types of data are available upon which to base estimates of absolute costs. Such estimates can at best be only rough approximations.

Tosdal and Carson (*op. cit.*, p. 9), made an estimate of personal selling costs for "outside" salesmen in 1949. The number of outside salesmen was estimated at 1,350,000. Making allowance for increases in income and in expense since 1950, the average figures of $6,750 for sales salaries and commissions, and $2,000 for expenses for travel, yield a current total of nearly $12 billion.

So far, retail selling personnel and retail advertising have not been included. In the studies of operating expenses of department stores of the United States, made by the Harvard Bureau of Business Research, one may secure figures on selling expense, which in 1955 included Direct and General

used alone from the standpoint of producing completed transactions. Personal selling effort can be adjusted in each case to
the needs and wants, as well as to the characteristics of prospective buyers, while advertising must be adjusted to some common
denominator of a group. In spite of the fact that personal selling
costs much more than advertising, it has escaped largely the

Selling, 9.6 per cent of sales and Sales Promotion, 4.45 per cent, or a total of
14.05 per cent. Applied to total department store sales of $11.5 billion in
1955, we get a figure of $2 billion.

In a similar study of limited-price variety stores in which self-service has
been spreading rapidly, large chains showed that the cost of salespeople
ranged from 7.81 per cent to 8.60 per cent of sales, regional chains from
10.59 per cent to 12.01 per cent. It appears that selling costs larger stores less
on a percentage of sales than smaller stores. In the absence of complete
data, one can only guess at an over-all figure. If a figure of 10 per cent is
applied to the recent $190 million figure of net sales, the total cost of retail
selling would be ca. $19 billion. Since this includes advertising estimated at
ca. 2 per cent the corrected total would be in the neighborhood of $15 billion.
If 5 per cent were used, then around $10 billion.

Another approach taking the number of persons employed in retail trade
and determining the portion engaged in selling, yields results depending on
the estimates used. In department stores, the number of selling people ranges
from 45 per cent to 55 per cent according to recent report. In smaller stores,
the proportion is larger; and in very small operations, nearly every employee
engages in some selling work. If 50 per cent of retail employees were to be
classed as sales employees, the total would be 3,750,000 (50 per cent of 7½
million). At $50 a week the total expenditure would be $9⅜ billion, not including any but sales personnel. Other selling effort beyond advertising and
personal selling is not included.

Printers' Ink, a leading advertising publication, estimates total advertising
expenditure for 1955 at slightly above $9 billion.

In arriving at a total, one should include several other items:

a) Supervision of outside salesmen (estimated at 20 per cent).

b) Equipment for salespersons, and for display.

c) Staff services, for direction of selling etc.

Leaving out of account (*b*) and (*c*) and other similar expenditures, and
estimating (*a*) at $2.4 billions we have as a total:

Advertising	$ 9 billion
Outside salesmen	12 billion
Supervision of above	2.4 billion
Retail selling	10 billion
Total	$33.4 billion

We have as a conservative estimate an annual expenditure of $33.4 billions—
a sum amounting to some 8 per cent of our total gross national product.

The statistical inaccuracy of such estimates will readily be conceded,
without affecting the only conclusions which are drawn, namely: (1) selling
effort (not marketing distribution as a whole) involves directly a large number of people, and all of us as consumers; (2) the costs are substantial from
any point of view.

type of adverse attention directed toward advertising. It may be true that salesmen have commonly so adapted their selling contacts and solicitation as to make them more acceptable to prospective buyers. Salesmen have thus been able to eliminate much of the irritation which comes from the use of inappropriate selling methods and appeals in advertising in their impact upon particular individuals. Certain it is that much personal selling is taken for granted in spite of incompetence of many salesmen, the crass behavior of others, and the abuses that have crept in. But personal selling is expensive, and it is the function of the businessman to work out that combination of personal selling with other selling activities which will secure the maximum result for minimum expenditure.

Advertising, that is selling in print or by voice or picture to large groups, does not need to be described in any detail here. It is clear that the purpose of advertising is generally persuasion to buy. Advertising does not, and is usually not intended to, bring about unaided completed buying transactions but rather to establish a base for more resultful personal selling or to enhance productivity of other types of selling activity that make up a part of the firm's selling program. Although it involves a smaller portion of our national income and less effort of our people than personal selling, advertising has been much more criticized than personal selling, because its abuses and bad taste are so forceably brought to the attention of people that no one can escape being cognizant of them. Whether one reads newspapers or magazines, travels the highways, listens to radio, or watches television, the faults of advertising are spread before all, the discriminating and undiscriminating alike.

The costs of advertising are also high in absolute figures; in the United States we spent $9 billions in 1955.[8] Firms vary widely in their expenditures for advertising from those which

---

[8] The most accurate estimates of total advertising expenditure are compiled by *Printers' Ink*. Cf. *Advertisers' Guide to Marketing for 1957*, August 24, 1956, Section Two, p. 38 ff. See also McCann-Erickson, Inc., "Total Advertising Volume Estimates: 1867–1954," in *Advertisers' Guide to Marketing for 1956* (New York: Printers' Ink Publishing Co., 1956), pp. 68–69, and *Printers' Ink*, February 10, 1956, p. 23. Preliminary announcements give the total for 1957 as $10½ billions.

spend nothing to those which spend as much as 50 per cent of sales. One soap company spends 5.5 per cent of sales for advertising, another 12 per cent. The largest electrical equipment manufacturer and the largest motor car manufacturer each spend about ½ of 1 per cent of sales. But a cosmetics company and a specialty food concern spend amounts over 30 per cent of sales for advertising purposes.

Personal selling and advertising each have special characteristics that require discriminating selection and usually avoidance of complete dependence on one or the other. The results in terms of buying action obtained by advertising alone or by personal selling alone cannot usually be completely separated from the results of other elements of a selling program. Therefore, the evaluation of advertising effectiveness in performing selling tasks is usually difficult and a far from precise process. It is generally accepted, however, that advertising under certain conditions can do portions of a selling task more economically and more effectively than personal selling.

The criticism that advertising and personal selling have their place only if used for informational purposes will be examined at length in a later chapter; but at this point it is not useful to make a sharp distinction between informational advertising and selling and persuasive advertising and selling because all forms are intended to induce buying action. In general, if buying action can be attained by informational techniques, those are used. If buying action can be brought about only by portraying satisfactions to be secured from the product or service, then it may be not only in the interest of the business but also in the public's interest so to proceed. Advertising and personal selling are both devoted to persuasion, whatever the means, although possibly advertising is more completely devoted to persuasion than the efforts of many groups of salesmen who frequently or on occasion perform technical and advisory tasks.

The business firm, large or small, compelled to sell its products or services in order to continue operations, must choose what means or methods or what combination of personal selling, advertising, and other means to use. Such a combination or mixture, which we shall call the sales program, may include only one or a few or many elements. The number of possible variations in performance is therefore staggering, at least from a theoretical point of view. In practice, the number of possible variations is enormous. To make the choice is difficult.

The usual basis for building the "selling program" is the experience of the business and of the executive personally in selling goods, although in some trades that experience represents the practice of the trade or the customer or that of individual competitors. In more recent years, increased effort has been made to apply experimental research and analysis in order to secure facts and to reduce the risks of making changes in selling methods or in adopting new programs. Preliminary tests as to particular programs may be made in selected territories; for instance, a company may experiment in the use of newspaper advertising in particular cities, comparing results with other cities in which such advertising is not used; or a particular type of salesman may be hired for work in one territory while other territories are used as technical control territories. The difficulties in possible types of pertinent research and experiment grow out of the obvious fact that conditions cannot be kept constant while certain experiments are made or research carried on. Usually the sales result is the outcome of factors that are more numerous and sometimes more important than the specific change being studied. To a limited extent, application of scientific analysis and experimentation to the development of sales programs has proved resultful; but, by and large, trial-and-error methods and trade practices have had to be used as guides. So far, relatively little has been accomplished in enabling the businessman scientifically to determine what combination of selling methods will give the maximum result at the lowest cost of distribution.

Only advertising and personal solicitation have been discussed as parts of a selling plan. To make the list of available methods more complete, one should include the manifold types of display and selling helps furnished to retailers, dealers, and wholesalers by manufacturers, as well as the extensive display efforts of middlemen themselves as, for instance, in supermarkets and department stores. Correspondence by sellers with buyers may in some situations become an important part of the selling effort.

Obviously the correspondence that begins to assume more standardized forms may at times approach direct-mail advertising. In some fields of trade and in some industries, the use of samples is extensive, in fact, universal. In other fields, occasional use of samples has been found to be effective in causing buying action. In the textile trades, the use of samples continues to be extensive in spite of the increased standardization of many fabrics and the increased and improved descriptions which can be used. Samples are, of course, used frequently in combination with personal solicitation, advertising, or correspondence.

Both in connection with industrial goods and certain types of consumer goods, fairs and exhibitions may play an important part in securing buying action or furnishing information and demonstration in situations where demonstration is not possible for the individual prospective buyer. These fairs and exhibitions range from small local affairs held in a suburban hotel, to extensive industry fairs that constitute the chief event in the year's buying-selling activities of an industry.

The use of auctions is important in marketing of some raw materials and perishable goods; but few manufactured products are sold by auction, except as an emergency method of disposing of excess supply. They constitute a regular device for selling raw materials, fruits and vegetables, and some other products. More important is the device of competitive bidding used to some extent by industrial firms in their buying, particularly for larger installations and for building, and used very largely by governmental bodies and public institutions under direct legal mandate. The place of selling in competitive bidding is, of course, more limited, although the efforts of a company to develop an impression of dependability may play a large part in determining those who ought to be permitted to bid on particular contracts. Not infrequently the nature of the specifications in competitive bidding is in part the result of the selling effort of manufacturers who have been active in the process of educating prospective buyers as to the merits of certain types of products.

Lastly must be mentioned reciprocity: that is, the practice of business firms of favoring in their buying those firms which are their customers. It is a practice that has been studied, praised, and condemned, opinions varying as widely as those of two different executives, one of whom classed it as "practical application of the Golden Rule," and the other as "business blackmail."

While there are relatively few broad classes of methods of securing buying action in a free economy, there are innumerable variations within classes and within combinations. Tens of thousands of publications carry advertising for sellers. Personal selling variations cannot even be counted, because they rest on differences in personalities, duties, training, attitudes, and conditions of work. With such a wide range of possible choices of sales programs, the businessman does the best he can. He selects a program on the basis of his best knowledge, but inevitably the elements of his plan are chosen with far less than complete assurance that the results achieved from the effort to secure the buying action will be adequate to keep his plant going and maintain the employment of his workers. By using experience of his own or of other executives and imitating competitors, or by applying research and analysis, he may reduce the hazard, but always he must assume the risk that the planned effort will fail to provide the results needed for successful operation at lowest costs.

SELLING BY MANUFACTURERS

Over 250,000 manufacturers in the United States produce primarily for the market, whether that market be industrial, business, or ultimate consumer. The manufacturer who produces for other manufacturers or businessmen must in some way see that prospective buyers are informed, and perhaps persuaded, so that they either buy his product or enable him to turn out products which they will buy. A manufacturer sells to the ultimate consumer in a few instances, as in the case of resident pipe organs; but the great majority of manufacturers of consumer goods is unable to reach consumers directly at any reasonable cost. Consequently, they sell to wholesalers or retailers, or shift the burden to brokers or specialized middlemen. This does not eliminate selling effort. It merely transfers in part the responsibility for securing buying action leading to ultimate consumption.

In order to do this selling, the means chosen to perform this effort and secure results will vary according to the type of buyers to whom the sales are to be made and the means available to the particular customer, the size of the task to be performed in selling the product, and many other factors. In selling industrial products to manufacturers, the producer will be selling frequently to firms which require that information be conveyed not only to specialized purchasing departments but frequently to technical executives engaged in production, inspection, or other technical activities. Furthermore, if the expenditures are of substantial importance to the company, negotiations with responsible executives who are endeavoring to keep the various parts of the business in balance may be necessary and require very substantial knowledge of the relationship of the desired buying action to the firm's general welfare. But the company may find that its program of introducing new machinery or securing replacement of standard types will be more effective if it also uses advertising in technical or trade journals, direct mail, and exhibits at recognized trade shows or exhibitions, and takes other action to secure an effective, well-rounded selling program.

If the manufacturer of consumer goods decides to sell to wholesalers, he may supplement his effort to sell wholesalers with extensive advertising directly to the consumer. The wholesaler, who may in some lines carry in excess of 25,000 or 30,000 items, cannot pay what he considers adequate attention to a single product or a very limited line of products. Therefore, the manufacturer of a specialty grocery product advertises soap or breakfast food or other lines directly to consumers, expecting that the latter will recognize the product and on occasion ask the retailer for it. The manufacturer may go further and have salesmen call upon retailers to solicit orders that will be filled through the wholesaler, or to see that retailers have stocks of the product, so that if and when advertising is executed, the consumer desiring to try the product will find it displayed in the retail outlet and easily available for purchase and trial. The manufacturer of roller bearings may advertise the excellence of his bearings, although few of those who read the advertisement will buy roller bearings directly. However, the manufacturer of an automobile will advertise the use of Smith's roller bearings as another bit of evidence of the excellence of the construction of the automobile. Consequently, the manufacturer may use direct methods in an indirect selling program to those who make the purchases from him or an indirect selling program to activate selling by those who do not buy from him directly but whose purchases will be effective in increasing direct sales of the manufacturer.

To describe more clearly what manufacturers may do in order to bring about needed buying action on the part of buyers, whether consumers, producers, or middlemen, brief descriptions of the selling programs of only a few typical firms may be outlined.

1) A sugar refining company shifts most of its selling work to a person or firm called a broker. The broker has a small organization, possibly only a helper, but he maintains contacts with large retailers, grocery wholesalers, and wholesale consumers, largely by telephone. He sells granulated sugar in carload lots or possibly a sugar solution for manufacturers in tank lots. Sugar manufacturers may advertise modestly a particular brand of product; but the usual selling programs consist very largely of personal and telephone contact with buyers. There is very little differentiation of product; those of competitors are almost precisely similar and priced at levels which generally yield low margins.

2) A manufacturer of prepared breakfast foods, on the other hand, operates an extensive sales organization with several hundred salesmen selling directly to larger retailers and wholesalers. He advertises widely in national magazines, sponsors radio and TV programs directed to children, and presents a constant succession of promotions, including small gifts, contests among consumers, and other features.

3) A producer of drugs and pharmaceutical preparations advertises in medical and trade journals and also places some institutional advertising in general magazines; but the main work is done by a force of highly trained selling representatives, who

solicit wholesalers and larger retail drug firms. Part of the work of these men and of a specialized force is called "detail" work. These representatives keep physicians and hospital administrators informed of new developments in the hope that they will introduce and later recommend or prescribe new products.

4) A manufacturer of radio and TV receiving sets sells exclusively through eighty specialized wholesale distributors, using twelve sales representatives as contact men. The distributors sell to selected dealers, using both their own and the manufacturer's advertising media to reach the consumer; but the principal selling activities of these distributors are performed through a force of salesmen who visit and work with dealers in the restricted territory. The manufacturer advertises not only in trade publications but also in consumer magazines and through radio and television programs.

5) A publisher advertises in magazines and book sections of newspapers and magazines and sends copies of new volumes to book editors as samples in the hope that they will be reviewed. He also travels a group of salesmen to solicit bookstores and bookstalls of department stores. To selected lists he sends circulars describing particular works. Contrariwise, a publisher of 25-cent paper editions distributes to a much wider group through special wholesalers. One such publisher uses 110 men to call on wholesalers and selected retailers. The company provides display cases, although distributing through jobbers, but does very little advertising in usual types of media. It was estimated that its books were sold in 125,000 retail outlets.

6) A furniture manufacturer has a limited force of salesmen who solicit retailers and wholesalers. Much of the selling is done at semiannual furniture shows held at Grand Rapids; Chicago; Jamestown, New York; and one or two other points. Some of his large competitors do a limited amount of advertising for special design or types of furniture, but this particular manufacturer advertises only in trade magazines. At the furniture shows, samples are displayed and salesmen and selling executives are in attendance to serve prospective buyers.

7) In the textile field the selling work is done primarily through personal contact by selling representatives. Many tex-

tile fabric producers transfer the selling to a so-called "selling house," which in turn uses salesmen to sell to wholesalers, garment makers, or larger retail stores handling piece goods. Garment makers sometimes sell through their own representatives, sometimes through larger retailers. They also provide for displays at buying centers. Advertising is done in trade publications, only seldom in consumer magazines.

8) In the industrial field such larger equipment as offset presses for producing newspapers, magazines, etc., are sold directly to printers by salesmen, many of whom are expert in printing and lithography as well as in the administrative problems of printers. One company not only operates a sales force but does trade-paper advertising, distributes calendars, and exhibits at graphic arts shows. Nevertheless, executives find it necessary to maintain a separate sales force to sell the chemicals required for offset presses and to use in their distribution a series of wholesalers, who in turn sell to printers.

9) A manufacturer of small fasteners, nuts and bolts, special lock nuts, and other small components of machines, particularly automobiles and airplanes, has a sales force which sells directly to larger users. But through them it sells also to a specialized group of fastener jobbers, who in turn send salesmen to smaller users. This company arranges for displays at trade shows, advertising in trade magazines, sampling, and the provision of technical data.

10) A company makes newer jet engines and finds that its principal market is airplane companies and the government. To get buying action, it must therefore provide for highly trained and experienced representatives in order to deal both with government buying officers and with the appropriate engineering and business executives of the airplane companies.

11) A petroleum company selling gasoline and lubricating oil through its own service stations and through independent stations, and selling specialized lubricating oils to industry, combines in its program many elements already mentioned in previous examples. The enterprise employs representatives who deal with the independent wholesale dealers; likewise, other selling representatives who solicit and work with the various sta-

tions to secure more effective sales performance. A specialized sales force calls upon industry to help with particular lubricating problems and to secure greater sales volume, while the company advertises in all principal types of media: radio, TV, magazines, and newspapers, as well as in the trade press for industrial products.

SELLING IN THE WHOLESALING FIELD

Wholesaling, with more than one-quarter of a million enterprises and over $235 billion annual sales, is a major economic and business activity in the United States.[9] In building the wholesale sales program, all the elements used by manufacturers and retailers are available to wholesalers, although all are obviously not available to each wholesaler. Since most wholesalers cover either local or regional areas, some elements of elaborate sales programs, such as national magazines and national network programs, are not available or appropriate. Yet even here, national advertising has been used by a few wholesalers.

A study of the common types of sales programs of wholesalers discloses the utilization of major selling methods already mentioned. Personal selling predominates, but advertising plays an important part in developing buying action. To illustrate:

1) A drug wholesaler in a Middle Atlantic city operates a typical selling program for a medium-sized concern. He employs some 14 general salesmen, each calling upon from 60 to 125 accounts. The men take orders, but routine order taking is handled largely by a highly trained inside telephone sales force of ten women. The salesman is expected to devote time to merchandising work with his accounts and to help them in problems of display and stocking of merchandise. Much of the company's selling effort is devoted to keeping these salesmen well informed on company programs and developments in the trade; but in addition the company sends mail circulars to retailers

---

[9] The wholesaling figures include manufacturers' sales branches and petroleum bulk stations; consequently, some of the statements made about manufacturers' selling practices apply to this group. Cf. U.S. Department of Commerce, Bureau of the Census, *1954 Census of Business, Wholesale Trade,* Series PW–1–1 (Washington, D.C.: U.S. Government Printing Office, 1956).

with announcements of special offers, new products, and other information. A limited amount of advertising in publications to which drug retailers subscribe is employed.

2) A paper wholesaler sells a line of cordage, paper, and paper products including boxes, gummed and wrapping paper, and cups and plates, primarily by means of twenty-five salesmen who solicit manufacturing enterprises and retail stores, together with hospitals, schools, offices, and other institutional buyers who comprise a large part of the market. Although a limited amount of trade-paper advertising and considerable direct-mail work is carried on, the company depends for its sales effort almost entirely upon its carefully selected, well-trained group of men.

3) An electrical wholesaler acts as a selected distributor for several leading manufacturers of electrical equipment in a single state. The company does not handle consumer appliances but specializes in products for sale to industrial concerns, public utilities, and large electrical contractors. Sales are made primarily through a force of nine men and include about 3,000 different items. The company secures the greater portion of its business through personal contact with dealers and customers. Advertising effort is of very minor importance, being confined primarily to direct-mail pieces, particularly a monthly mailing of blotters. Announcement of new products is made by sending descriptions to a mailing list of selected names. Since the job of selling equipment is one requiring technical knowledge, men with engineering degrees or background are preferred as salesmen.

4) An industrial distributor handling over 30,000 items, including a few specialized and franchised lines, travels a force of thirty men, who call upon manufacturing enterprises in the area. Beyond the catalogue, which is in part an assembly of sheets provided by the suppliers and in part its own catalogue of items offered, the company depends little upon advertising, using only a very limited amount by mail direct to prospects. Close personal contact and frequent calls of the salesmen upon factory superintendents, purchasing officers, and owners in smaller companies, and the service offered in terms of available

stock and delivery, are the factors that account for the company's volume of sales.

5) The other extreme is illustrated by a large drug organization which controls over sixty wholesale houses operating in most states of the union. The drug line includes some 17,000 items, of which some are purchased from the manufacturer for resale and some are manufactured in its own plants. The latter are advertised and promoted nationally. In such a situation one would expect, therefore, that all the methods and means of aggressive wholesale promotion would be utilized. National magazine advertising, radio, trade-paper advertising, direct mail, displays, dealer helps, samples—all are used, together with the efforts of general and specialty salesmen. Approximately 1,000 men sell the company's products to the retail trade.

6) A middle western wholesale dry-goods distributor, who formerly specialized in piece goods, operates now not only as a wholesaler but as a manufacturer and retailer as well. It controls thirty-five manufacturing and fabricating plants, five of which are wholly owned. It administers a dozen partially owned retail stores for experimental purposes. It sells dry goods, luggage, clothing, and notions under about 200 different trademarks. Some 300 men do most of the selling work. The company had not advertised nationally until recently, when it began promoting certain of its own manufactured and branded products in women's magazines. An unusual feature of its program is the development and offer of an extensive merchandising and management service to retail merchants, who regard this wholesaler as a major source of goods for resale. This includes advice as to layout, fixtures, and display.

7) A hardware wholesaler has a somewhat similar program adapted to its own special situations, again emphasizing both detailed and general help and advice to retailers. It uses some 250 salesmen to make contact with retailers and to become buying advisors as a means of securing eventually sound action.

8) Lastly, one may mention the specialty wholesaler who distributes consumer durables, typical of a large group of wholesalers distributing lines of radios, washing machines, ironers, refrigerators, home freezers, gas and electric ranges, etc. In

each line carried, the wholesale distributor customarily represents only one manufacturer. Sales are made to 900 dealers scattered throughout the area through a sales force consisting in part of specialty salesmen devoting attention to one line, and in part of salesmen who sell several lines to dealers. Each man works closely with the dealer to sell the products, to co-operate with national advertising of the manufacturers, and to utilize all the other elements of the manufacturer's selling program. To these he adds such help as he can in the effort to teach and induce the retailer to sell more goods.

These sales programs vary widely in their emphasis upon personal selling, advertising, and other features; but the examples are by no means inclusive of all types. They do represent, however, the major types of selling programs that characterize the wholesale enterprises in the United States.

SELLING IN RETAIL ENTERPRISES

Each of 1,748,000 retail stores in the country does something to induce buying action. Some of what they do is good and effective; much is of indifferent quality and effectiveness. Some is bad, incompetent, and inefficient, but no retailer under normal conditions can escape taking some action designed to persuade buyers to buy. That action may range from providing attractive and convenient displays of goods and highly trained and able forces of salesmen who give advice, down to offering no more than the services of a part-time worker or a proprietor dealing indifferently with customers who come into his store. In advertising, retail practice ranges from extensive national coverage to the occasional advertisement of the small-town retailer or the dodgers scattered over town by the schoolboy working after hours. In displays the range is equally wide, from the disorder of the cluttered general stores in rural areas to the carefully designed mass displays of supermarkets, demonstrators in department stores, and the artful displays in windows and interiors of specialty and department stores in the cities. All of them suggest thought and effort of retailers to induce people to buy. The effort represents one of the major items of expense in retail distribution. For department stores, sales promotion (including expenses for advertising and other selling effort exclusive of direct and general selling effort) amounted in 1955 to about 4 per cent of sales, ranging according to size of store from an average of 3.7 per cent in smaller sizes to 4.45 per cent in larger. The promotion costs of specialty stores ranged from 4.25 per cent to 5.15 per cent. Direct and general selling costs were over 9 per cent, the range being from 8.45 per cent to 9.90 per cent for the largest stores. Specialty stores also fell within this range.[10] Thus the total selling expense of these classes of retailers might be as low as 12.45 per cent or as high as 13.55 per cent but was likely to be in the 13 + per cent range. Specialty stores had selling and sales promotion expenses about ½ per cent higher. These figures are a reflection of the trend pointed out by McNair and Carson that salespeople constitute an increasing percentage of total employees of retail department and specialty stores.[11]

Even conservative interpretation of the available data gives basis for the assertion that selling by retailers costs the public 10 per cent or more of consumer purchases. In what the retailer pays for goods is included the additional expense of paying wholesalers, manufacturers, and possibly others for their selling efforts.

The specific steps which retailers take in order to sell vary because of the opinions of individuals involved, type and size of retailer, product, location, and size of operation. However, patterns develop out of experience and the force of competition, so that most retailers use very similar selling programs. Personal selling plays the largest part in most of these programs, but comparable advertising media and displays, plans, and devices appear in the different classifications of retail outlets.

The retailer, to continue to exist, must sell at a profit; but he may, and often does, sell without profit at particular periods. If he does not manage well, he may sell but make no profit because costs are too high. Nevertheless, it is absolutely clear that unless he does sell, he cannot make a profit and cannot survive. The failure rate of small retailers is very high. Apparent exceptions to the rule that retailers must make an effort to sell may appear where small retail stores constitute a way of life

---

[10] McNair and Carson, *op. cit.*

[11] *Ibid.*, p. 41.

for those persons who hope to enjoy some independence beyond that available to those who work for wages or salaries. A meager living may be secured until the small capital with which the business was started may be frittered away. Even in very small stores, some effort to be agreeable and to induce repeat purchases may make the difference between success and failure.

The bulk of our retail sales are made by medium-sized and larger independent stores, by chain and department stores, by mail-order houses, and outlets such as gas stations, etc. Each of these must sell more or less aggressively in order to maintain or improve its position in the competitive field. In all areas the retailer must compete for the buyers' favor. How the retailer does this is illustrated by the programs of the major types of retail institutions that most of us have had a chance to observe.

The small independent grocer may depend entirely upon personal selling and display. He may go further to use local newspapers and distribute dodgers. His window displays and other display material may in part be financed by manufacturers who seek to push their own product.

The chain store in the neighborhood with which he competes may use display more aggressively and artfully; but again, the chain has in the past depended largely upon personal selling. Both chains and independents may seek to adopt self-service plans in which access by consumers to goods and planned displays is emphasized and personal selling services are reduced to a minimum. The preference of consumers and the high cost of personal services, together with the possibility of lowered price to consumers, have combined to make this choice of selling programs the currently preferred one. But both chains and independents use advertising extensively, together with many other devices to bring potential buyers into the store, relying upon display, once customers are in the store, to develop buying action. They also try to make shopping convenient and pleasant so as to get buyers to repeat their purchases and become steady customers. Provision of such conveniences frequently imposes the requirement of a substantial volume of sales in order to bring costs within tolerable limits. It has been said that a modern supermarket needs sales of at least $1,000 a day to afford the services consumers desire. When we remember that not so many years ago, 27 per cent of our retail grocers had sales amounting to less than $5,000 in a whole year, we have some indication of the vast changes which have been taking place in the retail grocery field.

Department stores, in order to sell, choose preferred shopping locations for convenience of buyers, employ large sales forces and extensive advertising. They go further to provide services of many types in addition to the stocks of goods they believe will be acceptable to the consumers of the community.

Mail-order houses, at least the principal ones, now conduct two or more different types of operations, one of which resembles the department store operation at several different size levels and the other is like the original mail-order business, in which selling action is secured through the distribution of catalogues that are expensive but carefully planned, with selling text and complete descriptions of products. The long and intensive study devoted to the preparation and planning of catalogues furnishes an excellent illustration of the definiteness of the conclusions upon selling practice that can be arrived at where observation covers a sufficiently large number of instances. As an example, it is asserted that close approximation of a week's receipts can be secured by weighing the mail received on Monday morning, since a careful study of the relationship between weight and week's receipts has shown a fairly constant ratio. Likewise, the selling values of particular space and particular locations in the catalogue have been studied and have permitted very definite conclusions. However, such conclusions are not final by any means, and from time to time consumer freedom of choice shows up in particularly large and unexpected orders for one commodity and failure to buy others.

SELLING BY AGRICULTURAL AND OTHER ENTERPRISES

Either directly or through an association or co-operative, the farmer-producer also encounters the necessity of selling. If he belongs to a co-operative such as the California Fruit Growers

Association, Cape Cod Cranberry Association, or any one of thousands of others, the selling will be conducted more or less aggressively by the marketing organization. When organizations may be represented at central points, large-scale advertising may be carried on in order to persuade people to buy more of the particular product. Witness the campaigns of the California Fruit Growers, Land o' Lakes Dairy Co-operative, and others. Selling is carried on by representatives at principal market centers. Experiments in the use of vending machines are being made.

The individual farmer may deliver his grain or cotton to a terminal market, taking what is offered for it, but on the other hand, the fruit or vegetable grower may try to sell to retailers or even set up roadside stands to sell to passing consumers. He may occasionally process and sell his product in a more acceptable form. Especially with staple products, little or no initiative has to be taken by the farmer, for there is a ready buyer at some price or a subsidy buyer under government provision. In some cases, buyers will even come to the farm to harvest the crop on an income basis. In this situation, the farmer is very much like the manufacturer who decides that he does not want to engage in selling and shifts the entire burden to some middleman who will, for a price, sometimes a large one, assume the responsibility.

In one way or another service enterprises, such as banks, may and often do provide for persuading people to buy their services. A bank vice-president may have the responsibility of persuading individuals to become clients. He may use advertising to accomplish the task of getting new deposits or new borrowers of the funds the bank has available for loans.

Many other examples might be cited, but they all confirm the conclusion that commercial enterprises, large and small, in the vast majority of situations, must and do take steps to persuade people to buy. If successful, the firm may flourish; if unsuccessful, the existence of the firm is endangered. Obviously, the failure of business firms in buyers' markets is evidence that adequate buying action in selling presents problems that never can be easily solved and that some men cannot and do not solve at all.

HOW MUCH SELLING EFFORT IS REALLY NEEDED

Much criticism of advertising and selling in business emphasizes the idea that advertising and selling effort is expensive and that the amounts spent for securing buying action on the whole are not warranted. Whether the amount of selling effort or expenditure is excessive from a social and economic standpoint will be examined later. From the standpoint of the seller, no more effort is employed than he thinks is desirable to make immediate sales and facilitate future sales. To spend more than necessary to accomplish his purpose would be a foolish subtraction from his profit. To spend less than needed may be equally wasteful, although not so easily detected.

But the limitations of the businessman's knowledge as to how much selling work will be required to accomplish a given result, makes it likely that with the best of intentions some waste will develop. One cannot know precisely what will result from a given combination of selling efforts, because changes in product, demand characteristics, social, economic, and political climates, and many other factors may affect the final outcome in an unpredictable manner. The businessman tries to allow for these, but occasional failure is to be expected. Failure to get results may end in unemployment and in a series of happenings that can be argued as being less desirable than possible waste in using more selling effort than finally proves to be necessary for the planned accomplishment.

However, it cannot be argued that the forms of selling efforts with which businessmen attempt to secure buying action are necessarily the most efficient. The lack of detailed knowledge, which grows out of the fact that we are dealing with the various aspects of human behavior that are only vaguely understood, makes some waste inevitable—wastes that may be losses to the employer, to the public, and to the salesman himself. Employers estimate that it may cost from a few hundred to thousands of dollars to train a new salesman. Careful observers have found that salesmen in general, in part for reasons not under their control, utilize their actual selling ability for only a limited portion of the working day. Personal deficiencies may account for this in part; but even where incentives are high, as in commission plans of compensation, it is evident that there is inefficient utilization of salesmen's time. The public loses through inefficient salesmanship by having to pay more than necessary for goods. It may be consoling but not constructive to point out that in any form of human leadership, hindsight reveals wastes that retard progress toward desirable goals.

The great spread between cost to the producer and the consumer's buying price is due in no small measure to the high cost of selling. Yet current efforts to reduce this high cost only emphasize the general conclusion that lack of detailed knowledge of human behavior limits the extent to which such efforts can be effective. The fact that selling costs and resulting volume may, and often do, lower manufacturing and production costs more than proportionally is one aspect of the justification of selling effort in business. But the need for reducing selling costs is obscured in sellers' markets. Only in free and unrestricted competition can we obtain needed healthy pressure to find better ways to sell effectively.

Chapter III

SELLING AND CONSUMER DEMAND

⌐⌐⌐

SELLING IS essential in a free-enterprise economy because human beings act the way they do. In our highly organized democratic society, the concerted action of many persons is needed if social progress is to be achieved. Little can be done without leadership to instill, maintain, and often intensify the desire for improvement so as to result in progress, whether in politics, religion, or economics.

The central energizing force in the American economy is consumer demand. It is not a vague general desire for a high standard of living nor is it a desire for money or riches or power. It is a specific dynamic force, a moving desire for improvement as embodied in specific material goods and services. It is a strong desire for a wide range of material and immaterial satisfactions—desire that acquires compelling force because its realization is within the limits of possibility. Persons wishing the satisfactions that can be secured from products or services can do something directly or indirectly toward their attainment. This is something different from the "effective demand" of the economists, which has been defined as demand plus purchasing power. The demand we are discussing is effective demand "plus"; plus knowledge that no serious social or political obstacles will prevent enjoyment. It is demand based upon the hopes, optimism, and productive work of consumers.

It is argued elsewhere[1] that the aggregate objective of the selling process in our economy is tantamount to high and rising standards of living for all the people. To achieve this objective through influencing people to buy involves the complex phenomena of consumer behavior, attitudes and behavior of business executives, and the whole functioning of our production and distribution organizations. However, it is clear that the consumer demand that will serve as an energizing economic factor must first of all be strong enough so that some action is taken, either directly toward purchase or toward bringing about the acquisition eventually of means of purchase. The desire must be such that it not only causes persons to work but also to demand an appropriate share of their production as a reward. Again, to achieve the largest amount and widest range of goods and services, consumer demand must be sufficiently uniform to permit most efficient production. The employment of mechanical, electrical, and biological processes where most appropriate in large-scale production is limited in effectiveness unless goods so produced in quantity will be purchased and consumed.

A third essential characteristic of consumer demand and consumer buying actions essential to progress is timeliness, particularly in relation to the survival and success of business enterprise. The timing of that demand must be related not only to the needs of the consumer but also to the needs of those who distribute goods and to the requirements of producing firms for successful and continuing production. Firms cannot survive long without some balance of expenditures with income; if what they produce and offer for sale is not sold within relatively short periods, losses are suffered and even failure may follow.

To the requirements of intensity of consumer demand, uniformity of desire, and timeliness of buying action must be added the desire of consumers for freedom of choice. The consumer in our competitive system has continuously enjoyed considerable freedom of choice. While he may not have been able to buy all that he wants at the moment, he has been free to buy now or save for the future. He has been free to buy or to

---

[1] Cf. Chapter IV.

refrain from buying, both because choices were available and because his income enabled him to buy much beyond mere necessities. The incomes of North Americans have, in a large proportion of cases, furnished a sizable margin above the bare requirements for existence. Statistical records show that the "disposable" or "discretionary" income of the American people has risen steadily until today it is the larger part of total consumer income.[2] Even since 1940, taking into account increased taxes and present costs of necessities—food, clothing, and shelter —discretionary income has increased over fivefold. Under such conditions, freedom of choice becomes meaningful. Under subsistence levels, freedom of choice means little.

Thus the American consumer has been free to buy one product instead of another or to choose one make of refrigerator instead of another. He has been free to choose among brands or types of food, even though the necessity is upon him to buy some food. He may buy one baker's bread instead of another's. Furthermore, as his standards of living have risen, he has found an increase in choice among the various satisfactions his income will give him; and as his real income has increased, he has shown a willingness to purchase new goods and services and to enjoy new satisfactions.

Where consumer freedom of choice prevails, the producers' continuance in business eventually depends on buyers' desires. If a buyer's decision is favorable, he may develop a profitable and prosperous business. If a buyer's desires are unfavorable or if the seller fails to bring his goods to the attention of individual buyers, he will learn to his sorrow that success is not automatic. Thus the nature and characteristics of buyers' demands are of vital concern to every producer and every distributor, just as they are of major concern and interest to economists and other social scientists.

It is in the characteristics of demand and in the requirements for high production and high productivity that we find the

[2] See *Economic Report of the President* (Washington, D.C.: U.S. Government Printing Office), for statistical details.

Also "Sales Outlook, 1956," an address before the New England Sales Management Conference, Boston, January, 1956, by Arno H. Johnson, vice-president, J. Walter Thompson Company, New York.

basic explanation and principal justification of selling effort, and selling expenditures. Contrariwise, it is in the inadequate assumptions as to the nature of consumer demand that we find not only an explanation of the failure on the part of businessmen to understand the psychological basis of selling but also some explanation of the attitudes of the economists and other social scientists.

The force of educational activities in improving standards of living does not invalidate the assertion that selling is necessary. Education influences demand by establishing ideas as to acceptable patterns of consumption and by making people who have lower standards acquainted with higher standards and their merits. Direct courses in consumption, in home economics, in automobile use and care, among consumer goods, and in the use of business machines, engineering, and related fields, all have to be taken into account, even though only a fraction of consumers participate. While courses in cultural and recreational fields affect consumption, the greatest impact of education upon consumption comes from raising the sights of buyers and creating a desire for improvement. It is against the background of environmental and educational influences that selling does its most effective work.

THE STUDY OF CONSUMER DEMAND[3]

The need to understand what the consumer wants or can be induced to want exists at several stages of industrial development; but that need is most pressing in the society which aims to give its members freedom of choice as consumers and high standards of living through the utilization of advanced techniques of large-scale production and distribution. Today a large proportion of the products that form the basis of industrial and commercial enterprise in modern states is produced or distributed by large-scale enterprises. Large-scale production requires prior judgments upon direct consumer demand or upon

---

[3] Much of this material is based on an earlier essay by the author entitled, "The Study of Consumer Demand in Relation to Capitalistic Society," published in *Business and Modern Society*, edited by M. P. McNair and H. T. Lewis (Cambridge: Harvard University Press, 1938).

derived demand based upon ultimate consumption. Large-scale distribution likewise compels manufacture and purchase in advance of express demand. Administrators and executives of both large- and small-scale business enterprise must, therefore, make decisions as to the quantity, type, quality, design, style, and other characteristics of products to be offered for sale or allotted to customers. To translate these decisions into working plans for the enterprise requires knowledge not only of the general characteristics of consumer choice but of a vast amount of detail concerning the goods the consumer wishes to buy. The time periods involved in these decisions will vary from a few days in highly flexible productive processes to a score of years or more. Certain of these decisions must be made at the time the enterprise is started. The more highly specialized the enterprise and its equipment, the more binding its initial decisions. For instance, the building of a plant to make rayon yarn implies a judgment as to demand conditions with respect to rayon for many years. After the enterprise is started, it is confronted more or less continuously by other problems relating to consumer demand. The rayon spinning mill will have to follow demands for color, finish, and weight. The weaving mill will constantly be changing operations and yarns to be in accord with consumer preferences. The manufacturer of old-type electric toasters will try to meet the growing preference for automatic devices. The manufacturer of simpler electric generators will try to produce more efficient turbo-generators to meet the desire of manufacturers of utilities for lower-cost power and likewise to meet more remotely the demand of household consumers for lower-cost current. The manufacturer of automatic machine tools or electronic control apparatus has to make decisions concerning the development of new high-capacity tools and automation on the ultimate basis of consumer needs for the products of such machines. In all of these cases, judgment must be made with reference to the limitations imposed by initial decisions and by many other factors. No enterprise escapes entirely the necessity of having to make decisions relating directly or indirectly to what and how much a consumer will choose to purchase and consume.

The direct contact between producer and consumer that characterized the handicraft system of production and that presumably enabled the craftsmen to make exactly what the consumer wanted had been replaced to a considerable extent, even before the industrial revolution which ushered in the factory system. The growth of the merchant entrepreneurs and the putting-out system brought about a new situation in which the contact of the producer was an indirect one through merchants who bought materials, brought them to the craftsmen, and took the finished products to markets and to buyers with which the craftsmen were more or less unacquainted.

The great movement toward separation of producer and consumer came, however, from the growth of the factory system and the development of production entirely foreign to experience either of the handicraft period or of the transitional period that followed. The industrial producer began to turn out goods for a market of which he knew little or nothing. Necessarily, he began and continued to produce goods of the same general types as had been produced by craftsmen in earlier periods, modified by the requirements of factory method and occasionally by information relayed from the market to the manufacturer. He produced at costs so much lower that vast new strata of the market were tapped for goods that previously had been rare luxuries. At the time when the use and application of machinery was new and great social changes were taking place, it is not surprising that the tendency appeared to shift practically the entire burden of distributing the products of the factory system to middlemen. Necessarily, the chain of intermediaries between producer and consumer in certain industries lengthened and the difficulty of getting firsthand information as to consumer demand was enhanced.

The changes in marketing structure and function during the nineteenth and twentieth centuries have not altered the essential fact that producers and consumers are separated in an industrial structure composed to a considerable degree of large-scale enterprises that cater to large numbers of more or less geographically dispersed buyers. The development of general and specialized wholesale institutions, the introduction of various types of intermediaries between manufacturer and whole-

saler, the rise of newer types of wholesaling and retailing institutions, the continued expansion of large-scale industries, and the
development of large-scale distribution organizations have added
to the efficiency of the performance of many necessary functions but have not greatly simplified the problems of consumer
demand. That increased speed of communication and distribution and the tendency to decrease the number of middlemen
by integrating marketing institutions in large-scale enterprises
have not solved the problem is apparent after brief reflection;
for the consumer demand for goods and service has likewise
kept pace with these developments.

To those who hold to the theory that discovery and invention come in response to need, the limits of our present knowledge of consumer demand, appraised from the standpoint of
its usefulness as a guide for decisions of economic and business
administrators, would lead to the conclusion either that the
problem was so complex and so far-reaching that sufficient time
had not yet elapsed to have provided the discoveries required
for a satisfactory working basis or that the need for such
knowledge had not been felt so strongly as to bring forth the
effort to find out. Both explanations appear to have at least
partial validity. The complexity of consumer demand is in part
the complexity of human nature. The slow progress of psychological science in the study of human behavior and in the
development of bases for the prediction of that behavior is
evidence of the size and difficulty of the problem.

On the other hand, the urge on the part of business to
supply the informational connection between producer and consumer has, for a variety of reasons, not been so strong as to
bring insistent and concerted efforts to solve the problem
through the past century and a half. In the first place, broadly
speaking, a sellers' market existed during the period preceding
World War I; until a relatively recent period, in fact, the
emphasis of businessmen was placed upon problems of production to a considerably greater extent than upon problems of
marketing and distributing. The relative recency of marketing
study as compared to the rise of instruction in subjects pertain-
ing to production may be cited as one bit of evidence.

The consumer has been compelled to accept goods offered

in the market place because he needed and wanted goods, and because the goods produced and offered for sale constituted tolerable compromises between the ideal but unprocurable goods and those products which were more or less unsatisfactory or more expensive. The refusal of consumers to buy, an effective weapon in enforcing demands, was limited to the most serious mistakes of producers or middlemen and to exceptional rather than ordinary conditions.

The need of intensive prosecution of basic studies of consumer demand likewise appeared less urgent in the earlier period because of the slower rate of change in consumer demand up to the twentieth century. Past experience was therefore somewhat more reliable as an indication of what consumers would buy than later was the case. Many factors in the last fifty years have brought about an increase in the rapidity of change— more rapid speed of demand, more rapid change in the wants of buyers, more frequent change of styles and designs. The spread of educational facilities, the decline of immigration, and other forces all are to be considered in explaining the greater rapidity. In a former day, when style might be crystallized into a native costume, the problem of the fabric producer was simple; but when styles last only a few weeks or a few months, when the demand for a commodity may suddenly flare up and almost as suddenly subside, the manager's problem with regard to demand cannot be solved by any simple application of past experience.

A third factor in delaying the study of consumer demand was the relatively low standard of living prevailing in many of the more important industrial countries up to recent times. Consumer freedom of choice assumes vastly greater importance and is much more freely exercised to express approval or disapproval of products offered for sale when the standard of living is high. Persons whose income includes a more or less sizable margin beyond the means required to purchase necessities are able to exercise pressure in purchasing or refraining from purchase. It is only in comparatively recent times that the pressure exercised by the consumer upon the producer to make the latter ascertain more closely what to make or sell has assumed major proportions. But that there has been a rise in the standard of living and in margins which permit consumer choices to be made admits of no reasonable doubt.[4] A society predicated upon free private enterprise and upon consumer freedom of choice and desirous of achieving qualitative and quantitative adjustment of production to consumption through the interplay of demand and supply factors in the price system must not only avail itself of technical advances in production and distribution but must reduce the waste inherent in any system in which faulty and incomplete knowledge of basic consumer demand factors is widespread. The determination of consumer demand through the price system is largely a process of trial and error in which, for the most part, businessmen, producers, and intermediate holders of products have been unable to dissociate and to study individually the numerous factors involved in the success or failure of products offered to the market. The consumer's purchase of products is likewise bound up with the conditions of the offer and with environmental and other factors relating to the consumer himself, in total so numerous that the balance against the offered product at one time may be turned in its favor at another. It is clear, therefore, that improvement in the effectiveness of the service of business to the consumer is vitally dependent upon filling, at least partially, the informational gap that has existed between producer and consumer. For if the business executive who wants to discharge his social obligations of producing or distributing the most socially desirable commodities cannot find out in advance what commodities or how much of them to produce and sell, much criticism of the failure of business to produce what the consumer wants is beside the point.

The study of consumer demand for the purpose of furnishing direction to American business is becoming ever more pressing in the United States and has brought increased explicit and implicit emphasis upon consumer study. Studies of consumer motivation, surveys and analyses of markets, the widespread redesigning and market testing of products, the improve-

---

[3] See Chapter IV.

ments in methods of analyzing past experience, all constitute efforts to learn more about consumer wants and needs and about ways and means of influencing them effectively.[5] It is a hopeful sign that both social scientists and businessmen have more recently perceived the importance of learning more about consumer demand and have supported and undertaken studies to advance knowledge of consumer motivation and consumer behavior. Numerous studies have been made by university research centers and consulting organizations and more are in process. They serve to disclose the immensity of the task; but many are proving to be sufficiently explicit and concrete to reduce the probabilities of error in demand appraisal. Studies by Dr. George Katona and Dr. Rensis Likert of the University of Michigan deal directly with phases of consumer behavior. Other studies by Dr. Burleigh Gardner, executive director of Social Research, Inc., and his associates have more or less direct bearing on the subject. The books and articles of Kurt Lewin, Dorwin Cartwright, and others, present challenges to those who hope to bring social research to bear concretely and specifically upon problems involving consumer demand.

WHAT BUSINESSMEN KNOW ABOUT CONSUMER DEMAND

Mainly through experience, and to a growing extent through research and controlled experiment, businessmen have arrived

---

[5] Such studies as those of George Katona, Program Director of the Survey Research Center, University of Michigan; and the essays and studies in the volumes on *Consumer Behavior,* edited by Lincoln H. Clark and sponsored by Consumer Behavior, Inc.

See, for instance, *Consumer Behavior,* Vol. II (New York: New York University Press, 1955) and Katona, *Psychological Analysis of Economic Behavior,* Part II, "Consumer Behavior" (New York: McGraw-Hill Book Co., 1951).

In most of the essays in the former volume, selling and advertising appear to be taken for granted. In the essay by Professor Robert Ferber entitled "Factors Influencing Durable Consumer Goods Purchases," (p. 75), the extensive advertising and selling programs of durable goods manufacturers are not discussed as a factor. Implicitly, therefore, they are accepted as a constant factor, a treatment which raises some question. But see in *Consumer Behavior,* Lincoln H. Clark, editor, "A Study of Purchase," by G. Katona and E. Mueller, pp. 30–87 (New York: New York University Press, 1954); also J. S. Dusenberry, *Income, Saving, and the Theory of Consumer Behavior* (Cambridge: Harvard University Press, 1949).

at certain generalizations concerning consumer demand that appear to be sound. The necessity of making detailed and specific decisions has also led to the utterance of unsound and fallacious statements as well as to mistakes and errors of judgment. These are to be expected in view of the limitations of our knowledge. Economists have also indulged in broad generalizations without adequate proof or sufficient observation.

Among the propositions accepted by businessmen, a number are pertinent to our inquiry into the demand basis of selling. They agree, for instance, that consumers tend to develop buying habits so that to some extent one may predict future consumer buying action from observation of past behavior.[6] Consumers buy certain types of products to fulfill needs and wants and to give them desired satisfactions. If this satisfaction is secured in sufficient measure from consumable products, the consumer is disposed to repeat the purchase. If the product is identified by brand or otherwise, the repeat purchase tends to be directed toward the product so identified. Likewise, consumers are inclined to repeat purchases from those vendors who furnish satisfactory products and services. Thus consumers tend to develop buying habits as to product, brand, and vendor.

The strength and persistence of these buying habits varies from indifference or mere recognition to preference, and from preference to insistence upon repetition. At one end the consumer insists on buying a particular product from a specific vendor. At the other extreme, the consumer is indifferent to product type so long as he secures the satisfaction desired, possibly even to the type of satisfaction secured among several offered. He may also be indifferent to the maker or vendor or to the identification of the product. Between these two extremes exist all shades of preference and all degrees of strength of habit. Few products command the insistent demand of consumers. Few sellers in competition command the insistence of any large proportion of their customer lists. One corollary of the fact that most products offered to the consumer are not "must" products is that preferences may be modified,

---

[6] Various essays in *Consumer Behavior, op. cit.*, describe studies which support this proposition.

shifted, created, by various influences but particularly by selling leadership and by the influence of personal selling, advertising, demonstration, and display.

Businessmen and other students of consumer demand for specific goods and services have frequently employed such terms as necessities, comforts, and luxuries. It is obvious that the strength of demand for specific goods which enter into a standard of living will vary widely. The classification of goods into necessities, comforts, and luxuries is indicative rather than precise and represents only approximate patterns of consumer behavior. It is obvious that the demand for some so-called necessities compels actions to produce purchases, or work to enable purchases to be made, and that it leads at times even to appropriation and theft to maintain life. But the definition of necessities has frequently been so broadened that many goods not necessary to maintain physical life are considered necessary to maintain a social status to which persons cling tenaciously. Thus many products may be classed as necessities because people will sacrifice much income and convenience in order to secure them.

The classification of comforts refers initially to physical comfort and convenience rather than biological necessity; but likewise here there is often a high degree of social conformity. The line between comforts and luxuries also becomes quite confused. At one standard of living, those products classed as luxuries may be considered merely necessities at a higher stage. But wherever the line is to be drawn, there are differences in buying behavior and differences in the influence to be exerted to cause people to take the buying action necessary to improve standards of living.

The businessman of today recognizes, furthermore, that the consumer can, and does, change his habits and his preferences. He changes his preferences for products or vendors. He may seek new satisfactions by buying new products. He may decide not to buy now but rather to save funds for future transactions or to give voluntarily to some charity. Substitutions may take place because both in his environment and personality, the buyer undergoes change from day to day and from year to year. Furthermore, there are many external influences involving buying action: for instance, education, example, and selling leadership, which will be reflected in the changes in the consumer's buying habits and the preferences for products or vendors.

A seller soon learns that the consumer does not know today precisely what he will want next week or next year or in the more distant future. He may have more or less precise ideas on a few things. He may know that he will want foodstuffs or clothes of certain types very shortly. He can be fairly definite on such things; but for other products he has only a desire for the satisfaction without any precise knowledge or opinion as to how or what products will satisfy that desire. For still other satisfactions, he has only a latent desire that must be aroused before he will undertake buying action or preparation for buying action.

The consumer generally expects to make choices, both among the types of satisfactions he will try to secure from buying action and among the offered goods or services necessary to supply these satisfactions. But he expects to make these choices at the time that he will take buying action, just as he expects then to make choices as to the sources of supply. The consumer expects to have offered to him at convenient locations types of garments or of cloth or television sets or frozen foods, and a thousand other items from which he may make choice whenever he feels that he wants to buy. He does not expect generally to make these choices in advance, certainly not at the time when production planning and manufacture of these goods begin. The consumer of today does not and will not commit himself to buy what has to be started into production at once in order to be ready for delivery a year or two years from now. He does not want to commit himself for the purchase of a 1960-model automobile of particular design because he does not know what he will want in 1960. Fortunately, in the present organization of our economy he does not have to do so, because the manufacturer himself takes the risk of preparing to serve him. He can afford to do so only because he can utilize selling leadership and selling effort to reduce this risk to tolerable proportions. As discussed elsewhere, one of the prime reasons for the inadequacy of buyer initiative on the part of consumers as a basic principle of organization of our economy and its commerce and industry is precisely this inability, or at least reluctance, to plan ahead and to make commitments for purchase in order to get production processes started and continued.

Thoughtful enterprisers realize that it would be humanly impossible to produce large quantities of goods which would completely satisfy the individual tastes of consumers. If the consumer does not know accurately what he wants so as to be able to order from producers in advance of production, the producer himself will have to do the best he can to anticipate wants. The consumer, in the exercise of his freedom of choice, will select from types of products available those which will best serve his wants and satisfy his needs. But it is conceivable that available products will not satisfy the desires of many consumers who have developed their own definite ideas of what products should be. Perhaps fortunately, consumer wants are generally not so definite but that buying action can be directed by selling effort to available types of products.

The necessity of making compromises between what would be ideally suited to each particular consumer's needs and wants, and what is available, is inescapable in view of the fact that large-scale and economical production requires that many products with precisely the same characteristics be turned out and sold. Thus the manufacturer incorporates those features which he thinks will be most acceptable although they may be ideal to only a few. Moreover, even when cost or price limitations are not involved, the consumer may desire conflicting qualities. He may want a very lightweight shoe and at the same time one that possesses great durability; but light weight and durability may be impossible to combine at a particular stage of technical development. Durability may have to be secured at the expense of greater weight, and light weight may be achieved at the expense of durability. And so with many other products.

The most commonly recognized compromise the consumer

is compelled to make is that between satisfactions to be secured by particular buying actions and the alternative uses of income, either for other products of the same type or for other satisfactions. Desires and tastes for products and services are not subjected to the same influences as income and do not necessarily move in the same degree upward or downward. It sometimes appears that tastes and desires for goods and services tend to increase more rapidly than income. However, when wants are sufficiently compelling, action will be taken to secure the income that will enable the purchaser to buy what previously he could not afford. For the people as a whole, there is clear evidence that both by pressure to get a larger share of what is produced and pressure to produce more, more is produced and more is earned with which to make purchases.

The consumer cannot, and frequently knows that he cannot, appraise the satisfactions to be obtained by the acquisition of many goods and services at the time he takes buying action. He must assume the risk that the goods and services he buys may not give him the expected satisfactions. There is some risk that sellers may have misled him knowingly or unknowingly, or that his desires may have changed before or during consumption of the goods purchased. The buyer, depending upon the seller and his representations, can have somewhat greater confidence because the seller generally has to depend upon repeat purchase actions by the same customers to make a profit. He is therefore disinclined by his own selfish interest to mislead his customer.

Finally, the basic and central characteristic of consumer demand that businessmen must recognize is this: Consumer desires for the goods and services that enter into a high material standard of living are most important economically in our free-enterprise economy when they are of such compelling strength that buying action follows or steps are taken to secure the purchasing power with which to buy. Consumer demand of sufficient intensity does not develop automatically except under compulsion of necessity to secure bare essentials for living—unless consumers are influenced to want the additional products and services required for higher levels. Habit, education, example, and social pressures all influence consumption and purchase, sometimes to the point of compelling action. It is to be noticed that habit may have been started and maintained by selling; education for consumption is influenced by selling; the purchases of community leaders and their example may be due to selling; and in a rapidly changing, dynamic society, social pressures may be influenced by selling. Consequently, it may well be argued that selling leadership has been a principal means of making consumer demand an effective force in our economy.

While the leadership necessary for higher standards could conceivably come from the people who are buyers or from government, a detailed analysis of the alternatives shows that the logical and economical source is the seller and selling initiative. From a social point of view, this is the preferred source of necessary leadership toward higher standards of living. Selling leadership develops the motivating force to make people want high standards of living so that they produce them. It causes them to release those energies and initiative which increase production, improve productivity, and encourage creative innovation.

THE LIMITS OF CONSUMER DEMAND FOR HIGH STANDARDS OF LIVING

The need for selling leadership receives support from the historical record. Selling as we know it today is a recent development; much of modern selling is a development of the twentieth century—and the history of aggressive selling can practically disregard the period before 1850. We know that seller initiative except to a limited extent in fairs, exhibitions, local markets, and artisans' shops played a very small part up to the Industrial Revolution. We know that as late as the seventeenth century strict rules were in force in many artisans' guilds forbidding any sort of seller initiative. Production was largely for household use; production for market use was extremely limited, and most selling was the house-to-house variety.[7]

---

[7] Cf. H. R. Tosdal, *Principles of Personal Selling* (Chicago: A. W. Shaw Co., 1925), pp. 15–26 and references cited therein.

Demand was also very small. If one examines the not-too-plentiful evidence as to living standards, he finds that for most of the recorded history, relatively high-level standards have been the privilege of the few, not the many. The aristocracy and ruling classes, a few landowners, the wealthy merchants, have been those who enjoyed relatively high levels of living. For most of recorded history and most of the countries of the world today, the standards of living of the bulk of the population were low and for a large number barely above the subsistence level.[8] Serious students of living standards declare that for thousands of years there has apparently been little change in the standards of the bulk of the population and that those standards hover around the subsistence level, sometimes above, sometimes below.

Even for the top few, the students of economic history can find little evidence of basic progress in living standards for centuries at a time. An occasional genius craftsman produced furniture, silver, jewelry of exquisite design; but in the majority of cases these were produced for the wealthy patrons. For most aspects of living, even the comforts and luxuries of the wealthy could not yield for them a standard of living which would match that of our average workman in the United States today. Professors Mitchell and Leys of Cambridge University in England, in an extraordinary historical study of living standards in England, have given evidence that over the period of many centuries the changes in standards of living, even for the upper classes, were relatively small.[9]

This slow development of living standards is, of course, the resultant of many different factors. One of these is the tendency where social class distinctions are marked to develop typical patterns of consumption. Members of a social group exert pressure upon new members to conform, not to go below the consumer's standard, not to go above it. For instance, in certain

---

[8] The Food and Agriculture Organization of the United Nations has reported that in areas containing more than half the population of the world, people do not get enough food and those who have enough do not always get foods in the proper proportion. See W. S. Woytinsky and E. S. Woytinsky, *World Population and Products* (New York: The Twentieth Century Fund, 1953), p. 303.

[9] R. J. Mitchell and M. D. R. Leys, *A History of the English People* (London: Longmans, Green & Co., 1950).

worker groups in England and France, the purchase and ownership of an automobile is not "approved" by the group. The
recalcitrant may even be socially ostracized as a result. The
rigid stratification of consumption patterns that grew up rather
early tends to perpetuate itself with the help of the ruling
groups of church and state, and even industrial leaders. But
the almost total absence of effort to increase wants has only
been noticed in passing. In fact, such evidence as has come
to hand shows that the ruling classes thus enjoying high standards of living viewed with alarm any evidence that people
wanted more than adequate food and clothing. They were
accused of trying "to ape their betters" and of not knowing
their place in society.

Anthropological studies point in the same direction. It appears
from such studies that levels of living were not only low
but that they have remained low for centuries, even for mil-
lennia. The leadership of priestly cults as well as certain types
of political leadership of totalitarian cast has generally aimed
at maintaining the *status .quo*, not at high and rising levels of
living. Furthermore, it is clear from the studies of contemporary
indigenous peoples in the many parts of the world that present
standards are little higher than those of centuries ago.[10]

The evidence is overwhelming that the standards for the
masses of the people have remained consistently and persistently
low for thousands of years prior to the nineteenth century.
How is this to be explained?

Even the Industrial Revolution of the eighteenth century did
not of itself bring high standards of living. Some few products
made by the factory method found their way into the living
levels of some people, such as cheap cotton cloth and a few
other items. Beyond this, progress was very slow for decades
after the Industrial Revolution started. Demand did not exist
to warrant rapid increase in the quantities of production; the
new industrial enterprises did not seek to expand demand but
generally shifted selling to existing classes of merchants, whose
selling activities were generally of a passive nature.

---

[10] See International Labor Office, *Report on Indigenous Peoples* (Studies
and Reports, New Series, No. 35), Geneva; and reports of the Food and
Agricultural Organization of the League of Nations on nutrition.

The slow progress in the elevation of living standards of the masses of the people in the western European countries and the British Isles must be attributed in part to the absence of a climate favorable to such an advance and in part to the slow rise of business, and particularly selling, leadership, interested in selling more goods to more people. It was not the lack of natural resources and the limitations of resourcefulness in the people themselves, but rather the lack of desire on the part of the people for high levels and the lack of desire of those who directed production that lay at the root of the existing situation. Economists as well as businessmen and workers themselves accepted the crystallized consumption patterns, as contempory literature of the eighteenth and early nineteenth centuries shows. The Malthusian theory could only have been developed at a time when common observation indicated the clear tendency of living standards to continue at a subsistence level.[11]

The lack of desire that characterized all groups up to well along in the nineteenth century could possibly have been changed by selling under favorable conditions; but to secure the intensity of desire that stimulates buying action and that, as a preliminary, requires pressure on the employers to share increased productiveness, necessitates, in addition, the breaking of long-established consumption patterns.

Under such conditions, even selling could do little more than maintain existing standards; and since these were low, little could be accomplished to warrant more than very limited selling effort. Even today, the acceptance by many European businessmen of the idea that only a given amount of product can and will be sold limits production and selling activities. Their conclusion is that the firms in an industry should agree to divide up the market, cartelize, get high prices, discourage new entrants into the field, and avoid the effort and strain of active competition. The effort is directed toward keeping the workers content, since the employers themselves are satisfied with the situation. The idea of disturbing the workers by increasing their wants for a high standard of living under such conditions becomes repugnant to them.

---

[11] Woytinsky and Woytinsky, *op. cit.*, p. 285.

This is a philosophy of static demand. It represents the lack of regard for the mass of people who make up the bulk of the population. It is a philosophy of privilege, of assuming that the good things of life are for the few, not for the many as well. It is the attitude that adds to the inclination of common people of many western European, as well as Asiatic, nations to view with favor the glittering promises of communism and to judge skeptically the capitalism that so far has given them so little opportunity to improve their standards of living. The modern business manager, the modern entrepreneur, expects to benefit along with the workers, not by a process of tearing down and redistributing the wealth of a few, not at the expense of any group of workers, but by the simple but only effective process of producing the goods and services that make up high standards.

COMMERCIAL AND INDUSTRIAL DEMAND IN RELATION TO SELLING

It is not sufficient in our economy to depend solely upon the wants and desires of consumers to energize our economic system. Just as businessmen have learned that consumer demands must be influenced, expanded, and intensified in order to have meaningful effect, so they have learned that in trade and industry, in banking and finance, in mining and agriculture, desirable buying action generally requires that the seller take the initiative in influencing buyers. Commercial and industrial buyers of medium-sized and larger enterprise often exercise initiative in buying, but even the largest firms are influenced by sellers in one way or another.

The retailer or wholesale merchant buys goods to resell, and in lesser measure he buys goods and services needed in order to perform his reselling functions. What the retailer buys is based upon his judgment of the types and quantities of goods he thinks customers will buy. The wholesaler likewise purchases what he thinks the retailer will buy. Thus for finished consumer goods it is clearly consumer demand, actual or prospective, that determines what is bought and sold. The demand of wholesalers or retailers for such goods is thus derived from consumer demand.

The merchant, whether retailer, wholesaler, or other middleman, must anticipate consumer demand in order to have goods available when the consumer wants to buy them. If he has anticipated correctly, he finds it possible to sell the goods he has bought and make a profit. If he has been mistaken, he loses. The consumers, retailers, and wholesalers exercising their democratic freedom of choice thus largely determine the degree of success insofar as sales income is concerned. If consumers fail to buy at profitable prices, retailers must take losses on unsold stock and learn from experience. A few losses may be borne, but multiply these losses and bankruptcy follows.

"Derived demand," as economists use the term, refers more specifically to the type and range of demands for varied goods and services that emerge as the result of the consumer demand for finished products. The desire for machinery to manufacture blankets grows out of the consumer demand for blankets. The purchase of cotton or wool or manufacturing supplies is undertaken because the demand for finished fabrics requires those products. The demand for machine tools is a consequence of the demand for automobiles or for railroad transportation or for other metal or plastic products. So also the demand for various business services for buildings and maintenance supplies. At the base of all this varied demand for industrial goods, which ranges from locomotives to tiny recording instruments or from cleaning compounds to engineering consulting services, is again this energizing consumer demand, whether that demand be individual or family, or the demand through collective groups such as a government endeavoring to furnish services of defense and other services to a democratic people.

The buying action based on derived demand is no more automatic than the buying action of the ultimate consumer himself. Choices must be made, decisions arrived at. Some of these choices may be briefly indicated by the concrete example of a machinery manufacturer in the Middle West who secured the patents to make a new, faster automatic loom that could be used to increase various types of cotton cloth. In spite of some free publicity, prospective buyers did not besiege the manufacturer nor did he expect them to do so. The loom producer realized in the first place that textile manufacturers must decide whether they wanted to replace existing looms or add new looms to their equipment. The desire to replace or expand in capacity by buying new looms might have to be created. A board of directors might have to be persuaded to authorize the capital expenditure necessary for replacement or expansion, after considering the company's needs for new looms as related to other needs and availability of funds for such purposes. The loom manufacturer also realized that the prospective buyer might continue to use his old looms, in which case capital costs on depreciated equipment would be lower, although operating costs might be substantially higher, than on the new looms. Furthermore, he realized that the prospective buyer, if he bought carefully, would study the offerings of several other loom manufacturers who might have made somewhat similar claims, before deciding which looms to purchase.

The loom producer believed that selling effort was clearly needed, not only to bring about consideration of the new loom, but also to influence the selection of the loom to be purchased. In making his buying decision, the customer would probably be less influenced than many ultimate consumers would be by emotional factors in their purchase. Nevertheless, the need for selling initiative and effort was fully as great and as essential for survival as in the case of consumer goods. The selling effort would consist to a much greater extent upon specialized advice and information presented by persons who knew thoroughly the types of products they were selling; the necessity of taking the initiative in furnishing such advice is a fact which many producers have had to learn at great expense. Technical types of selling such as this are expensive. Such salesmen or sales engineers are apt to be among the more highly paid and the cost per transaction in absolute figures is higher—although low in ratio to sales. In such selling, advertising tends to play a smaller part; its costs are likely to be lower, because advertising is directed not to a mass market but to limited groups of prospective buyers through media of limited circulation.

Merchants need to buy in order to sell. Manufacturers need to buy in order to produce output. But both of these need to be persuaded to buy particular goods at particular times, even though the purchase will be beneficial to them as well as to their customers. This is shown first by the fact that selling organizations or selling executives appear practically necessary for every machinery and industrial manufacturer. Many a producer wishes it were not necessary to sell or to incur the expense of selling, but he has been compelled to learn the facts of economic life.

In addition to universal recognition among industrial goods producers of the need of selling, there is clear evidence that even with that selling much needs to be done to persuade industrial firms to buy essential machinery. A recent survey of the *American Machinist,* a McGraw-Hill publication, states as key findings:[12]

1) More than one million machine tools—out of a total of less than two million in the metalworking industries—are at least ten years old. Many of these, after day and night operation during the war years and the recent rush to rearm, are actually much older production-wise than their age in years indicates. In most cases, these machines are unable to produce goods as efficiently as modern equipment can, thus needlessly increasing costs.

2) Almost one out of five machine tools is more than twenty years old. Most of these machines are so outdated by modern standards that they have little more than scrap value. And an even larger portion of our metal-forming equipment (presses, breakes and shears, bending and strightening machines) has passed the 20-year market and is beyond normal retirement age.

3) Two out of three machine tools are of designs predating World War II, though many of them have been built since the war. Thus, two-thirds of our machine tools fail to incorporate the many major postwar improvements in design and operating methods.

4) Never before has outmoded high-cost equipment been so widely diffused throughout American industry. In every one of fifteen major divisions of metalworking production, more than 45% of the machine tools are at least ten years old.

5) Not since the depression days of the 1930's has the average

---

[12] "A Message to American Industry," *No Room for Industrial Complacency,* by McGraw-Hill Publishing Co., Inc. See also, H. J. Loberg, *Machine Tool Selling* (2nd ed.; New York: McGraw-Hill Book Co., Inc., 1953).

age of machine tools risen so rapidly as it has in the past four years. Today, 55% is ten years old or older, compared with 43% just before Korea.

Surely, in the face of such an inventory, one cannot contend that industrial firms buy up-to-date machinery automatically or that good selling is unnecessary.

SUMMARY AND CONCLUSIONS

Selling leadership is necessary to motivate the current and future production of goods and services needed to provide a high standard of living for all the people. Without such leadership the American people would not want a high level of living intensely enough to produce it. The statement by economists that human wants are limitless or that wants are indefinitely extensible seems plausible; but such assumptions have little significance if they refer to uninfluenced desire. The only wants that have economic significance are those which cause people to take either present or future action. Psychologists will assert that no action such as buying action takes place unless desires and motivation are sufficiently intense.

Buying action is the immediate objective of selling, but it starts a whole series of actions and reactions in our economy that energize and develop our productive facilities. To illustrate, let us trace the influence of the family purchase of a new automobile. First the salesman secures the order, thereby earning salary and possibly a commission enabling him in turn to buy goods of the types that he wants for himself and his own family. Second, the dealer secures a margin over his buying costs of the automobile, which enables him to maintain his place of business, pay the employees who operate the agency, and pay his executives. Perhaps a profit remains to furnish interest on capital invested and to give him a net yield on operations. But that profit remains only if his expenses are not too high and if he handles his trade-ins in such a way as not to lose money. Third, the dealer's orders and commitments for automobiles given in advance of the beginning of the selling year combined with the orders of other dealers, are expected to dispose of the planned output of the factory. Its representatives maintain relations with dealers, help them to improve their business operations, and induce them to sell more cars. Obviously, in periods of shortage, the promotional efforts of the factory need to be very much less than when demand is at a low ebb.

The factory, having established a plant, has possibly bought many new machines and tools, and has employed engineers and designers. Many millions of dollars have been spent on preparing new models for the approval of the public. One large automobile manufacturing group was said to have spent $275 million in 1956 in retooling for new models, and another firm $100 million for such purposes. Thus the firms making tools, dies, and equipment for manufacture have previously made sales because the automobile makers planned and prepared to produce automobiles that they expect to sell. The automobiles to be introduced in the fall of 1957 were planned and some commitments made as early as 1954 with increasing commitments in the succeeding years. In addition to the preparations for production, obviously materials and parts have to be purchased and labor hired, trained, and directed.

Sales representatives and even executives of materials and equipment firms have been at work to help plan and induce the purchasing officers of motorcar manufacturers to use new equipment, new or known materials and supplies. Such selling may have been going on for months, even years, until choices are finally made and products ordered. One might carry out the description in much greater detail, tracing the sales efforts of the representative of materials and equipment and those who sold to the equipment producers. It is sufficient, however, to point out the need for buying action and the points at which selling effort has been applied.

One conclusion to be drawn from any such analysis is this: The manufacturer of motor cars can plan to produce in quantity and can make plans to equip for sufficient production only because he believes that by selling leadership, his organization of dealers and branches can dispose within the model year of the quantity of production necessary to warrant these commitments and expenditures and yield a profit. He knows that if selling effort were to be eliminated, demand and buying action would decrease to a point where he would have to cease production. Even with available selling effort, he may fail in competition, because there is no assurance that a consumer will buy, any more than the politician can be sure of converting a particular individual to his own brand of thinking; nor can a manufacturer be sure that he will sell enough to keep alive if his products or his selling cannot hold their own with competitors.

Here is production planning and selling under a free market system. The manufacturer of automobiles knows that he must sell in order to survive; he plans his product and his selling effort to realize profitable sale of his production. But he also knows that he assumes risks, sometimes huge risks, because of his limited ability to forecast the effectiveness and extent of selling effort, and the reactions of auto buyers to the product and to that selling effort.

It is easy and tempting to imagine that some wise person or group of persons could plan production with perhaps some leadership of consumers so as to avoid the alleged wasteful competitive selling and advertising; but the experience of so-cieties that have tried it lends no support to the assumption that there are such planners. It seems to support the conclusion that no planners are wise enough to design the complex economic structure and direct its functioning so that all the people will be motivated to produce for themselves the goods and services which make up a high level of living; nor has it been shown that planners can make any progress by means that yield high results without slavery or substantial loss of freedom.

Clearly the demands of our people and their capacity to consume with benefit are not fixed in totals. Clearly such demand if strong enough may increase and motivate increased production.

Business firms in the United States have operated on the theory that consumer demands can be expanded and intensified into action and that desires can be stimulated for the benefit of all concerned: owners, employees, workers, and consumers.

And the results to date attest the soundness of this philosophy.

Thus high in the list of requirements for high standards of living has been placed a psychological factor—the desire for improvement in material welfare. It will be admitted that most men and women desire to improve their lot; economists assert that human wants are insatiable. It should, however, be repeated that the desire for the improved standard of living that is here under consideration must possess special characteristics. It must be of such intensity that men and women are willing to work to secure the purchasing power with which to secure the goods and services that make up this standard of living. When standards of living were so low that they included little beyond subsistence and biological requirements for nutrition and shelter against the elements, obviously the pressure to work was terrific. As standards of living have been raised, as attitudes of peoples and government have changed to make it possible for those who do not produce to get at least a minimum living, the pressure of starvation on people to work has less effect. What men work for today is not primarily the minimum essentials for living on a low scale but the desire for comforts and luxuries, which in emergencies they could dispense with— even for longer periods, a fact which war and depression experience have emphasized.

Persons vary widely in their desires for goods and services. Desires for many things that enter into present levels of living have been acquired. They are not the results of childhood environment, although more and more this is becoming the case. They are the results of leadership and of the influence of habits and environments that have been acquired because of selling effort. It is an incontrovertible fact that some people must be led to want progress in any field. Unless these people are led to want to the extent that they will work productively to attain high standards, the whole effective use of large-scale production, of advanced technology, and of skillful and professional management is reduced or even made impossible. As a consequence, costs go up, and even those who are willing to work for high standards of living find their effort brings them a lower standard than they might otherwise have attained.

The effort to induce people to want those goods and services enough to work for them appears to be desirable in the general social interest, and in terms of the welfare of the individual and his family. Failure to work and work productively injures both those who do not desire a higher standard of living, therefore, as well as those who do. It is desirable in the general interest of society to induce them to participate in production, because as our society is constituted, no large segment can be unwilling to share that productive effort without having effect upon all the people. Unless of course the workload is excessive, the individual who is led to work to get better food, better housing, and better equipment, or to pay for educating his children is benefited and so is the society of which he is a member.

The desire for improved living conditions where standards have been very low may be, and has sometimes been, intensified and channeled into social protest and acceptance of communistic promises. People may come to espouse more or less violent measures to bring about relief to the underprivileged at the expense of the "rich." In the redistribution of wealth, violent expropriation may occur, but more likely, gentler but more insidious measures will be adopted. The rapid introduction of social benefits, desirable as many of them may be, may involve taxation to the point of lessening production, productivity, and enterprise. Too late, the lesson may be learned that redistribution quickly reaches its limit, and that high standards for all the people may be achieved only if all the people produce them for themselves.

Chapter IV

OBJECTIVES OF SELLING

SELLING LEADERSHIP must be judged by its objectives, its methods, and its results, just as any other form of leadership. If selling influences people generally to want a better life, it deserves credit, the more so if it leads to action to achieve a better life. If political leadership aims to bring about greater good in man's relation to man, it deserves credit, especially if it induces action to achieve that advance.

But in any form of leadership one must distinguish between immediate objectives of those who practice the leadership function and the sum total of the individual objectives. We must distinguish in selling between the immediate objectives of the individuals and firms engaged in the process of influencing the public and the broad final results of the millions of specific leadership efforts. Higher standards of living should be the eventual result, just as good government should be the end result of political leadership. But this end result has been brought about by a vast multitude of individual actions and influences exercised by persons of varying position, varying capacities, and varying motives.

NATURE OF SELLING OBJECTIVES

The objectives of selling may at first thought appear to be very simple. Some individual or business firm is endeavoring to influence other people or firms to make purchases for the selfish benefit of the seller. But there is much more to the function of selling than this. The objectives ascribed to selling and to those engaged in selling are too often based upon limited experience, observation, and contact. True, the immediate objective of selling is to make sales and to develop buying action on the part of prospective or potential buyers; but most sellers are also under heavy economic pressure to deal with buyers or those who influence buying in such a manner that future transactions will be facilitated. Most sellers are looking forward to making repeat sales, that is, to inducing future purchases by the same customers, because the bulk of business transactions takes place between buyers and sellers who have had previous buying and selling relationships. The seller must, therefore, direct his effort so that the buyers will want to repeat the experience. Where freedom of choice prevails in our competitive economy, that repetition will not occur unless the buyer is "well satisfied" to use the words of the Supreme Court. Thus "enlightened selfishness" tends to influence the seller to establish himself as a good source of supply and to avoid methods and practices which would harm the buyer.

Any careful examination of the objectives of selling, however, must go beyond such enlightened selfishness to reach a basic understanding. It is the failure to penetrate more deeply into objectives and results that has contributed to the misunderstanding of selling. As is so often the case in studying social phenomena, it is easy to fail to see the forest for the trees.

It is helpful in the process of the study of objectives to distinguish between individual and group objectives and to separate the purpose of the individual and the private firm from the general social objectives and goals of the total selling process. That selling has as its ultimate purpose a social goal is not quickly apparent because we do not attempt to look at the over-all purposes and results. There is need, therefore, to outline the scope of these objectives and to relate the conclusions derived from limited observation and embodied in common opinion to the broader facts of the selling situations and their significance. The objectives of selling to be discussed will be grouped therefore under four major headings:

1. The objectives of selling effort carried on by individuals, directly engaged in selling activity whatever the form.
2. The objectives of selling effort on the part of the firms and corporations in relation to those doing the selling work in those firms and in relation to the owners of the selling enterprise.
3. The objectives of selling effort in relation to our economic structure and its functioning.
4. The objectives of selling effort in relation to our society as a whole.

Objectives of Individuals Engaged in Selling Work

The objective of selling activities generally is obviously to secure buying action, to cause purchase of goods and services by buyers. This leads eventually to higher consumption by many people, although higher consumption may or may not be the objective of a particular seller. Any careful examination of the objectives of selling must lead to the conclusion that the objectives of individuals who are engaged in the practice of selling may differ widely in type and emphasis. Among these objectives are the following:

1) To make a living. From the standpoint of the individual salesman whose income and success depends on his efforts to cause people to buy, it is evident that selling constitutes a gainful occupation at the practice of which he hopes to make a living. His ambition may extend to achieving advancement into executive ranks. This ambition may in turn be motivated by desire to secure the ownership of business that will give him the income desired for the benefit of himself and his family, the enjoyment of luxuries, or the acquisition of power.

It is certainly not assured under the usual plans of compensation that salesmen will make a living, much less go beyond that. Many a young man who has started out to sell aluminum utensils, magazines, or hosiery from house to house, has found out in a very short time that he could not make a living and has given up in despair. He has learned that selling is not easy and that earnings are not automatic, particularly in normal buyers' markets. A substantial proportion of those who try selling fail for want of aptitude, industry, or basic interest in and respect for their work. Some fail also because what they are trying to sell is not wanted.

Those who work in the field of advertising or display, or who perform many other supplementary and staff duties, find that ultimate success in their jobs depends on the estimated contribution that their work makes to selling. They have the same ambitions, the same desires as those who are directly in contact with the prospective buyers. But the difficulty of measuring their contribution to selling results is a handicap to some, perhaps an advantage to others.

We cannot, offhand, condemn the motivation of the individual in trying to make a living and improve his lot in life as purely selfish and antisocial. On the contrary, one's first economic responsibility is usually to himself and family; and unless he meets this responsibility, he cannot ordinarily serve society well. But serving society may be the best way of serving himself. A possible conflict between his obligation to society and private interest may exist; but in selling it need not and usually does not. The salesman who persuades a manufacturer to install a new machine to make a better product or to cut costs is contributing to a higher standard of living, in spite of the fact that the motivation of the salesman may be to increase his own standard of living and that of the manufacturer who, in installing the machine, increases profits and avoids loss. Eventually his purchase will contribute to lower costs and higher scales of living for the people. The salesman who sells an electric washing machine to the housewife is generally raising the family's level of living.

Because selling involves a form of leadership, because it requires those practicing selling to influence other people, selling has frequently furnished a training ground for other positions in business. Selling leadership is persuasive leadership, a type of leadership that is both appreciated and greatly needed in democratic societies.

2) A second objective of those who perform selling work is likewise understandable. It is the desire to secure satisfaction from the work itself. Salesmen who believe in their products and in the benefits those products will convey to buyers feel satisfaction when they make sales, entirely apart from the contribution that such sales make to their personal welfare. In fact,

success as a salesman is usually predicated on a firm belief in the merits of the product sold in terms of the satisfactions to be obtained by the buyers. There is no evidence that salesmen, any more than any other group, wish to make a living without regard to the service performed in return.

3) Again, there are special satisfactions from successful sales work which attract and hold a good many workers in the selling field. That is the desire to secure the excitement and thrills from successfully influencing people to take the desired action. Obviously, to the salesman who is ethical in his conduct, such thrills and satisfactions must be the result of selling that is mutually beneficial.

The ease of selling during periods of shortages brought about by global war has for many years obscured the fact that selling in a competitive economy is a difficult task requiring intelligent, often exhausting, effort. In a competitive economy with high standards of living, with many products both old and new, the difficulty of making particular sales at a particular time will furnish a challenge to the keenest brain, a challenge that is paralleled only in other areas of human activity where democratic liberty prevails and freedom of choice obtains. The intense satisfactions which men have often reported at the successful conclusion of a selling project need to be experienced in order to be fully appreciated.

4) Serving buyers and customers. Since most selling is done on a repeat basis, sellers get to know buyers and become friendly with them. Particularly in the sales of technical and complex products, the salesman develops friendships that cause him to serve his buyers and customers to a point substantially beyond the length required by cold and calculating type of enlightened selfishness. The salesman who furnishes selling or merchandising services to customers is adding to the satisfactions that both his firm and the customer feel as the result of the purchasing transactions. But he also derives personal pleasure and satisfactions from the relationship with customers.

5) Lastly, except in the general desire to be engaged in useful work so that the earning of a living or the accumulation of capital for personal or family improvement is accomplished in

an honorable manner, one does not expect that many salesmen will engage in such work with vague altruistic ideas of serving society. The man who believes in his product and acts honorably in bringing about a sale that leads to mutual satisfaction is actually serving society, whether the goal he seeks to reach is explicitly service to society or the same goals as characterizes other vocations: to make a living, to develop security, to furnish the means for cultural or other development, to attain power, or any of the other objectives that men may hope to reach, directly or indirectly, through a chosen field of effort.

The motivation of the individual may differ from that of his firm. Sometimes the differences in that motivation are not important in the performance of a useful function for society. Sometimes they are. The behavior of the salesman who engages in sharp practice or even the use of illegal means of influence may go beyond anything either permitted or encouraged by the firm itself. In other cases, the standard of the salesman may be merely a more concrete reflection of the carelessness or low standards on the part of the executives of the selling firm itself. It is unlikely that the sales organization in its contact with the public will rise above the character of the top management, but it is also possible that top management with a large and scattered field sales organization may not be able in all areas to control the behavior of those who are exercising influence at the point of the contact with the public. The parallel in political leadership is quickly apparent; it need not be spelled out. One may only mention the contrast between some top political leaders and the ward bosses of certain cities. Fortunately, checks upon "bad behavior" and unworthy motivation, inherent in selling in our economy, seem to be more quickly operative than in the political field.

Selling Objectives in Relation to Business Enterprises and Owners and Managers

The business enterprise which is devoted to the production of goods or services, or both, sells for various reasons, some of which are obvious and some not so apparent:

1) In the opinions of a good many businessmen, selling is

fully justified if one can show that selling is essential to the survival of an enterprise in competition. In our economy distinguished by large-scale production for national or even international markets, the cessation of selling effort would, except under war shortages or monopoly of necessities, mean more or less rapid failure. If one will examine the balance sheets of many firms, he will find that if the income from sales were cut off, the firm operating at its previous level would consume its capital in a very short time, even where heavy capital investment was involved. Obviously the cessation of selling effort would not cut off all sales, because some buying would take place based in part on connections and past selling, and in part upon need for the sellers' products. Generally, however, the decline in the volume of goods disposed of in the absence of selling effort would be disastrous. For that decline in most industries is likely to be much more than proportionate to the possible decline in costs, thus quickly bringing losses because of the insufficiency of income from sales to cover costs.

To the experienced businessman, it is quite evident that production does not create demand. Sales do not come automatically and purchases are not made automatically despite implications in some economics texts. Basically, survival of the firm is the condition of continuing private profit, but it is also the condition of continuing service to society. Just as in politics the most competent man with the best motives may be forced to pay attention to his survival in office if he is to be able to carry out his program, so the businessman will look to profitable sales as a condition of real and outstanding accomplishment and growth.

It is obvious that for most business enterprises sales transactions constitute the sole source of income. Sales provide the income out of which wages and salaries can be paid and the requirements met for goods, machinery, supplies, and taxes. Without sales income, firms cannot long continue to make these payments without dissipating assets, endangering chances of restoration to economic health, and suffering eventual failure.

2) Businessmen sell in order to secure return on investment. The business executives who are responsible to a board of di-

rectors and to stockholders may aim through selling to provide the income necessary for return on investment. They realize that only an adequate volume of sales, made at a profitable price, can provide the dividends, allowance for depreciation, and reserves necessary for continuously satisfactory operation. If return is not earned for a considerable period of time, the difficulty of securing further capital is increased and becomes eventually impossible.

3) Businesses and business executives sell in order to have the satisfaction of achievement. Business executives and leaders take pride in the building of enterprises and look upon the work of building a going concern as a worthwhile economic and social objective.[1] They know that the building of large enterprises is seldom a one-man job. The planning necessary for successful sales operations, the execution of sales plans, and the overcoming of obstacles, thereby contributing vitally to bringing into full operation an enterprise that produces useful goods and services, is an accomplishment worthy of credit. In the United States more than in some other parts of the world, such men think of businesses not only, or even primarily, as a means of

---

[1] This attitude and objective is described by Franklin J. Lunding in an address delivered at the National Business Conference at the Harvard Business School, June 7, 1952:

"It can be said without qualification that the typical business manager of America today is not working primarily to get rich. In the first place, it's virtually impossible, at least in the formerly accepted sense of the word, and he knows it. No matter how high his salary goes he is not going to become an immensely wealthy man under present tax laws. Furthermore, he would be likely to find great wealth embarrassing, even if he could acquire it. The opulence which characterized the great business leaders of bygone years is out of place today.

"The chief motivation of today's business manager is a desire to build a sound, healthy organism, financially strong, competitively alert, able to progress steadily and to weather whatever storms might lie ahead. His objective is a smoothly-running, tightly knit, cooperative organization to which everyone from the president to the floor sweeper contributes his enthusiastic best and from which each draws his due share of material reward and spiritual satisfaction.

"Such an organization, he is convinced, operates more profitably and offers the best prospects for steady jobs at good pay, for the growth and development of the business and of each individual in it, and for the pursuit of happiness and life's satisfactions for all concerned. The business manager wants all these things for the people who work in the business as much as they want them for themselves. His primary job is to get people to do things cooperatively so those goals may be achieved."

deriving purely personal and family benefit. They often regard these businesses as living organisms which bring benefits to workers, users, and owners as well as to the managing groups. These benefits are realized, developed, and expanded by selling.

4) Public benefit is the ultimate goal of most selling. The objective of serving the consumer public, whether the consumers be ultimate consumers or firms or institutions, constitutes a rarely expressed but implicit objective even beyond the necessity of selling in order to make a profit. Many a businessman who disclaims altruism in his business conduct actually performs a greater social service by what he does in his own business than he could possibly perform in participating in community affairs or in his gifts to educational or charitable institutions.

The obvious connection between selling and employment constitutes a working objective that is a powerful incentive to many businessmen. Selling requires production; production requires employment. Or, to reverse the statement: Employment results in production that must be disposed of for money or other goods. Disposing of goods for money requires selling effort. "Sales means jobs" because without the continual flow of buying and selling transactions, the entire basis for attaining high and rising standards of living and for maintaining those standards which have been achieved quickly disappears.

5) Both owners and executives will, of course, share the range of objectives relating to family and personal ambitions and to standing in the community, in the industry, or in the general economic structure of the nation. The interests of the individuals in management selling and ownership may, therefore, be parallel to those of the enterprise; but at times and in varying degrees they may be divergent. The evidence is that most successful executives identify their own interest with that of the firm with which they are connected. Nevertheless, when the motivation for selling is power or is unworthy, the possibilities of abuse exist and may result in injury and harm to the buying public until correctives are applied. But in this respect as in so many others, selling leadership does not differ from leadership in other fields.

Ultimate Objectives of Selling

One must constantly keep in mind that the basic objective of decent selling effort is to sell goods and services, to influence people to purchase and consume the food, clothing, shelter, the machines and materials—all the millions of items—required for an industrial civilization intended to furnish high levels of living for all the people. In other words, selling effort in all its manifold forms has as its immediate objective buying action taken by people as individuals or as part of a business or other organization. Such action represents the buying of those material goods and immaterial services that make up the economic level of our living. The amount of household production tends to grow less as living standards rise. Only in the early agrarian, pastoral, or hunting stages of economic development could family production satisfy more than a small portion of its needs. Most of the wants of an advanced industrial society such as ours must be satisfied through purchase, because the productive efforts of the family are specialized and may produce directly nothing that the family uses or desires. But only by such employment can workers be productive enough to have their work yield a high standard of living. The fact that selling effort is directed toward all people, not just toward a few privileged persons, needs special emphasis. It aims to sell automobiles not only to the wealthy but to the workman in the factory, to the farmer, or to the teacher. Selling is not the only influence, but it is the most powerful influence to take the type of resultful and productive action that will bring automobiles to the people. It has been the major influence in bringing into operation over 60 million automobiles for 160 million people. It has placed electric refrigerators in more than 90 per cent of wired homes —and one might cite many other instances, to support the fact that it is the many, not the few, who have obtained the increasingly high levels of living.

Successful selling effort obviously implies that people have been led to buy, both for consumptive and productive purposes, those goods and services needed for the continuance of high and rising levels of living. The performance of individuals and firms in persuading many people to buy thus achieves the objective of raising actual levels and standards of living if the persuasion to buy causes people to produce desired goods and services. Therefore, it does no violence to the facts to assert that the *aggregate objective of selling effort, taken as a whole, is to raise living levels and standards of living.* It is the objective of selling not only to bring about high and rising levels of living but also to raise the goals toward which people strive so that when relatively high income levels are attained by the majority of people, there will still be a gap between levels attained and levels desired. Standards are established in a dynamic economy that are a spur to the people to attain still higher levels.

The achieved levels of living in the United States are high for the population in general, higher than anywhere else in the world. They are unique in the history of the world, even though a small portion of our population still endures substandard levels. More production is needed to bring these people up to standard. Higher standards would require even greater productivity and production.

On the other hand, it is to be remarked that the attainment of these higher levels in the United States has not been accomplished by longer or more exacting labor. Rather the reverse. High levels requiring high production do not necessarily increase the amount of time and effort involved. If it were true that high levels could only be secured by longer hours and more exacting work, the question would soon arise as to whether those levels warranted the additional effort. For high levels of living, a balance is required between the work necessary to turn out large amounts of goods and services and the requirements for health and social and spiritual growth, all of which are and should be a part of broadly conceived high levels of living. The reconciling factor, which gives greater production but shorter hours and less exacting labor, is the development and application of technological and management skills and equipment to bring about greater productivity. That this has been done is clear from the record, which will be cited below. That it will continue to enable the reconciliation to be made between greater quantities of goods and services and the burdens of labor is possible but not automatic. Automation is intended eventually to reduce the human burden of producing goods and distributing goods. Nevertheless, although much has been accomplished along this line, it must be stressed that increasing social adjustment in other than economic fields to our high material standards is required before the highest levels of living can be attained.

Logicians will quickly point out that concomitant variation is not a proof of causal relationship; that high living standards in the United States may be due primarily to other causes rather than selling, or may even have occurred in spite of it. Some economists have implied that the high standards of living come first and enable us to bear the "waste" of much selling effort.[2] But it can and will be shown that there is a definite causal connection between high levels of living and selling, which becomes clear from a realistic study of the behavior of buyers and sellers, of businessmen, executives, and the buying public.

STANDARDS AND LEVELS OF LIVING

What Is Meant by Standards and Levels of Living?

If we are to set up as the objectives of selling leadership, the attainment of high and rising levels and standards of living, we need both to define what we mean by the terms and to show that they are worthy objectives. In an excellent definition, Joseph S. Davis, director-emeritus, Food Research Institute, Stanford University, says:[3]

1) For some 20 years there has been a spreading conviction that "raising standards of living," or helping people to raise them, deserves to be taken as a basic goal of national and international policies. The UN and its specialized agencies are devoting special efforts to this end. But progress is hampered by foggy thinking

[2] Cf. John K. Galbraith, *American Capitalism* (Boston: Houghton Mifflin Co., 1952).

[3] From manuscript by Joseph S. Davis, June, 1953. Also see two articles by the same distinguished author: "Adam Smith and the Human Stomach," *Quarterly Journal of Economics*, Vol. LXVIII (May, 1954), p. 275; and "The Population Upsurge and the American Economy, 1945–80," *Journal of Political Economy*, Vol. LXI, No. 5 (October 1953), p. 369.

about what "standards of living" are to be raised and how to recognize and roughly measure achievements, as well as by uncertainty as to the means by which desired results can be achieved. Fortunately, this weakness is now increasingly recognized.

2) In the interest of clearer thinking, it is necessary to make a number of distinctions: between *consumption* and *living*, between *levels* (or planes) and *standards* proper, between *actual standards* held by a people or group and *normative standards* set up by specialists, between standards for *current, near-future,* and *deferred attainment,* and between *program targets* and *ultimate goals.* All these more specific concepts are of importance, especially in considering problems of "raising standards of living" in low-income countries.

3) In my view, *levels* are experienced realities, while *standards* proper are levels desired with sufficient urgency to lead to efforts to attain, maintain, or regain them. Each is made up of many components, and balance or harmony among the components is an essential element in the whole. Individuals and groups are more or less vaguely aware of their levels and standards, though very few are articulate about either.

4) The importance of the distinction lies partly in the fact that the "gap" or spread between a people's standard and its level, whether of consumption or of living, has high significance. A moderate gap spurs them to raise their level toward or to the standard. A wide gap tends to breed despair, at worst to paralyze effort, at best to call for radical alteration of the current standard. Moreover, understanding of the composition of the standard held by a people or group, and the specific deficiencies in their level in relation to it, can indicate where a specific gain can most improve the level. And there are great differences among groups of peoples in the composition of their standards, and greater clarity about standards can be of high importance in appropriately and economically raising corresponding levels.

5) Consumption is everywhere essential to living and a fairly important part of living. It includes whatever goods (and services) an individual, family, group, or people uses up in the personal satisfaction of wants, including the services of durable goods, free goods, and public goods, whether self-produced, home-produced, purchased, or received gratis. The personal consumption level of a group of people is the per capita (or better, per capita adjusted for age and sex differences) volume of consumption. Approximate measurement of this is very difficult, but not impossible.

6) Living includes consumption, but in terms of outcome—rather than "input"—in nutrition, health, education, efficiency, security, etc. It includes other components by no means wholly de-

pendent on consumption. Such are working conditions, hours of labor and leisure, freedoms, security, opportunities, social and spiritual atmosphere, and the balance among all components. The level of living of a group of people is this complex combination of such components, in per capita or adjusted per capita terms.

7) Rising or raising standards of living is inadequately interpreted to mean rising or raising consumption levels, even in the U.S. where consumption looms relatively largest in the level of living. The desired objective is a balanced advance in levels of living in accordance with the standards of the people concerned. This is especially important in considering the problems of low-income countries. "Progress," in its most significant meaning, consists of advances in levels of living, in contrast with growth in population, output, or capital.

Are High and Rising Levels of Living Desirable Objectives?

If it be agreed that the increased consumption of wanted goods by all the people, coupled with consumer freedom of choice, are the actual objectives of selling, and that successful selling effort brings higher economic levels, there still remains the question as to whether or not such objectives are worthy. Is the accomplishment of selling in increasing levels of material consumption and production a socially desirable achievement? Are those who do selling work entitled to feel that they are engaged in an essential and socially useful work?

The answer is decidedly affirmative—even though the activities of some specific individuals or firms may be fraudulent, antisocial, or harmful, and abuses exist in selling leadership as in any other form of leadership. The objective of achieving high and rising levels of living is a worthy one, because it aims at attainment of freedom from want and the achievement of increased material welfare as a condition of increased total human welfare. The objective is worthy not only because it seeks to give people food, clothing, and shelter, but also because it seeks to furnish greater opportunity to all the people to lead "the good life," embodying a balance of spiritual, cultural, religious, and other aspects of living, and a balance of work and leisure such as ideals may call for.

It is significant that high and rising standards of living are almost universally desired. Low living standards have been the cause of much of the world's unrest in recent decades. There is evidence that the tendency of many countries to embrace communism is based upon existing low standards and the communist promise of better living.

Nominally at least, even the Soviet government has set up as a goal the material well-being of the people. As Mr. Voroshilov put it in an address on the thirtieth anniversary of the Bolshevik revolution in a speech to the fifth session of the Supreme Soviet:

The Soviet government considers as their main task in the field of international policy the care for the people's well-being and the steady rise in the material well-being of the workers, collective farmers, intelligensia, and all Soviet peoples.

In accordance with this the party and the Government have lately adopted a number of important decisions, the implementation of which must insure a sharp rise in the production of consumer goods, further mighty development of agriculture, an appeal for the improvement of Soviet trade and a great increase in trade turnover, the expansion of house building, and a number of other measures.

All these decisions are permeated with the profound solicitation of the party and the Government for the well-being of the people so that in a short time the standard of living of the workers in urban and rural areas will be raised considerably.

These historical decisions indicate a new development of the Soviet economy, when we, parallel with the high speed development of heavy industry, set ourselves the task to raise sharply the branches of national economy which directly serve national consumption.

Elsewhere in that speech, he remarks upon the problem of obtaining adequate production saying:

The successful solution of the great task of creating an abundance of consumer goods in the country depends directly on the improvement in the work of our industry. . . . We have still not a few factories and works which do not fulfill the state's tasks for the increased labor productivity, which tolerate faulty goods, which fight badly for high quality production and for the reduction of costs.

Thus even within this speech, there is evidence to support the headline which is of interest to the careful student of Soviet conditions: namely, "Soviet Consumer Gets Promises but Few Products."[4]

That higher levels of living are almost universally desired requires little further discussion. There is need, however, for greater clarity as to what we mean by higher levels in terms of more explicit objectives. We may include in our broad objective the following:

1) Elimination of substandard levels for all who produce for themselves, their families, and dependents.

2) The raising of standards of living for all income classes but especially those in low- and medium-income classes above substandard levels.

3) Raising quality standard of consumption for all levels of income.

4) The increase of productivity so that with less human effort and more machine effort, we may have higher consumption with less work.

5) The provision of more satisfaction in productive work.

6) The increase of leisure needed to improve health and to develop a well-rounded life with hobbies and intellectual, artistic, and spiritual interests.

7) The provision of acceptable standards for those who through incapacity, disaster, or for other cause cannot contribute to social production or secure purchasing power to attain such standards.

These all represent economic and social progress. The objective of high and rising standards for a whole people is really unique; it can only have fullest meaning in a democratic, fluid, and essentially classless society such as we have in the United States and Canada.[5] High levels of living have prevailed in many societies—for the few—never for the many. As has been remarked, our museums are filled with the beautiful and luxurious

---

[4] *New York Times*, August 16, 1953; November 7, 1953. It is significant that promises of Voroshilov were re-emphasized by Malenkov after Stalin's death. But Malenkov's policy of higher living standards for the people was put into discard when he was succeeded by Bulganin.

[5] Frederick Martin Stern, *Capitalism in America; A Classless Society* (New York: Rinehart & Co. Inc., 1951), chap. vii, p. 41.

possessions of the wealthy.[6] What is not so apparent is that the high standards of living they indicate were the privilege and possession of a very few—the many lived in abject poverty. And in a large part of the world today, the masses are at or below subsistence.

The objective has been given lip service in other parts of the world, but the means used in the United States and the accomplishment are unique in their scope and success. Selling has brought more things, new products to the American people. It has enabled them to buy these new satisfactions, by increasing both productivity and incomes and by lowering prices of the things they buy, in spite of the costs of selling effort. How it does this, how it attains the higher productivity are discussed in subsequent chapters.

The accomplishment in the favorable economic and social climate of the United States is huge, but not without faults. It has not escaped adverse criticism of those who realize that some members of our society are not well fed, clothed, or housed; from others who dislike the methods employed; and from still others who believe that the objective of higher consumption is open to question.

What selling and our economic system does that is not appreciated, is to give to the people generally on a larger and more comprehensive scale than ever before in world history, the opportunity to develop other than economic areas of human living. The accomplishment of higher standards of living with less work has occurred in so short a period, and really has compressed a revolution of first magnitude in standards of living in little more than a half century, that we have not had time to learn that balance between material welfare and general welfare which eventually we shall accept as a goal. And as a people we still have far to go before we have achieved a degree of economic welfare that will make further effort to raise standards of living questionable.

The objective of high and rising standards of living is a

---

[6] W. S. Woytinsky and E. S. Woytinsky, *World Population and Products* (New York: The Twentieth Century Fund, 1955), p. 266.

worthy one, not only in its emphasis upon economic and social welfare, and the fuller opportunity for individual development, but also because the actual achievement of high standards for all must be based upon high production, high productivity, and socially equitable distribution of goods and services. Our political parties, governmental agencies, economists, social scientists, and other groups are all agreed as to the desirability of raising standards of living. They may disagree as to the ways and means of achieving high levels, but there can be no sound disagreement that high production is required.

Conversely, the existence of low standards has been shown to be an incentive to the acceptance of ideologies that are in practice inconsistent with high production, such as those of communism, and forms of socialism which lay major emphasis on redistribution of existing wealth but fail to provide incentive or to secure higher production. Furthermore, it will be readily conceded that there may be a wide divergence between the announcements of policies and promises to furnish better standards of living and their actual attainment. The declaration of governments that economic and social welfare is their prime objective must be regarded with more than a little skepticism in view of the universal appeal of better standards of living and the danger that that announcement is mainly political strategy. Such policies or policy announcements are meaningful only if definite and potentially resultful steps are taken to produce and distribute the goods and services that go into high levels of living for all the people. At the present time, only free countries can show substantial accomplishment; and the United States and Canada show the outstanding development.

Historical and statistical record is woefully weak in describing in detail the standards of living of the common people in earlier societies and is not too illuminating for more recent periods. Considerably more has been learned by patient search concerning the living standards of members of upper-income classes. Few detailed descriptions of living levels of serfs and peasants exist in Russia or anywhere else. Descriptions of living standards in the earlier histories of the United States are in large part based upon travelers' accounts. Such information is scattered, limited, and generally too meager to permit easy comparison. However, a few general observations as to living standards emerge from an examination of varied historical and statistical materials.

1) By any standards which we choose to set up, a large portion of the people of the world have suffered low standards of living throughout recorded history. As late as the early part of the last century, Malthus, the economist, postulated as the basis of his research that the population would increase and press upon the means of existence. He observed that the bulk of the population of his time was living at subsistence levels, and he came to the conclusion that that would always be so. Today, low levels of living still rule in most of the world, and as a United Nations study shows, half of the earth's population is made up of persons whose annual income is less than $100 a year.[7] Two thirds of the world's population, 1,600,000,000 persons, live in underdeveloped regions at or below the subsistence level. An Indian observer, speaking to a university seminar, points out that the average per capita income in India was $57 and that levels of living involved deficiencies even in the satisfaction of elementary wants for food, clothing, shelter. In a recent article, John Gunther, asserting that the annual income of many African natives amounted to no more than $10 a year, refers to "miserable" housing, "usual undernourishment," poor medical services, and other aspects of abject poverty. One can only conclude that even today, much of the world is undernourished, poorly clothed, and badly sheltered.

2) In every society, groups of rulers, professional or military people, and landowners, have enjoyed a relatively high standard of living. These groups have been relatively small, apparently not more than 1 per cent or 2 per cent of the population. The objective of a high standard of living for all the people was unknown, except to "crazy dreamers." The very idea of allowing people of the lower classes to improve their living standards

---

[7] Refer for instance to Woytinsky and Woytinsky, *op. cit.*, pp. 303–9. See also International Labor Office, *Report on Indigenous Peoples* (Studies and Reports, New Series, No. 35), Geneva; and reports of the Food and Agricultural Organization of the League of Nations on nutrition.

was considered dangerous and foolish. One will find occasional reference, even up to the nineteenth century, to workers' desire to wear better clothes, to eat better foods.[8]

3) Living levels for both upper classes and lower classes changed only very slowly over the centuries. In historical descriptions, the lapse of hundreds of years seems to have made little difference in the way people lived. While in many regions there were political and religious changes, the Renaissance, which set off an intellectual rebirth and a revitalized appreciation of artistic endeavor, did not noticeably affect the material welfare of the general population, nor were the material standards of living of the upper classes substantially affected. It was not until production increased as the result of the application of labor and the application of power and machinery that goods increased in amount and became available to lower- and middle-income groups. But those groups did not benefit greatly from the higher productivity until a larger share of the increased production was secured in response to demands of the workers themselves, at first by unorganized labor and later by unions. The example of enlightened employers played its part. And labor legislation tended to enforce minimum standards upon the unenlightened. It is only in comparatively recent times that belated recognition has been given to the idea that high standards of living were beneficial not only to workers and society but also to employers, owners of industry, and business generally.

4) Historically, therefore, high standards of living as an objective and as an accomplishment for any sizable proportion of a population are a relatively recent phenomenon. The major part of the improvement in our standards of living has come in the last three quarters of a century. The rapidity of improvement in standards of living, particularly in the twentieth century, is in sharp contrast to the earlier slowness of change in living standards. The peasant of the early eighteenth century in England lived little if any better than his forebears of a thousand years earlier. The economic organization for producing goods and services operated at low speed even in the early nineteenth century, and did not begin to bring the production wherewithal

---

[8] Cf. Woytinsky and Woytinsky, *op. cit.*, p. 282, for an example.

for high living levels until after our Civil War. It is more than a coincidence that the acceleration of production of goods and new productive capacity accompanied the growth of selling effort after 1850.

Objective of High and Rising Standards of Living Further Examined

The attainment of high and rising standards of living for the entire population must include, first of all, bringing the substandard levels of living of portions of the population up to acceptable levels for our society. With all the accomplishments in the direction of rising standards of living in the United States, a portion of the population does suffer from what we consider substandard living, even though they may, at that, average considerably higher than the average of total populations of most countries of the world. What constitutes an acceptable level and what constitutes substandard levels are obviously matters of opinion.

In the United States, those who have substandard levels of living are likely to be low-income receivers due to lack of productivity.[9] The causes for lack of productivity are varied, namely, the lack of essential skills, lack of application, and deficiencies in mental or physical health. To a constantly decreasing extent, low incomes are due to the vicious circle set up by maldistribution. Clearly, if the worker does not get the food, clothing, and shelter he needs for effective production, we generate a cycle of low production and low incomes, low standards of living because of low incomes and deficiency in strength, vitality, and willingness to work. Disaster and illness, bad habits which interfere with useful productive work, addiction to drugs or alcohol militate against high production and

---

[9] *Economic Report of the President, 1956,* recognizes this need (p. 63). A special report entitled, *A Program for the Low-Income Population at Substandard Levels of Living* was published as a Congressional Document, Senate Report No. 1311, 84th Cong., 2nd sess. It summarizes the situation with respect to the low-income families. There are no accurate figures as to how many of these are living at substandard levels; but the highest estimate is less than 20 per cent and the total may be much lower. Whatever the figure, the fact that 80 per cent or more has higher standards is a unique situation.

high productivity. So also do the practices and policies of some unions and labor organizations and of some individuals. The mistaken belief that the principal means of securing improvement in the lot of the worker is through securing redistribution of the results of past production likewise hinders production. Finally, but not necessarily independent of the above, are those situations where a low standard of living has been due to the loss of the breadwinner of the family. Here the conditions may call for subsidy and relief, even though there are still persons who prefer to endure substandards rather than to accept relief.

It is clear that in this respect the task of raising levels of living in the United States differs markedly from that of raising levels in many foreign countries. Bringing substandards up to standard is entirely within the bounds of possibility, and society encounters no insuperable obstacles to the development of ways and means of bringing at least acceptable standards of living to all our people. Contrast the situation in the United States with that of a country noted for the low level of living standards for the masses: India. A prominent Indian businessman, analyzing the situation at the University of Calcutta in 1952, asserted that the standard of living in India involved the most important question of the times.[10] He pointed out that the Indian population received a very low per capita income, no more than one fifteenth of the average income of the United Kingdom and one twenty-seventh of the average income of the United States. The levels of living in India involved great deficiencies. Food was poor and inadequate. The average daily caloric content the laborer received was 1,700 as contrasted with an estimated 3,170 in the United States. In protein content Indians received less than half that in the United States or the United Kingdom. Consumption of clothing in India was one fourth that in the United States. This lecturer did not mince words, asserting that not only did higher standards of living depend on bigger production but also that it depended upon a slower rate of growth of population, referring to the large families and the lack of feeling of responsibility of family heads for the improvement

---

[10] B. T. Thakur, general manager, United Commercial Bank, Ltd., in the Taraparasid Kahrtan Lecture Delivered at Calcutta University; published in the Supplement to the United Commercial Bank, *Review*, August, 1952.

in the welfare of offspring. Particularly significant was the emphasis on the will to work, upon "know-how." He pointed out that a much higher sense of responsibility was needed among workingmen and their supervisors and stressed the fact that the production process was a huge interconnected mechanism that required that each do his part. He explained the will to work as an important, although not exclusive, cause of the low standard of living.[11]

The will to work, which finally appears in any study of low productivity in various parts of the world, is obviously affected by the health and energy of a population. This is based in part on the adequacy of nutrition. Evidence in Germany, France, and other areas indicates that where food is insufficient in type and quantity to maintain health and energy, production decreases. Beyond the necessity of good nutrition, incentives to work are affected by attitudes, philosophies, and desires. Evidence the world over seems to indicate that the will to work for higher standards is also clearly and directly affected by the strength of the desires a person feels can be fulfilled by work.

The objective of raising standards of living in substandard countries differs markedly from that of elevating levels in countries that already have achieved high standards. Under high-level conditions, the problem presents special problems because consumer freedom of choice is involved. As the level of living of a society rises beyond minimum standards, choice becomes possible and important. There is the tendency not only to increase the quantity of consumption but also to try to raise the quality by new products and by improving the types of goods used for basic satisfactions. The capacity of the human organism to consume food is limited, but there are no such strict limits on the taste for variety, the desire for less common and

---

[11] It is interesting also that another Indian student, speaking in the United States recently, mentioned the failure of an over-all government-ordered increase in wages to accomplish the expected improvement of standards of living except that of increasing the amount of drinking and gambling. He looked upon this clearly as an indication that the vague desire for higher standards of living among those who received the higher wages raised by government decree was not a real desire for the things that would make up higher standards of living. He argued that the average Indian had not been led by philosophic, religious, or other leadership to desire those things that go to make up high standards of living.

higher-quality foods. We spend, as a consequence, much more of our incomes and much more than the necessary minimum for nutrition in order to be well fed. Furthermore, the quantities that must be consumed in order to maintain and raise levels of living for a population involve the goods and services required for increase in population. The problem of providing for such increases takes on a different aspect when the rate of increase takes a turn such as it has done in the United States since 1940. The predictions of a stationary population to be reached probably as early as 1960 have had to be completely revised. The net increases in population have been such as to compel re-examination of production and distribution requirements in all aspects of our economy. Because the basic facts are everywhere observable, a detailed description of present levels of living is superfluous.

Selling, supplemented by other influences, is the obvious dynamic solution of the problem of raising standards for advanced societies predicated upon free enterprise and consumer freedom of choice. The selling, properly applied, will render pointless the fears that the rapid increase in our production facilities and the enormous advances in our technology will yield a flood of goods and services we cannot sell. Also, except for passing maladjustment, consumer demand will determine the rate of production and eventually the rate of growth of facilities.

The philosophy of a demand that is not fixed but can be expanded by selling and low prices has its value also for societies which suffer from low standards of living. But often drastic governmental and social movements are needed to break the vicious circle and establish more favorable conditions for release of individual initiative.

SUMMARY AND CONCLUSIONS

Since the avowed immediate objective of selling is to influence people to buy more goods and services, selling effort therefore logically brings it about that people do buy more of those goods and services. If the goods so bought furnish satisfaction without disproportionate sacrifice, the level of living has been improved. If the goods and services are bought by all the people, the general level of living has been raised. If by lowering prices more people are induced to buy, more people will enjoy higher levels of living and they will develop rising standards. People are caused to want better living standards and are induced to work for them, so that not only are levels raised but also the standards toward which these people strive.

Since the objectives of the individuals comprising the selling forces of our nation add up to high and rising purchases of those goods and services that make up high and rising levels of living, and since the demonstrated results of that action have been high and rising standards for all our people, we are justified in asserting that the aggregate objective of selling activity is to bring about high and rising standards of living.

High and rising levels and standards of living are worthy objectives of selling, whether viewed from a private or a social point of view. The objective is one in which those who participate in selling leadership may develop satisfaction and take pride. Selling is only one of the types of leadership aiming toward high standards of living; but it is the one most directly concerned with that objective, and it is the most effective of all the forms of leadership directed at least partially to that objective.

Several aspects deserve repeated emphasis. The objective of selling includes the entire population. As any economist or social scientist knows, or as any historian has observed, in most countries at the present and in the historical past for which we have sufficiently detailed records, certain more or less limited groups, comprising a small proportion of the population, have enjoyed high levels of living. Both in modern and historical times, some small groups have enjoyed extravagantly high levels. Land holdings by a few wealthy persons have generally insured high living standards. In more recent times and in most countries, industrialists, large merchants, and financiers are the principal limited groups that have enjoyed the high standards, together with ruling and military groups. The objectives for selling in a modern economy set as a goal a decent and rising level of living for every man, woman, and child in the nation.

Next it should be re-emphasized that the objective of high and rising standards of living refers primarily to economic and material standards. These are important and are broadly recognized by social scientists, by reformers, and by governments, as worthy standards. Nevertheless, in the argument set forth throughout this volume, it is recognized that economic and material standards and consumption of goods and services are not the whole of life. Not only is it recognized that the human costs in terms of working hours, energy required, and health must be considered in the definition of levels and standards of living; it is also recognized that cultural, spiritual, and other activities must have their due share of attention in the lives of men. The goal requires not only higher production of goods and services, but also higher productivity of labor and of the equipment that helps labor to produce more. Thus less and less labor, both to make up the components of a high level of living and to develop, create, and make the equipment for higher productivity, becomes imperative.

Lastly, the selling objective of high and rising standards of living is a dynamic one. It is in sharp contrast with ideas that have prevailed for countless generations, ideas that restrictions of wants and limitations of consumption were "among man's highest virtues."[12] Selling is opposed to the scale of values that has been typified as "Spartan" or the ideas on consumption of the Schoolmen of medieval times or the ideas of Gandhi of our modern age. The objective of selling is likewise opposed to the ideas of those who from their positions of power, wealth, and influence, regard a low level of living as the right and proper level for the world's "lower classes." The idea that any particular group has an inherent or divine exclusive right to high standards of living to the exclusion of all other groups in the economy is inconsistent with the goals of selling in the United States. The idea that certain limited groups shall appropriate high standards as the rightful, proper, and peculiar perquisite of the wealthy and powerful, whether these represent industry, agriculture, aristocracy, church, or state, is undemocratic and contrary to the ideas of a fluid or classless society, which is a condition for reaching the highest standards of living.

---

[12] Woytinsky and Woytinsky, *op. cit.*

Chapter V

BASIC REQUIREMENTS FOR HIGH AND RISING STANDARDS OF LIVING

HIGH AND RAPIDLY RISING living standards in the United States have been achieved under conditions favorable to that development. Such conditions are not the peculiar possession of a few countries, but they do enable economic leadership and the special leadership of selling to make their greatest contribution to the elevation of living levels. Favorable conditions can be grouped easily into several broad classes.

First, there are natural resources and natural factors favorable to production and productivity. Here are to be included the availability of agricultural, mineral, and animal resources, together with sources of power and climate favorable to human effort and to the maintenance of vigor and health.

A vigorous and healthy population is a second important favoring factor. For the developing, maintaining, and effective functioning of an economic organization, man-power resources must be available of the required types, abilities, and training. Management skills and technical competence should be on call if a people is to develop that production and productivity which alone can bring and maintain high levels of living.

Next, a basically favorable political climate is essential if high standards of living are to be attained within reasonable periods of time. A government must encourage or at least not discourage enterprise. It must encourage individuals and groups to take the initiative; and it must assure those individuals and groups that they will be permitted to retain enough of the results of successful enterprise and innovation to constitute real incentive, not only to continue in business but to go further.

A favorable social climate contributes to improved standards of living and to the rate of that improvement. Socially, the objective of high and rising standards of living can have real meaning only in a society in which there is no dominating social opposition to the enjoyment of those higher standards and in which there is mobility and fluidity of social groups.

Closely related, and part of the social climate, are the attitudes of those who are engaged in the production of goods and services as owners, managers, executives, staff, and workers. Their attitudes toward the work they are doing and toward each other become an important part of the social environment.

An attitude of employers and managers favorable toward the sharing of the benefits of greater productivity with the workers and consumers is helpful. For if higher standards of living are to be achieved for all the people, all the people must benefit from such advances. They must secure such benefit either under the compulsion they place upon employers and managers or by decisions of those managers and owners based upon their own attitudes and conclusions as to long-run advantage.

Finally, a strong desire on the part of the people themselves for high standards of living energizes production and tends to overcome other adverse conditions. If workers are fully satisfied with the existing standards, the difficulty of getting more productive work is enormously increased. On the other hand, even if workers are not satisfied with their existing lot but expect to achieve improvement by a process of redistribution of the returns of labor, by collective bargaining and other compulsions, high living levels may not be achieved, because the limits of improvements without increasing productivity are quickly exhausted. The only fruitful long-run combination is that of higher wages and income based upon greater productivity, so that prices need not be increased and may even be lowered while wages are raised.

From a broader point of view, economic effort necessary to produce high and rapidly rising standards of living is likely to be forthcoming only if there is added to the desire for such higher standards the hope of attaining them. A hopeful, optimistic people can make rapid progress toward such goals. On the other hand, a people whose leaders are permeated with a philosophy of despair, in which they are joined by the rank and file, makes little if any progress. The vicious circle—despair, lack of effort, lack of production, low standards, leading to despair—is not easily broken. But success in raising standards, even in limited areas, generates optimism, particularly if that optimism is supported by increased production and productivity and not for temporary periods merely by redistribution of existing production.

It should be noted that not all business and economic requirements for high and rapidly rising levels of production are of like importance. Inherent in the listing of these factors is the need to release the energies and initiative of those who are to produce the necessary goods and services. Unless that is accomplished, higher standards cannot be achieved, and the failure to achieve high standards of living in many parts of the world has been to no small extent the result of the failure to unlock human potentials.

NATURAL RESOURCES IN RELATION TO LIVING STANDARDS

Everyone will agree to the proposition that the availability and possible possession of natural resources are factors favorable to the attainment of high standards of living. Controversial questions emerge, however, when one explores the detailed relationship of selling and high standards of living to these resources. History shows and current conditions confirm beyond doubt that ample natural resources are not automatically accompanied by high standards of living for the masses of the people. Russia, China, Africa, South America, Mexico, all furnish examples of countries with high material resources but low levels of living. Undeveloped regions in various parts of the world that possess natural resources have suffered in the past and continue to suffer from standards of living that sometimes fail to meet even the requirements for subsistence.

Again, the relation of specific natural material resources to high standards of living is a changing one. The need for and use of particular materials for important products in the material standard of living are both changing and subject to continued change. These natural-resource requirements for production occupy much attention on the part of both government and industrial leaders. The government is concerned lest war cut off essential raw materials; consequently, government policy is to stockpile and encourage the search for synthetics or substitutes. In times of crisis and under shortage pressures, that search becomes a vigorous one. In an unstable and contentious world, the possession of raw materials enables industrial production to be carried on in spite of war or restrictions. But while shortages restrict production, they encourage search for other solutions, so that we developed, in World War II, substantial independence of foreign sources of rubber as we did for indigo and other dyestuffs in World War I. In the case of indigo, the synthetic has almost entirely supplanted the original source. In the case of synthetic rubber, the steady improvement in its manufacture has made it superior for many specialized uses, even though for others natural rubber continues to have some claim of superiority.

No country possesses within its borders all the requirements for raw materials that might be used industrially. Some have large supplies of vital materials toward which attention is usually directed. Others have very limited supplies. We tend to direct our attention to the so-called strategic or scarce materials rather than to the broad flow of materials and the changes in uses and needs for such materials.

To examine another aspect of the problem, it appears that a people could produce a relatively high standard of living without great raw-material resources if under conditions of free markets, such materials were available in commerce. An alternative would be the orientation of its economy toward the production of services, toward "refinement" industries rather than those which consumed large amounts of raw materials. It must be remembered that with quite inadequate natural resources, England built an outstanding industry and an empire. And today, advances in transportation and in the technology of war expose every country to risks of shortage of supplies.

Shortage of power in the form of coal, petroleum, or water power may delay and handicap production, but that handicap is not an unsurmountable one if other factors are favorable. Some Latin American countries with large natural resources lack power sources; but their failure to develop high standards of living for the bulk of the people is accounted for not by such deficiencies but by many other factors. The lack of social fluidity, the ideas of dictatorial governments and employees, have perhaps had as much to do with discouraging enterprise as the lack of raw materials. Nevertheless, the potentials of atomic-power sources for power-deficient countries stagger the imagination. Power shortage no longer becomes a factor or excuse for low and static production. But the availability of power, like the availability of other natural resources, is in itself no assurance of high standards of living for the peoples of a country. Power resources are not self-motivating toward higher standards of living.

Some observers have strongly warned that our raw-material resources are insufficient to support a much higher standard of living or even to continue the present standards indefinitely. They have been concerned that the rise of standards of living, even in a portion of the world, would be limited by a world scarcity of some raw materials. It is true that certain statistical tabulations indicate that we are consuming certain materials out of which tens of thousands of items are made more rapidly than we are finding production sources.[1] The pessimistic conclusion drawn by some of these writers is that we shall quickly

---

[1] For instance, see Samuel H. Ordway, Jr., *Resources and the American Dream* (New York: Ronald Press Co., 1952). Also Sir Henry Tizard's address in *Mid-Century* (Cambridge, Mass.: John Ely Burchard, 1952).

come to a point where we must abandon any hope of rise in the standard of living because of these shortages.

Such statements obviously are at present unproved conclusions. Furthermore, the possibility that for other reasons we may arrive at a point where further quantitative consumption of raw materials may not be desired deserves careful consideration. It is conceivable that our material standards of living may reach a point where quantitative increase is not the objective but rather qualitative increase. Mere quantity of consumption is not the only determinant of the level of living. It may be argued that now, and even more in the future, the greater productivity we achieve will be directed toward securing fuller enjoyment of high material living standards and the fuller development along other than economic and material aspects of the "good life." That objective would require more "leisure" and more productivity, but not necessarily more consumption of raw materials.

However, there are other reasons for believing that such pessimistic conclusions can be disregarded for the purposes of this study, even if we are to pass over the broad laws of the indestructibility of matter. The rate of scientific advance, for instance, in the atomic field, the conversion of minerals and metals, the development of new organic sources of materials, tend to make one less inclined to draw rigid conclusions on the basis of past statistical trends. If one were to go into the history of raw-material supplies, one would discover that for a number of basic raw materials, such as iron and petroleum, warnings of immediate exhaustion have been uttered from time to time. Somehow there has in each case followed a discovery of new sources so that the available sources of such materials appears to be greater now than they were even a short time ago. However, to dismiss the possibility of temporary and embarrassing shortages would be unwise, even though there seems to be little danger in the foreseeable future that high and rising standards of living will become meaningless because of raw-material deficiencies except in the case of war and temporary interruption of supply.

Furthermore, the discovery of raw materials and of new

processes and new substitutes tends to come in response to demand, although it would be naïve to assume that the timing of discoveries could be so precise as to avoid even temporary interference with our growth. Many inventions and discoveries have occurred in response to great need. Witness the quick early development of atomic energy when the need seemed to be extremely pressing. In fact, relatively short time limits are placed by scientists on the development of atomic energy for civilian and peacetime purposes.

To conclude one may ask:

Is there, therefore, an upper limit to high and rising levels of living imposed by the lack of raw-material resources, by rising population numbers, or by other factors? For many decades, positive statements have been made as to such limits, only to be disproved by actual developments in another generation. In a careful scientific study by the Director of the Food Research Institute of Leland Stanford University appears the statement:[2]

We have no present basis for setting upper limits to life expectancy or to our national production potential, or forecasting the course of the birth rate, the productivity per worker, and the changes in the make-up of the *standard* of living (not the consumption level per capita) that influences the choice between consumption goods and children—to say nothing of numerous other significant factors. Statements on these subjects that aroused no emphatic dissent when they were published during the past 30 years now appear clearly wrong. We have no safer basis now, except for saying that certain important potentialities are clearly in evidence and that others may come to light in the course of time.

Harold Moulton's recent work (*Controlling Factors in Economic Development*, Brookings Institute, 1949) merits critical examination in this connection, and especially his striking conclusion that a doubling of population in 100 years, with an eightfold increase in the per capita consumption level, is within the bounds of *economic* possibility, though he by no means predicts that this will occur. If this staggers our imaginations, let it be recalled that much

---

[2] Joseph S. Davis, *The Population Upsurge in the United States* (War-Peace Pamphlets, No. 12) (Stanford, California: Food Research Institute, Stanford University, December, 1949), p. 70. See also an article of the same title in *Journal of Political Economy*, Vol. LXI, No. 5 (October, 1953), pp. 375–79.

of what has occurred since 1850 would have seemed incredible to persons then living, and that what has happened in the past 10 years would have seemed incredible to most of us in 1939.

MAN-POWER REQUIREMENTS

No matter how developed a technology, high production and high productivity depend upon human labor. That labor may be less exacting and less exhausting than in the days when machines did few of the tasks, but the work may be more exacting in terms of training and the attention required, and in the penalties for failure. A vigorous and healthy worker population is a factor that favors the high production and high productivity required for high consumption and high levels of living. Material welfare makes possible the development and maintenance of that healthy working population. The extent to which the levels of living are raised in terms of the good life depends on how rapidly a population learns to live and use the results of increased productivity.

A low standard of living tends to perpetuate itself. An undernourished worker is not likely to be productive. He produces little and gets little because he produces little. Studies of the relationship of diet and production, even in more advanced countries as, for instance, in the coal mines of West Germany, have shown a clear relation between productivity and food in a heavy industry using considerable manual labor.

In addition to the influence of climate on natural resources, it is obvious that climate influences the productivity and production of people. Temperate climates favor production, while excessively high or humid or cold climates tend to discourage production. The latter introduce a handicap for the human being that needs to be overcome. The agricultural resources and exchange that enable a nutritious diet to be obtained by the worker are, of course, of basic importance. Workers whose food intake is substantially inadequate are not in a position to develop the health or vigor needed for most productive industrial work, even with the same machines and the same know-how and management.

The highest productivity requires not only bodily health

but also healthy attitudes. Such attitudes, of course, are in part the result of political and social environment, but the desirable attitude is one which seeks improvement for self, family, or community. The man who because of poverty sinks into an attitude of despair, which contains no hope for more than continuance of the daily drudgery and scant existence, is not in the frame of mind quickly to become productive. The healthy mind has generally worthy and attainable goals, which are consistent with public welfare. The gap between the levels and the standards to which he aspires are well within the points of attainment if he exerts himself. His expected reward, a fair share of what he produces, is worth fighting for; likewise, an increased share of his productivity is his due. However, he has not fallen into the error of thinking that higher wages alone can bring the high standards of living. Such standards in the United States have not been accomplished by leveling off, not by pulling down the few who have the highest standards, but by increasing total production.

A FAVORABLE POLITICAL CLIMATE

In a democratic society predicated upon private property, private initiative and private enterprise, individual liberty and opportunity, the requirement of a favorable political climate becomes a complex one. Government must seek to secure the maximum benefit to its citizens from the resources of the nation and from the initiative and abilities of its people. It must make use of the incentives of personal and general interest while reducing to a minimum the injury to the public that may be caused by fraud, greed, or destructive selfishness not otherwise checked by business and industry itself.

Private enterprise and private initiative mean little unless individuals and firms perform services of value to society and take risks in hope of reward. It is in the interests of the public that improvements in products and production methods and in the productivity of workers take place. We benefit by new projects, by new enterprise, by innovation, whether the result is lowered costs of production and lowered prices or more products or new satisfactions. However, excessive reduction of rewards tends to discourage initiative, invention, and desirable change. Our patent and copyright laws are based on the concept of reward to those who contribute something new. These and other laws are partial evidence that the need of opportunity, of providing rewards for successful service or successful innovation, is fundamental to improvement.

It is in the development and maintenance of conditions that enable the businessman to secure reward for successful service or innovation that government functions for good or ill. If the tax system tends to deprive the firm or individual of so much of the earnings of success as to leave an amount insufficient to warrant the risks involved as compared to other alternatives, it is obvious that some will be deterred. Threats of expropriation, of government seizure with inadequate compensation, discourage new ventures.

Effective also in discouraging enterprise is the attitude of government servants that success is somehow culpable, that business can be used as a "scapegoat" for political aspirants, who have discovered the voices of business are too often inarticulate and unable to present the position of business enterprise effectively. The idea that business success is to be deprecated on the ground that wealth cannot be secured honestly and in harmony with social welfare is injurious to the very people whom it is alleged to benefit. While the discussion of profit motivation will be taken up elsewhere, the opinions of detractors, when in positions of power, lead to excessive taxation, so that successful enterprise is penalized and new enterprise discouraged. When a successful businessman under a socialist labor government is compelled to pay regular taxes amounting to 114 per cent of his income and another has to pay 103 per cent, the fact serves as a warning that conservatism rather than innovation and expansion and risk taking are preferred. But venture and initiative are the more beneficial to an aspiring people who are not living under the illusion that high and rising standards of living can be achieved without increasing production and productivity.

More specifically, the difficult question as to how far to go in regulatory legislation to correct abuses of business may be resolved in a manner that discourages initiative and enterprise rather than the abuses of business. Some regulatory action is needed—but enterprise and initiative thrive best in an environment of freedom, where restrictions are aimed at limiting abuses, not at destroying initiative. Broadly, such a favorable political climate can exist for the people only where the rights of individuals are recognized as dominating. The prevailing philosophy of government must be that the government exists to facilitate the full enjoyment of opportunity and individual liberty and to guard the exercise of such liberty by individuals within the limits necessary to preserve the rights of others. Such a philosophy is not characteristic of those governments which hold that people exist for the state. A favorable political climate does not of itself assure high production or high levels of living. But on the whole, a favorable political climate is one in which the political roadblocks in the way of high production, high productivity, and high and rising standards of living either do not exist or have been lowered to consistent levels. However, this does not mean complete absence of regulation of abuses nor does it mean *laissez faire* or license.

In nondemocratic societies, the height of political barriers to production, innovation, and enterprise depends upon the rule or whim of a dictator or a governing group. Attitudes may change rapidly and arbitrarily as is apparent from the historical record in communistic Russia and Nazi Germany. Generally, however, such societies learn to give economic freedom to selected individuals or groups of individuals to encourage initiative for the benefit of the ruling group, as for instance in the recent history of atomic-weapon development in Russia. Special rewards and encouragement of initiative to increase production and productivity have long since been accepted as necessary to get such results, contrary to the fundamental tenets of totalitarian or authoritarian societies. But little such interest has been evinced in connection with raising the living standards of the average worker.

Freedom from excessive political control is essential for rapid elevation of standards of living. An editor puts it well when he writes in general terms:[3]

The idea of a free economy has never lacked competitors and detractors since it had its first stirrings in minds oppressed by the rigid controls of feudalism. Yet where it found fertile soil—in the Dutch Republic, in England and above all in America—its flourishing began to give men their first hope against their ancient scourge of poverty. Its record against the societies where neither freedom nor competition was welcomed is hardly obscure.

Nor is its record today. You can go through the list of nations, from Soviet Russia to the United States, and find that success in their assault upon great economic problems can be charted by the amount of freedom in their economic affairs from the hand of the state. Great Britain, Belgium, Holland, France, Spain—in proportion as they have restored economic freedom or prevented it, so is the prosperity of their people determined. Nowhere, perhaps, is the contrast made plainer than by the line that divides the heart of Germany.

It would not seem necessary today for the jury to understand the abstruse arguments of the theorists in order to render a verdict where the tangible evidence is so plain in every household.

A FAVORABLE SOCIAL CLIMATE

The incentive to work is most effective when men have assurance that they will be rewarded, when the man who seeks to raise his level of living or to advance can find no insurmountable bar to that advance if he is successful in his work. In the United States we can be proud that there has been a constant progression from the lower to the higher standards. When a worker buys an automobile for his family or an automatic clothes washer for his wife, there generally is no occasion for questioning the propriety of his action. The high progressive income taxes have tended to level down higher incomes where, as one journalist puts it, the "United States is fast becoming a one-class market of middle-class people."[4] The possibility that workers by their own efforts may rise in the social scale is a

---

[3] *Wall Street Journal*, October 20, 1954.

[4] Cf. Stern, *op. cit.* Mr. Stern emphasizes the same point in chap. iv, "America Sheds Class Distinctions."

powerful incentive to work for higher standards. High fluidity of social movement is unfortunately to be found only in a small part of the world and particularly in the free countries such as the United States, Canada, Australia, and to a lesser extent, in certain western European countries. The incentive that exists in a fluid society for the ambitious man to work more productively in order to rise in the social scale is apparently absent or at least much weakened, not only in the far eastern and eastern lands, but also in much of continental Europe.

The English economist, Graham Hutton, in an analysis of the findings of more than fifty productivity teams that visited the United States and studied the American economy concluded that the real secret of American productivity was that American society was imbued with the desirability, the rightness, the morality, of production. Among the most important reasons for the high productivity and high levels of living in the United States was the high fluidity of American society;[5] in other words, the relative ease with which successful producers in any economic field could move upward from one social group to a higher social group.

He found that many more such incentives to higher production and high levels of living were operative in the United States than in Britain. It was his conclusion that the efficiency of work was highly rewarded in America. Not only were workers rewarded, but the rewards meant more in the way of real income, for more could be bought with income. Furthermore, he pointed out that more leisure was available in which to buy these things and to enjoy them. He went on to declare that since the rewards from greater efficiency depended in many cases upon the firm or department or team effort, greater awareness of team spirit existed, which in itself was an incentive. In another chapter, the author asserts that American society is far more fluid than European. It has expanded more rapidly and its incentives are different. Furthermore, he emphasized the productiveness in all walks of American life and the existence of a legal and institutional framework devised to

---

[5] Graham Hutton, *We Too Can Prosper* (London: George Allen & Unwin, Ltd., 1953).

foster and secure competition in business. He concludes by saying that there is no particular secret of American high production and productivity and practices that could not be carried out elsewhere with good management, good human work, and good equipment. In his further discussion, however, while he perceives the favoring factors, he has failed to recognize the need of an energizing influence, a dynamic influence, for he says the only real problem of productivity is that of securing the required degree of "goodness" of management. Undoubtedly good management enhances productivity. It does not produce high standards of living for all the people unless that management and many managements provide the energizing force to start the economic machine and to keep it going in high gear.

The absence of rigid patterns of consumption in the United States is certainly a favorable factor, the value of which cannot be easily measured. But it can be said that in the United States, people are generally free to buy what they can afford, either in their own opinion or in the opinion of those who extend credit to them. The day laborer may buy a new car if he wishes without causing commotion among his neighbors. If a new car is too expensive for his income, he may buy a second-hand car, some one of which is pretty sure to be within his budget. There is no occasion to fear that he will be criticized adversely by his friends for going beyond class custom, because no rigid class customs exist. His friends and neighbors also want to buy or indeed may have already done so. Furthermore, his employer sees nothing reprehensible in his purchase, although he may think the man has not used good judgment.

How different where rigid patterns cover people's actions! The influence of such patterns is verified by an advanced investigator studying entrepreneurship in France. There he found that workers accepted relatively low standards of living without complaint, much lower than corresponding standards in the United States. The work was no less taxing in energy output and hours than the work done in our own country. None of these workers possessed automobiles. Their attitude was expressed in the statement that "automobiles are for the bosses, not for the workers." Questioning of the owners of business elicited general statements in agreement to the effect that "automobiles were for the bosses." They accepted as only just and right, even ordained, low standards for the workers, together with high standards and the right to accumulate wealth as the perquisites of the bosses.

The investigator in the course of his study interviewed labor leaders as well as workers and employers. One French labor leader said that in his efforts to help the workers attain a high standard of living, he was confronted with apathy and indifference and low productivity. The workers did not want high standards of living nor expect them. It was difficult to arouse them to demand high standards; thus little pressure was exerted on employers to give workers higher wages. This labor leader made the illuminating statement that he believed he could get higher standards, even automobiles, for French workers if they would only demand them and put forth the productive effort to earn them.

The obstacles of custom to rapid rise can be traced both historically and geographically. One need not go very far back to find evidence of such patterns in much of recorded history. While much too little historical research has been accorded to the levels of living of the common people, one obtains the impression that not only were the standards of living of the masses of the people very low but they remained low for thousands of years, even as late as the eighteenth and nineteenth centuries. The effort to secure even modest levels in living were regarded as unseemly or abortive. Woytinsky quotes from an eighteenth-century author who was in the small minority of those who were articulate in defense of raising standards. He reproduces a page from a pamphlet published in 1796 that really described the conditions of life of English workers at that time. The author is seeking to exonerate workers of the accusation that they eat white bread and drink tea. In the last paragraph of this page occurs the statement:[6]

Small indeed is the portion of worldly comforts now left them. Instead therefore of grudging them so small an enjoyment as a

---

[6] W. S. Woytinsky and E. S. Woytinsky, *World Population and Products* (New York: The Twentieth Century Fund, 1953), p. 282.

morsel of good bread with their miserable tea; instead of attempting to show how it may yet be possible for them to live *worse* than they do; it well becomes the wisdom and humanity of the present age to devise means how they may be better accommodated.

One recalls in this connection a classic quotation from John Stuart Mills' essay *On Liberty*.[8]

The despotism of custom is everywhere the standing hindrance to human advancement, being in unceasing antagonism to that disposition to aim at something better than customary, which is called, according to circumstances, the spirit of liberty, or that of progress or improvement. The spirit of improvement is not always a spirit of liberty, for it may aim at forcing improvements on an unwilling people; and the spirit of liberty, in so far as it resists such attempts, may ally itself locally and temporarily with the opponents of improvement; but the only unfailing and permanent source of improvement is liberty, since by it there are as many possible independent centres of improvement as there are individuals. The progressive principle, however, in either shape, whether as the love of liberty or of improvement, is antagonistic to the sway of Custom, involving at least emancipation from that yoke; and the contest between the two constitutes the chief interest of the history of mankind. The greater part of the world has, properly speaking, no history, because the despotism of Custom is complete. This is the case over the whole East. Custom is there, in all things, the final appeal; justice and right mean conformity to custom; the argument of custom no one, unless some tyrant intoxicated with power, thinks of resisting. And we see the result.

One further element in the social climate favorable to the attainment of the basic objective of selling needs to be noted in addition to the absence of social barriers to advancement and the breaking down of stratified consumption patterns. It is the need of attitudes that we characterize by such terms as "optimism," "hope," "hopefulness," "the spirit and will to improve," and "forward looking." A prominent banker recently addressed himself to two questions: First, will our country be able to retain the momentum of its recent economic life, will we move ahead or will we fail to make full use of our resources? Second, can we continue to develop means by which we can work with our allies in achieving a common defense and improving living stand-

---

[8] Fifth edition, London, 1874, p. 126.

ards throughout the free world? He went on to say that certainly one of the principal characteristics of American life—and one that is notably stronger than in the thirties—is the feeling of a strong forward movement, a sense of continuing growth and change, which brings with it new opportunities and steady improvement. He mentioned particularly the high rate of growth of our population, the rise of economic and technological changes through research—but without further analysis and with the usual nonrecognition or implicit acceptance of selling as a dynamic force.

Along this line any intelligent observer who travels in Europe, talks with the people, reads their literature, and compares notes with the United States must appreciate the differences in attitudes that reflect the hopefulness of people in the United States, a hopefulness which persists in spite of the relative pessimism of many other countries. The actions of our businessmen in planning expansion, the attitudes of our consumers in buying on installment terms, the results of studies of buying intentions, are evidences of that hopeful anticipation. Interesting also in this connection is the series of studies by a noted university colleague in which groups of young men from ten different countries were asked to project their autobiographies to the year 1980. Once seriously undertaken, such an exercise compelled young men imaginatively to set forth what they expected of the future and its effects upon them personally. The results have shown an amazing difference in those expectations. On the whole, American young men have been optimistic, while Europeans displayed attitudes of indifference and more commonly, pessimism, often pessimism as to the future of civilization. Certainly if such attitudes were typical, as they appear to be, they are not conducive in Europe or elsewhere to the formulation of new ideas, the establishment of new enterprises, or to the launching of new products and the acceptance of risks incurred in innovation and development in the hope of future profit.

As one of our very able businessmen has written after an extensive study of European conditions:[9]

---

[9] Clarence B. Randall, *A Creed for Free Enterprise* (Boston: Little, Brown & Co., 1954).

But in Europe the economy is torpid and sick, kept alive for the most part by blood transfusions from the healthy arteries of our industry. Over there the young men seek security and have a depressing sense of fatalism about the future. They doubt whether there is anything they can do about themselves in particular or the world in general. Among the older businessmen are many who are very wise and many who often seem to have a clearer understanding of the world in which they live than their counterparts among us, but there is a lack-lustre look in their eyes. They are defensive, sensitive to criticism, and more proud of what has been than of what is to be. Their spirit is not that of the risk-taking entrepreneur, but of the conservator of what their fathers and grandfathers have passed on to them.

ECONOMIC AND BUSINESS CLIMATE

The best efforts of people will be enlisted to realize a high standard of living if work is effective in bringing high real wages and other satisfactions to those who participate directly or indirectly in production. This means that workers must work productively, that managers must manage so as to enhance production and provide the tools to make work productive. Researchers, innovators, teachers, financiers, and many others must all contribute. However, because workers compel or because employers see long-range advantages in sharing, owners and managers must share with workers the results of greater productivity. While the business climate in some measure is determined by government and political action, an economic and governmental milieu that fails to offer those who venture and those who work a fair share of increased production is a discouraging factor. Enterprise, innovation, advancement in management skills, new applications of technology, offer a considerable risk and will be retarded unless there is reasonable opportunity to secure return. There need not and cannot be assurance of return, but there must be a reasonable chance of profit.

The favorable climate is created and maintained by good human relations, good teamwork among those engaged in the enterprise. The great accomplishment of American business has come about through tapping the resources of many such people and securing the results of the brain power, ability, and energy of these people rather than depending solely, as in most other parts of the world, on a small segment of society to furnish direction and ideas. The realization of the capacity of the population is to be secured only if there is widespread incentive and hope of reward. Selling leadership makes its greatest contribution in providing these incentives to effective economic action.

The attitude of employers in the United States toward the teamwork already mentioned illustrates clearly the vital difference between ours and the climate in which the European worker finds himself. European productivity teams appear not to have grasped the full significance of our conception of teamwork. To them good teamwork consisted of able leadership coupled with implicit obedience of the workers to a boss who does the planning and ordering. The informal give-and-take between workers and bosses in which the interest and contribution of workers, foremen, and higher officials are sought was often taken for lack of discipline and the informality for impertinence of workers and lack of respect.

The absence of any real desire or feeling of compulsion on the part of employers and owners to share the increased productivity with the workers characterizes some employers in the United States but appears to be common in western Europe and other parts of the world. The employer's interest too often does not extend beyond his family. Frequently he feels that he has fully carried out his social obligation by paying his relatively low-producing workers according to the standards of the area in which he is located. The idea of improving the productivity of the worker so that he may share the improvements of productivity with the worker, so that his standards of living may be improved, seems not to be taken in friendly spirit. In fact, if one employer desires to raise wages so as to bring about the cycle of activity that brings higher standards, he is likely to find himself encountering the active opposition of businessmen, bankers, and competitors. For instance, an article in the *New York Times* points out one employer who applied new techniques to making shoes, coupled with a profit-sharing plan. He was able to reduce selling prices and raise wages substantially.

When he wished to borrow money, his bankers refused to finance expansion, although the success and profitability of his actions and philosophy had been thoroughly demonstrated.

LIMITATIONS OF FAVORING CONDITIONS

Examples already cited indicate that high and rising standards of living have not necessarily been achieved where favoring conditions exist and that the possession of large natural resources does not of itself guarantee elevation of living standards. Potentially and actually vigorous populations endure low living standards. Low standards are found in salubrious and stimulating climates. Even under seemingly favorable political conditions production may languish. It appears that no one of these favoring factors alone produces high living standards, nor does the possession of several achieve economic welfare for the people. Take the case of France. Economically France would appear to have all the requirements for prosperity and for high and rising standards of living for the people. A student of French affairs points out that:[10]

Except for petroleum, she is rich in natural resources. Her population of 42,000,000 is highly skilled. There is an even balance between industry and agriculture. Most peasants own their land. Employment is high but the economy is on a 1910 model. Firms and farms are small, models and machines old, sales techniques clumsy; all the usual signs of dynamics—heavy capital investment, big advertising, bold new ventures—are absent from the French economy. Basic adjustments are necessary but the present economic balance in France has led to a high division of conflicting interests. Each conflicting group wants the other to adjust.

In the study of French labor unrest,[11] another observer asserts that the unrest which has long troubled France is based on the low standard of living:

The cost of living combined with wage scales that even in ancient times of a stable franc have never permitted the French working class to keep more than a few steps ahead of poverty. . . . But out

[10] New York Times, August 16, 1953.
[11] Ibid.

of diversity and the statistically muddy picture comes a generaliza-
tion that everyone is sure of. That is that in one of the most highly
sophisticated and intelligent countries of the western world the
standard of living of millions of its citizens is woefully low. It is
affirmed both by unions and by Premier Joseph Laniel who is not
"labor's man."

More important than the affirmations is the tangibility of this
low standard. It is seen in budgets that stretch so thin between one
monthly pay day and another that they often break and leave a
family living on cheap bread, soup and potatoes for the last two
or three days of the monthly grind. And it is seen in the fact
that there is little money for clothes (many families make their
clothing at home), that gas, electricity and the tri-monthly rent
bills present problems of financial ingenuity for harrassed house-
wives, that ordinary distractions such as movies are rare and some
months nonexistent.

It is seen in the dilapidated apartments filled with simple furniture or in hovels and hotel rooms where families live cramped together because there is a housing shortage and those with the least
money get the least housing. It is seen in the fact that the refrigerator is a luxury that is not only out of reach of the working class
but is a difficult object for middle-class families to acquire.

What produces this standard and maintains it at its low level?
A currency pushed downgrade by two great and impoverishing
wars has sent prices in exactly the opposite direction, as those with
goods to sell have attempted to compensate for less and less reliable
money.

Mass production is still in the first timid stages in France where
the gigantic United States production system is regarded as dangerous for French individuality. The artisan is still highly regarded
here. He makes undeniably beautiful objects, but because of their
price they grace neither the person nor the home of the workman.
French manufacturers, in addition, are reluctant to take the risks
involved in creating and supplying a mass market with high-volume,
low-price goods. Many manufacturers putting out many brands of
the same item stick to the safer method of low volume with profit
on each item correspondingly high. In a way they are encouraged
in this by consumers who want objects just a little different from
everyone else.

The conclusion is inescapable that political and psychological
factors are usually more important in the achievement of high
levels of living than material factors. The desire for better living, the possibility and probability of achieving it, and the polit-

ical freedom to produce and consume goods and services that make up high standards are basic and essential.

NEED FOR ENERGIZING INFLUENCE

The basic fact is that high and rising levels of living have been achieved and will be achieved only if the people have intense desires for the goods and services required to satisfy that demand. High levels of living of all the people mean that in one way or another all the people must produce. There are no exempt classes. There are no privileged groups depending upon the masses of workers producing at low or subsistence levels for themselves and high levels for the few. Higher incomes and higher wages for all who produce, which permit higher standards of living, are implicit in the philosophy based upon high production and high productivity. In no other sound way can high and rising standards of living be developed and maintained. There are, of course, other ways in which a democratic society may for a time help some people or certain classes. Redistribution of existing wealth, compulsion to pay high wages, not matched by productivity, heavy taxation for welfare without corresponding production—all of these may for a time permit some increase in average standards of living. It has been observed, however, that in more and more countries of the world, redistribution of wealth in these forms has not brought continuing rise in levels of living. Production is likely to be neglected and productivity declines as a result of these measures.

To repeat, progressive rise in the standards of living must come from past or current production. The philosophy that redistribution will bring high levels of living fails to recognize to how large an extent redistribution has already taken place. Some redistribution may be highly beneficial to the whole economy. This has happened in the United States. In 1929 the richest 5 per cent of the people had about 30 per cent of the total take-home pay. Today the figure is less than 15 per cent, due particularly to the leveling effect of a progressive income tax.

The large increase in the share of lower-income groups has been due to higher wages and in part to the increased employment compared to earlier depression years. Few persons who hold jobs today can be said to fall in the low-income groups or to have a low standard of living. Wide variations in standards of living from lowest to highest, such as characterize certain South American countries where most people exist at low levels and where there is a relatively small middle class, tend to increase the indifference and apathy that reduce effort or even kill desire. Low-income groups in this country do not consist in the main of those who work but rather of old people, those who are ill, or women with families widowed by death, desertion, or divorce. This is the reason why wage increases rarely help the low-income groups. Fortunately, those groups have become smaller and smaller.

The desire that leads to continued and rising production of goods and services required for a high standard of living does not emerge automatically and is not a part of our psychological make-up. That desire must be intensified if it is to provide the dynamic force. Our people can have and continue to have a high and rising standard of living if they want it enough. The prime function of selling is to intensify desire to the point of buying action and subsequent production.

What happens in a highly developed country when people do not have this intense desire may be illustrated in British experience.

In an article in the London *Economist*,[12] entitled the "Riddle of Prosperity," the editor after studying the reasons for low productivity in England, even in situations in which equally good machinery and equal "know-how" were involved, says:

It begins to look as if we have been dealing with the surface symptoms of poor productivity and that the real causes lie deeper. For a few years after the war, it was possible to ascribe a great deal to the lingering effects of the disorganisation and the exhaustion of the war itself. But that excuse serves no longer. For a time, it was believed that productivity could be increased by exhortation. It had a little effect, but only here and there, and for short periods. Exhortation will work only when it can act as a lever on a firm fulcrum of faith; and in this country, it appears, faith in the merits—one might say in the morality—of economic achieve-

[12] Vol. CLXVIII, No. 5733 (July 11, 1953).

ment is dim. Then there was the phase of believing that the trick could be done by more and newer and better machinery. There is something in that too. But as an immediate stimulant to British productivity it suffers from two defects. There is a shortage of savings to pay for the machines. And machines will do little without the will to use them. In the last eighteen months, monetary discipline has been tried, and its effects have been considerable. But no one would claim that monetary policy can change the basic shape and spirit of a nation's economy.

Slowly, therefore, the conviction has been growing that the essential element has been missing. That element is the human will. Unless the ordinary man or woman sees the virtue, or at least the necessity, of producing more, more will not be produced. Even the Communists, who are taught to regard human beings as machines, are beginning to learn this truth. Certainly in a free society, it is basic. And perhaps no set of people more badly need recalling to it than the professional economists.

The editor concludes:

How does a nation set about changing its own frame of mind? That it needs to be done will not be denied by anybody who realises what the economic hazards of the future mean for a people situated as we are. That it can be done will hardly be denied by anybody who reflects upon the enormous change in precisely these attitudes that has occurred in the last two generations or so, much of it the direct result of deliberate teaching. How shall we set about restoring some belief in the rightness of effort, the morality of success? How shall we make the British people determined to be prosperous?

CONCLUSION

One is compelled to draw the conclusion that prosperity in terms of high levels of living for people generally does not rest principally upon natural resources or climate or other natural factors, but upon the abilities, capacities, attitudes, and behavior of people. And it is in the differences in behavior that the explanation of the differences in the rate of economic growth is to be found. A useful analysis, made by Professor Walt Rostow of the Massachusetts Institute of Technology[18] suggests

[18] W. W. Rostow, *The Process of Economic Growth* (New York: W. W. Norton & Co., 1952), p. 285.

that the basic determinants of the rate at which an economy grows as between one country and another, or between one time and another, are the six fundamental functions:

1. The propensity to develop fundamental science (physical and social).
2. The propensity to apply science to economic ends.
3. The propensity to accept innovations.
4. The propensity to desire material advance.
5. The propensity to consume rather than to save.
6. The propensity to have children.

One may disagree with any such list, but it is not only interesting but significant that if all or most of these are high, economic advance will be rapid.

The role of selling in relation to these functions is discussed at many points in this volume. It will suffice to point out that selling tends to develop and intensify the propensity to consume and the propensity to desire material advance. In subsequent chapters it will be shown that selling performs essential services in developing and intensifying the propensity to accept innovations, and in furnishing incentive to apply science to economic ends. The fact that science can be applied to economic ends and yield rewards to those who make the application encourages and provides the means for more rapid development of fundamental science. But the incentives and rewards for rapid economic progress depend upon selling to an extent that becomes apparent upon careful study of the thinking and bases of action of business and industrial executives.

Chapter VI

PRODUCTION, PRODUCTIVITY, AND SELLING

THE ROLE of selling in elevating standards of living would be of minor consequence if selling stopped with creating strong desire for more and better goods and services. Selling must and does do more than that. Selling in its various applications motivates people to produce more in going enterprises; establish new enterprises; develop new products; carry on industrial and economic research; originate, develop, and improve industrial and distribution processes; and place into the hands of the people more goods at lower prices. For selling is the energizing, dynamic force which enables all these to be brought about. The result is large and rising production and high and rising productivity, without which the objectives of better living cannot be attained. The fact that the rise in production and productivity has taken place concurrently with rise in the volume and force of selling effort is no mere coincidence. A definite and provable cause-and-effect relationship exists.

Clearly, the goals of high and rising standards of living for all the people require great quantities of goods and services if people are to have:

Supplies of known and established types of goods;

Adequate supplies of new products to satisfy needs and wants.

Furthermore, rising productivity of the whole producing organization is required if:

New and old products are to be turned out in greater quantity with less work;

Prices are to be lowered so that real income of people is increased;

Satisfaction in the work of producing and distributing goods is increased; and finally if

More leisure to enjoy these goods and services and to develop a balanced life is to be attained.

That our economy has achieved a great deal toward realizing these objectives can easily be observed and is demonstrated by careful statistical study. The accomplishment has been described in popular terms as it affects the consumer in a Boston newspaper editorial as follows:[1]

In the midst of wars, worries and alarms there is accumulating evidence that this nation is experiencing an extraordinary upsurge of cultural, scientific, and economic achievement.

It is possible, indeed, that here in this Western Hemisphere there may already be a reborn Golden Age whose fruits belong to all the people rather than a single, favored class.

There is, for example, a deep, genuine and expanding musical interest in this mid-century in America—creative, performing, listening. Here in this area there is all sorts of evidence of it—young people cross-legged on the floor of Harvard's Fogg, listening to chamber music—MIT students forgetting stresses and isotopes and mathematical formulas in orgies of classical records in Hayden Library—public library record exchanges—community orchestras and choruses, neighborhood quartets—new compositions and scores being written.

Last year some 30,000,000 persons attended concerts of classical music in the country, twice as many as before the war. And they spent more money to listen to this "long hair" music than they did for baseball.

When the Boston Symphony Orchestra was organized in 1881 it became one of a small handful in the country.

In 1951 there were 200 symphony orchestras, 89 more than in 1940.

Without becoming involved in arguments over the relative merits of bebop and Beethoven, it is possible to point to this as one element in what Fenton B. Turck in *The Scientific Monthly* called "The American Explosion." We are a society, he says, burst out in a

[1] *Boston Globe*, October 12, 1952; editorial by Frances Burns. By permission.

"flood of new ideas, new tastes, new standards . . . a fresh and exciting age, marked by changed attitudes, changed customs, changed goals. . . ."

The thesis of a new Golden Age which is "neither the product nor property of any particular class" but offers all its advantages and opportunities to the "average individual American" should not be surprising or novel to anyone able to look back on four or five decades of living in this country.

But the trouble is, we haven't much clear judgment about ourselves any more. We are prone to accept the sneers about our supposedly "materialistic philosophy."

Yet all the while the nation has been growing up in a manner that believes most of the popular ideas about it. Mr. Turck uses figures to prove this point.

Thus, he says, that while the real purchasing power of the American consumer was 53% more in 1950 than in 1940, the nation is buying new cars now only at a 10% greater rate.

But Americans increased in constant dollars their purchases of books by 96%, spent 140% more for toys and sports equipment, and 120% more for flowers and seeds than ten years before. More than half—54%—of the nation's consumers own their homes today and even after the surge of G.I. attendance had subsided there were 23% more students in institutions of higher learning last year than before the war.

All these statistics are impressive. But each individual is aware, if he stops to think about it, of that "explosion" in taste through the medium of his own experience every day. It is not too long since, outside New England, public libraries were uncommon and bookstores were to be found only in the cities. People who may listen knowledgeably today to Aaron Copland and Walter Piston, to Prokofiev and Beethoven and Vaughan Williams were satisfied then with Ethelbert Nevin on the parlor square piano and the Anvil Chorus and Toreador Song rendered by the high school glee club.

Even those who deplore esthetically the mass production of houses today admit their virtues in light and air and decoration and furnishings over the scrolled and jigsawed, golden oak and beaded curtain horrors of a half century or more ago.

If we are, indeed, in a new Golden Age of America the final spurt to growth has come in the ten years since World War II began. The seed was planted long ago—three centuries and more. It lay dormant, to be sure, for many years under the chill necessity of hard and unrelenting toil to survive in a new world where there was neither capital nor cheap and plentiful labor and no time and energy for "frills."

But the atmosphere of freedom from Old World restraints and

shibboleths provided plenty of nourishment for the first tender shoots when they finally pushed forth, and it is this freedom in which the plant has grown and flourished.

We have developed machines, harnessed power, created new substances from earth and air. In 40 years from 1910 production of electric energy jumped from 20,499,775,000 kw.hr. to 387,994,000,-000—

Tractors on farms from 1000 in 1910 (1,545,000 in 1940) to 3,825,000—and value of farm implements and machinery in 10 years from $1,265,000,000 to $3,060,000,000.

Production of petroleum from 26,286,000 barrels in 1930 to 2,042,686,000 in 1950.

There were 76% more constant dollars spent for newspapers and magazines in 1950 than in 1940—

For steamship and overseas aircraft fares an increase of 412%—

Life insurance assets increased 49%, group membership in hospitalization plans 900%, accident and health insurance 375%.

The atom has been split, nylon and other plastics developed, timesaving devices have become routine in our daily life, and all these technological processes have made possible a measure of leisure for vast numbers of people, while giving them means to enjoy it.

Students of manners know that there can be no arts without time in which to cultivate them—ask any housewife about it! Primitive people whose wants are few often have been more free to develop handicrafts than their busy conquerors. Even the great depression, sad as it was, saw an immense upswing in ornamental gardening and planting and widespread enjoyment of the less expensive arts.

The war certainly provided a booster for the "explosion." It lifted one of every 10 persons out of their familiar ways and set them down in strange and dangerous new places to fight. It moved millions more to new work. It took the brakes off old ideas of production and income and spending. It offered a new perspective on values.

And now here we are—the knowledge and achievements of all the ages spread out for everybody in such a harvest as the select few who have enjoyed other golden eras never dreamed—music, literature, art, science, freedom from want, even compassion and understanding.

What is lacking? Just one ingredient—Peace—in the world and the minds and souls of us all.

And that, in the end, each of us only can achieve for himself, whatever and wherever the reservoir from which we draw strength.

The part that selling has played in bringing this about can be only partially appreciated even if we recall the extensive selling efforts of such firms as the phonograph, radio, and television receiver producers; the continuous selling programs of the automobile industries and their distributors; the huge advertising and selling expenditures of electrical equipment manufacturers and power companies; or the fact that newspapers, radio, and television networks could not have developed as they have, either without their own selling and advertising solicitation, or the support of others who endeavor to influence people to buy.

Human and physical factors affect both quantity of production and the productivity of workers. Some of the physical factors must be accepted, but human attitudes and the human will, human capacities, human initiative and human ingenuity, all are basic and fundamental factors in attainment of production and productivity. It is with these human factors that selling is concerned. The impact of selling upon workers, employers, owners, and investors—in short, upon those who operate our productive system—is one of the vital forces that differentiates our free-enterprise economy from other societies that have failed to attain high living standards for the masses of people.

PRODUCTION AND PRODUCTIVITY IN THE UNITED STATES

Before we embark on an analysis of the forces that lead to high production and rising productivity, a brief glance at the course of developments in the United States, with some comparisons, may be useful; for we have before us high and rising production as well as high and rising productivity. It has been so concisely described and pointed up by Frederick C. Mills of Columbia University in the opening paragraphs of a report that one can do no better than to quote his words:[2]

Over the last half century the real national product of the United States increased five-fold, while population doubled. Output per capita of the population increased two and one-half times.

[2] Frederick C. Mills, *Productivity and Economic Progress* (New York: National Bureau of Economic Research, Inc., Paper 38, 1952), pp. 1–2, 21–22.

Here was the basis of a substantial advance in economic power and in levels of consumption. Over this same period the total volume of human effort going into production (measured by man-hours of labor input) increased by 80%. The great gain in total output was won with an increase in labor input well below the increase in population. Here is evidence of a gain in welfare in another dimension—a saving of effort and a lightening of the toil by which the material needs of life are satisfied.

The major instrument used in the winning of these dual gains was enhanced productivity. During this period there was an unbroken advance in average physical output per manhour of work done. Decade by decade the effectiveness of productive effort increased. In the final decade output per manhour of labor input was 2.81 times what it was fifty years before.

The movements thus briefly summarized reflect four basic trends in the growth of the economy of the United States (see table below). These trends are examined in the pages that follow. We there attempt to determine the magnitudes of some of the elements of growth, to outline the uses to which we have put our expanding productive power and, in so doing, to define some aspects of the pattern of progress over this half century of economic expansion.

REAL GROSS NATIONAL PRODUCT, POPULATION, LABOR INPUT, AND PRODUCTIVITY, UNITED STATES, BY DECADES, 1891–1950

Decade	Billions of 1929 Dollars	Relative	Population (Relative)	Total Man Hours of Labor Input (Relative)	Output per Man Hour (Relative)
1891–1900.......	294	100.0	100.0	100.0	100.0
1901–1910.......	455	154.8	120.6	126.1	122.8
1911–1920.......	603	205.1	143.4	140.5	146.0
1921–1930.......	838	285.0	165.4	145.1	196.4
1931–1940.......	843	286.7	181.9	122.8	233.5
1941–1950.......	1,493	507.8	201.4	180.5	281.3

Professor Mills in the last sections of his study goes on to conclude that a study of the pattern of economic growth of the United States over the last half century answers the criticism that it has delivered the goods necessary to furnish a high standard of living; but that it has gone beyond that. To quote further:

We have used our natural resources to produce a great and growing volume of goods and services. Apart from the protracted check that came in the thirties, the advance has been virtually unbroken. By far the greatest factor in this gain has been rising productivity. Machines, plants, administrative methods, and men have improved in productivity quality; equipment has grown in quantity; flexible power has been carried to assembly line and bench. These improvements, embodied in innumerable major and minor working methods, have brought an increase in output per unit of productive effort that is probably without precedent in our history.

Appraisal of the uses to which these tremendous productive powers have been put is not so simple. Noneconomic standards of judgment must enter if the moral issues suggested by Toynbee are to be faced. We have used some of these powers for destruction, a fact that may be charged to the ill fortune of our generation rather than to design and deliberate choice. Thanks to modern technology we have had to employ only a relatively small part of our resources to maintain and enlarge our productive plant. We have used most of our vast new powers to ease the lot of citizens at large through gains in leisure, and to improve it through diversified consumption patterns. Not all the standards expressed in this diversification might win a moralist's highest sanction. There are doubtless faults to amend. But the record leaves no doubt that much of our new productive power has gone, over this half century, to advance human welfare. In major degree, the benefits of industrial progress in the United States in this half century have served to lighten toil for producers and elevate living standards for consumers.

The record thus shows a continuous rise both in the volume of production and in the productivity of workers. Concurrently, there has been a steady rise in the real income of people generally. Two requirements have accordingly been met: first, that larger quantities have been produced, and second, that the work has required less exhausting and time-consuming effort. Workers have thus been able to enjoy the higher production. It becomes obvious that high and rising productivity is the key to high production in shorter work times.

The highest production and the highest productivity should be in the consumer interests of owners, managers, and workers in a modern enlightened capitalistic economy. Each shares responsibility for production, each shares responsibility for productivity. The responsibilities differ because each makes a different type of contribution. Each expects and should work toward adequate rewards. Owners, managers, and workers require incentives to do their best. Financial incentives in the form of wages, salaries, profits, dividends, and rents must come in largest part from sales income. And sales income is simply volume of sales multiplied by the prices received; and net profit is volume of sales multiplied by prices received from which expenses including taxes have been subtracted. For continuance of income and employment, the worker as well as the executive must depend upon sales volume; for continuance of return upon investment the owner and investor must depend upon net profit after taxes. For stability and growth, all groups must depend upon sales at a profit, preferably in steady, growing volume.

PRODUCTION, PRODUCTIVITY, AND THE OWNERS

The owners and managers of a business enterprise in competition with other business firms operate under three pressures. The first is the pressure to attain larger production at lower costs in order to increase profit. The second is the pressure from workers to secure higher incomes. The third is the pressure from consumers for lower prices. The pressures of owners for profit, of workers for high wages, and of consumers for low prices can achieve their objectives by means of better management, lower unit returns to owners, and higher productivity of workers. Owners face the responsibility of providing the proper equipment in the way of tools, machines, processes, and management if high worker productivity is to be secured. Obviously, for the highest productivity are required the best machines, the best tools, the most competent workers, and the most competent executives in the optimum size of the producing unit, all operating at optimum capacity.

The principal function of the owner is the contribution of capital for purposes of the enterprise. He furnishes fixed capital for buildings, equipment for long-range development of products, processes, and markets. He furnishes directly, or through borrowing on credit, working capital for the operation of the enterprise, desirably in amounts sufficient to give economical and effective production and distribution of goods and services.

The strikingly increasing capital requirements per worker in modern industry are indicated by the recent statement that the investment per worker exceeded an average of $14,000.

In corporate enterprise as in unincorporated partnerships, or individual business, ownership gives certain rights and imposes certain responsibilities. For successful enterprise, owners have to exercise the rights of appointing certain managing officials; but that selection imposes a responsibility to all the owners, a responsibility for selecting competent, able, and right-minded executives whose attitudes and philosophies lead to action consistent with good corporate citizenship. Out of this grows the responsibility for insisting that management adopt and carry out sound policies within limits imposed by the board of directors as representative of the stockholders. Directors also must take those steps which are needed to provide for growth and development, both in men and equipment. It quickly becomes obvious that in a changing economy, wise owners will not be unwilling to take risks to keep up with or even to anticipate change.

Finally, owners and their boards of directors carry the ultimate responsibility for sound policies relating to production and productivity insofar as wages, labor relations, capital improvement and research policies are concerned.

Owners, however, cannot economically furnish capital for large-scale enterprise or the equipment necessary for efficient production unless there is reasonable assurance that what is produced can be disposed of. Furthermore, if and when the goods are sold, that income must be enough to pay wages and salaries, cover raw materials and manufacturing supplies, repair and replace equipment, and yield profit. Wages must usually be paid from week to week; raw materials and supplies must sometimes be paid for in advance of receipt. Equipment must be paid for or rental paid on lease arrangements. Only temporarily can the well-financed enterprise continue to turn out goods if they cannot be sold, or if later sale is not assured. A firm may, of course, produce for seasonal demand or may produce for a time without profit but with expectation of improvement in conditions.[3]

The equipment for an "automatic" factory—automation—may cost millions, but it presents a similar set of problems to owners. Successful automation depends upon large-volume production of precisely similar products. The manager of one highly efficient automatic factory for electric motors has stated that it will take five years' of operation, twenty-four hours a day, turning out identical motors to amortize the plant—a highly inflexible operation. Quick response to changes in volume of demand is difficult and costly, for it takes an hour to start up that automated line and another hour to shut it down. More difficult is response to any changes in design and type.

More than ever, selling must assume the burden of disposing of this flow of motors. The sales department is expected to deliver orders at a regular rate in spite of market changes. If it cannot do so with reasonable effort, if it cannot sell the quantities produced except at disastrously high costs or at prices so low as to be ruinous, the owner's investment may indeed prove unwise from several points of view.

If one studies the problems of new enterprises, it becomes obvious that such firms cannot usually wait until by word of mouth or free publicity purchasers learn about the product and seek out the producer to buy what he produces. That process is slow—much too slow. If we are to judge by historical records, generations would be required to develop sufficient demand to warrant production of any large variety of goods in a factory system. Long before that, new firms would have been compelled to cease operations.

The survival of new enterprises depends upon the relationship between income and outgo. For relatively short periods, if expenditures exceed income from the sale of goods the enterprise suffers a loss, a reduction in its capital resources. Depending

---

[3] The role of expectations in the behavior of businessmen has been recognized by economists and others. Professor Keynes in his classic *General Theory* discusses the subject (pp. 46–47), distinguishing between "short-term" expectation as a determinant of daily output and "long-term" expectation as affecting purchase of capital equipment.

upon the size of the losses, the responsible owners may decide to continue at a loss in the expectation that selling will develop a total market sufficient to make the enterprise profitable over a longer period. But if selling is not effective or capital is too limited, as is often the case, then bankruptcy and failure may be the outcome, or a new ownership takes over.

Men start new enterprises to make goods or render services in the expectation that people will buy them either of their own volition or as the result of information or persuasion. The urgent need for income from products in order for a new manufacturing enterprise to survive can be satisfied only by getting buying action within clearly defined time limits. Instances are on record where workers have tolerated a delay in receiving payment, but usually payrolls have to be met promptly with cash—cash from capital, cash from loans made by banks or other institutions, or cash in the form of advances from individuals or other firms. Failure to obtain income in order to pay trade creditors or to meet loans or other obligations may constitute insolvency and lead to bankruptcy.

The retailer fails who does not sell what he buys for resale or if he does not sell within the usual credit periods. Likewise does the wholesaler or the chain store or every other distributor who buys for resale come under the pressure to dispose of his products within the time periods set up by the grantors of credit or by the requirements imposed by the limitations of his capital or borrowing capacity.

But it is not only for new enterprises that selling pressure becomes necessary. For established enterprises, likewise, selling becomes necessary to maintain the required volume for production and profit. When a firm decides to budget a particular volume of product, that firm decides upon its sales-volume budget, based in part upon past production and in part upon other factors, including changes in the amount and character of selling and advertising effort. Some firms sell to the capacities of their plants. Others have plants larger than needed immediately, possibly planned for future expansion. All hope to sell the amounts needed for economical production.

Without selling effort, the volume of products sold by most firms tends to decline and usually to decline to levels which make the firm unprofitable. There are several reasons for this. First, if a company ceases advertising and selling effort while competing companies continue their selling effort on the same type of product, the demand for the company's products will tend to decrease unless the product is necessary and vital. Again, if all companies ceased selling effort for a product not a necessity, other firms offering alternative products or alternative satisfactions are likely to take a share in the market. Third, if people are not continually urged to buy, the desire to purchase a particular class of products may decline and the total amount purchased is likely to decrease. People may buy other products to secure other satisfactions. They may cease buying particular products and save. For most people, incomes are insufficient to cover all the types they want to buy, and consequently the nonselling producer will find himself out of the running much more quickly than anticipated.

To summarize, for successful operation of a producing enterprise, selling must perform a vital task. First, it must dispose of goods in sufficient volume to meet the requirements of economical production and the utilization of the machinery available to the enterprise within the framework of size of market and company resources. Just as vital is the requirement that selling must secure volume buying action within time periods that enable the firm to continue operations. For both the basic creation and intensification of the desires of the masses of the people and the conversion of that desire into buying action are essential.

Second, production does not take place in advance of demand unless there is a belief that goods will be purchased. Demand created and sometimes embodied in buying habits of greater or lesser strength is likely only to a degree based upon biological essentials for food, clothing, and shelter. Few firms would survive even their first year without the possibility of definite and effective effort to influence buyers so that produced goods can be disposed of.

Thirdly, large-scale production requires consumption, sometimes in widely scattered areas. The larger the scale of production, presumably the more widespread area within which consumption must take place. Such consumption cannot take place unless people know that products are available or can be made available. How are they to know? To a limited extent the search of buyers for products may enable them to know about them. But basically it is necessary for the seller to tell buyers in personal contact, or by radio, correspondence, or by advertisement. There are, of course, some exceptions. A new product may fill so clearly an existing and felt need that limited production is disposed of without particular effort.

Finally, it is to be expected that in resolving the pressures upon owners and management, the rate of return to owners on sales will in general tend to be lowered, even though owners and management retain a share of increased productivity. The return on capital invested need, however, not be lowered if sales volume at lower prices to a better-paid group is increased to offset the effect of the lower rate of return. Firms will vary in competitive ability, but in competitive areas, the sharing of the results of increased productivity is forced by competition, sometimes by increasing wages, sometimes by lower prices.

PRODUCTION, PRODUCTIVITY, AND MANAGEMENT

The responsibilities of management are those assigned to them by corporate charter and bylaws and delegated to them by owners. The alert observer of current corporation operation will recognize that where ownership is widely scattered and inarticulate, executives of the management group may take or be compelled to assume some of the responsibilities of owners. There are, however, special responsibilities of management, such as the following:

First, management (used to indicate the responsible executive group) is responsible for quality and effectiveness of the administration of the enterprise, within the limits set by the owners or stockholders. Executives are expected to have the skill, knowledge, and ability to be competent administrators. In the terms of one large firm, which has made many special studies and uses the term "professional management," management is defined as:[4]

The process of conducting a business (1) within OBJECTIVES AND POLICIES that serve the balanced best interest of customers, owners, employees, suppliers, and the whole public; (2) through the LEADERSHIP OF MEN (the human resources of a business); (3) by PLANNING, ORGANIZING, INTEGRATING, AND MEASURING; (4) the use of all RESOURCES (men, money, and time); (5) to achieve optimum RESULTS.

Next, as a part of competent administration, management must be on the alert to find newer and better methods of production and distribution, using its collective ideas to distinguish between sound and unsound proposals for change. It must demonstrate willingness to accept the risks of change in adopting new techniques, in production, and in developing and marketing new products.

Furthermore, management must be willing to recognize and act upon the principle that rising productivity is desirable and that sharing the gains from increasing productivity, whether forced by demands of workers or not, is in the long run consistent with stability and growth of the enterprise.

In small and medium-size businesses, ownership and management are likely to be closely connected. In small enterprises, owners are often managers—and even in some large businesses managers are or become owners. But to an increasing degree, management in large enterprises must assume the responsibilities of both ownership and administration of the enterprise.

The profitable disposition of the goods and services turned out by the enterprise is a major function that, in most enterprises, deserves as much attention as other major functions. Few firms can provide profitable disposition of their outputs without selling.

---

[4] As presented by L. Byron Cherry in an address to the Conference on Sales Management, University of Michigan, March 20, 1953. For a fuller discussion, see the volume by the president of General Electric Company, Ralph Cordiner, *New Frontiers for Professional Managers* (New York: McGraw-Hill Book Co., Inc., 1956).

PRODUCTION, PRODUCTIVITY, AND THE WORKER

The selling of goods and services affects the working of groups in three ways. It induces workers to want these products, it influences them to work so as to obtain them, and thus enables the group to buy them, and it causes the group to buy and consume products that maintain and raise the level of living.

It is obvious if workers do not work diligently, production will decline or cease. If men generally do not produce in return for an equitable share of that production, unit costs of product will be increased and eventually prices must rise. If they do produce in effective manner, better wages become possible, or shorter hours for the same pay. Demand customarily falls under such conditions. The worker is therefore a key figure in the production process; without his co-operation the practical and effective application of technological progress and of management skills and know-how would be impossible. The sources of economic progress would remain unused and finally disappear.

Large-scale production, division of labor, and specialization of the work of individuals are basic postulates of high productivity. In order to produce goods and services needed for high standards of living, the worker is therefore confronted with very definite responsibilities that grow out of the nature of large-scale factory production and large-scale mechanized farm production.

1) The workers must work at definite places and for definite periods and at definite times. Essential factory production requires that workers be present and ready to work at the particular tasks assigned them when the machines and chemical processes are operating. For some production processes, continuous attention is necessary twenty-four hours a day. Here at least three successive shifts must be manned to obtain high and economical production. In other cases, a single shift or two shifts a day may be sufficient.

To allow complete freedom to workers to come and go at any time when progressive production processes consist of interdependent parts for each of which some individuals have responsibility, both in terms of output and in terms of timing, would either raise costs unconscionably or stop production. Obviously, some leeway must be arranged in the procedure for illness and occasional failures; but the provision of any such reserve is expensive and cannot be carried to the extent that it will greatly reduce or destroy the advantage of large-scale regular production.

The basic principles of the division of labor and of specialization imply the necessity of co-operation among workers, especially the co-operation among specialized workers, each of whom contributes his part to the completion of a finished product. What happens if the company workers in a specific enterprise absent themselves or go on strike has often been demonstrated. Not infrequently, a very few men can, by their own refusal to work, put hundreds of men out of work. Absenteeism, whatever the cause, is certainly a deterrent to high production. From time to time, strikes of small groups have been reported in the press, compelling the shutdown of plants forcing thousands of workers into idleness.

2) For highest production, the worker must be skilled at his job. He should have the mental and physical qualifications for the job, the training and experience in the tasks assigned, so that lost motion is reduced to a minimum. In addition to all these, there must be an attitude of willingness to work and a feeling of satisfaction in it, which leads to high morale.

3) Production will certainly be increased if the work itself is interesting or at least not disagreeable or overtaxing. The tendency has been to make many types of work more agreeable, to substitute chemical, mechanical, or electronic devices to take over exacting physical burdens and routine types of tasks. Nevertheless, it would be unrealistic to expect that in any foreseeable future we shall be relieved of all but the task of pushing buttons. The necessity of performing some repetitive tasks will probably continue. For some production, unremitting attention will be required in spite of "electrical brains," feedbacks, "electrical memories," and other widely advertised new develop-

ments. But certainly the human burden of work has been and will continue to be reduced. Mental energy and machines will supplant most physical effort.

4) The worker's output will be greatest if he is provided with the best tools and the most productive machines. Pride in workmanship has frequently caused the laborer in times past to provide himself with the simple tools he thought best. But that does not enable him in a factory job to substitute an automatic screw machine for simple tools or an automatic turret lathe for a hand-operated lathe. Nor can the office worker provide a tabulating system for payroll records, instead of old handwritten records, with the old-fashioned adding machine. In such cases the responsibility for providing the best, the most productive machinery and tools as well as methods of utilizing them, rests on the managing executives and owners.

It is both significant and interesting to note the difference between older attitudes of union labor and current union attitudes. In Congressional hearings on automation and in various other public pronouncements, union leaders have expressed themselves in favor of accelerated installation of laborsaving machinery. The attitudes are undoubtedly based upon the recognition of the productivity basis of higher wages and the belief that labor will secure its full share of the increased production.[5]

5) For high productivity, adequate motivation must be added to these factors of skill, equipment, and type of work. These factors merely enable the worker to produce more than he would otherwise *if he works*. But whether he does work regularly, industriously, and effectively or not, depends mainly on the incentive he feels to do so.

Incentives for Workers to Produce

The basic incentive is, of course, the necessity to make a living. But the incentive in our democracy arising from the threat of hunger or inadequate clothing or shelter has become more and more remote as our standards of living have been

---

[5] See also *Automation and Technological Change,* Report of the Subcommittee on Economic Stabilization to the Joint Committee of the Economic Report, Congress of the United States (Washington, D.C.: U.S. Government Printing Office, 1955), p. 5.

raised and as the amount of effort to cover food and a minimum of clothing and shelter has become less and less. The effort required for mere subsistence is generally far below that required to maintain our economy at best productive levels. Furthermore, it is commonly accepted that in our economy no one will be allowed to starve, whether he produces or not. Through relief, unemployment payments, and other social means, a minimum standard of living is provided for the unemployed worker as well as for indigent nonworkers—sometimes much more.

The worker who conforms to the requirements of large-scale production, previously discussed, does so not from any altruistic motives but because he expects to benefit by his work and his conformity to the work standard. Fear of discharge and the possible effects of unemployment upon himself and family have been traditional incentives to comply, but experience has shown that fear has very limited value in getting high productivity. This has been amply demonstrated, for instance, in the Soviet Union. A worker may be induced to work by fear of punishment to himself, family, or group, and the threats of a secret police, where the benefit the worker expects to receive from conformity are a low living standard and the preservation of limited freedom or avoidance of punishment in prison or labor camps. But even in the Soviet Union, it appears that greater productivity and greater production are increasingly secured by positive means, by promising the worker material rewards, goods, and services not otherwise procurable. The great incentive for the people is the hope of a higher standard of living, a hope that has been so long deferred that from time to time Soviet leaders have had to reaffirm their intention and take steps to give workers additional products as a promise of somewhat higher standards. For reasons discussed elsewhere, the political and social climate of totalitarianism is not favorable to high and rising production nor is it favorable to high productivity. The incentive to the individual worker to produce has not been sufficient. There have been many reports of the difficulty of getting production standards up to even a respectable fraction of those that prevail in the United States. Workers' failure is only one of the factors accounting for the situation, incompetence of management and direction being another. Above all are the limitations of governmental economic planning.

The level of production and the productivity of the worker are certainly affected by the work situation. If the worker likes his work and his co-workers, if he has respect for his superiors, and if he generally believes that his work situation and the enterprise he works for are good, he will tend to produce more than if poor conditions prevail. His work situation has to be judged in relation to other work situations.

But back of all the desire to work is the bald fact that workers work and conform to the requirements of effective production in order to satisfy their wants, whatever those wants may be in addition to minimum requirements for existence and health. These wants are for personal and family purposes that make up the standard of living that he and his family are willing to work to maintain or improve.

Selling in Relation to the Desires of Workers for Goods and Services

The standard of living that the worker strives to reach and maintain is one that is determined for him and by him. The influences discussed earlier all bear upon the workers' wants and desires: environment, ambition, family, education, and selling.

The wants and desires of the worker are of importance to production only if they cause him to do something about them. The desire for an automobile may cause the worker to work more regularly, to do more work productively with the equipment at hand, provided he sees in such work an opportunity to acquire and operate an automobile. In the United States, the social situation usually does not bar opportunity to use it for the satisfaction of himself and his family.

The desires for automobiles, refrigerators, washing machines, new homes, radios, and television sets, the desires in general for more and better foods, better clothing, better housing, and for various other comforts and luxuries, have been in part created by outside influences, and certainly they have been created and intensified by selling effort. The desire for shelter is a fundamental one; but the desires for special types of houses and for the equipment and furnishings have been vitally influenced both quantitatively and qualitatively by selling and advertising.

When the electric refrigerator came on the market, much effort was required to dispose of even the limited initial production. By continuous selling and advertising extending over a quarter of a century, the electric refrigerator has become a necessity in more homes than any other major electrical appliance. The people who have purchased and enjoy refrigerators are those who in a historically very short period have learned how to want them, to make them, and to buy and use them.

This is but one illustration of the rapidity with which relatively large and conspicuous items have been introduced in the standard of living of the whole population. The automobile furnishes another; the automatic washer is a third. It would be easy to cite other illustrations of smaller items such as nylon hosiery and even more recently, dacron in items of clothing; but these suffice to emphasize the fact that new and better items are constantly being included in our standard of living, sometimes displacing older items, sometimes furnishing additional satisfactions.

A few conclusions are clearly indicated by any such survey. One is that when such items have been included in the standard of living, selling effort has played a very large part. In some cases the work of thousands of people and the expenditure of millions of dollars have been involved in getting quick acceptance. Although after a time such selling effort has been supplemented by educational institutions, sometimes by government, the burden of persuading people to adopt a new product has fallen, by and large, upon private enterprise. People gradually have learned about new products through advertising, through observation, and through contact with those who previously have bought; but the process has been started by selling and is continued by selling.

Secondly, the conclusion is clear that because of this effort people have finally been led to want these products seriously enough to do something about it. Two types of effort were possible. One was to work more productively and to fit into the requirements of large-scale production; the other was to demand and secure the wages required to increase real income.

Finally, employers have been induced by the demands of workers to give higher wages and to provide shorter hours. Some employers have looked to their own long-run interests in expanding markets as a justification. Others have looked also to their desire to see a greater spread of high living standards among workers. Many wage increases undoubtedly have been granted as a result of the pressures exerted by union organizations, pressures based upon the desire for higher living standards and the unwillingness in the American system to accept traditional living standards or to be satisfied with stratified consumption patterns. Employers have sometimes foreseen, at other times learned by experience, the great profit-making possibilities of high productivity, low prices, and large volumes, while paying high wages. That philosophy has spread widely in the United States but is still to be accepted by more than a small fraction of employers in other parts of the world.

SUMMARY

The great production required for high standards of living for a large population requires the continuous and effective operation of many productive enterprises. For most of these, production must take place in advance of purchase or assured demand. Production does not take place in advance of demand unless there is a belief that the output can be disposed of at an acceptable price. Demand, created and sometimes embodied in buying habits of greater or lesser strength, is likely in only a limited degree to be based upon the biological essentials of food, shelter, and clothing. Few firms could survive without the availability of effective and definite effort to influence buyers so that produced goods could be disposed of and necessary income obtained. Established firms do not and cannot ordinarily continue to produce and stock products for which demand cannot be developed.

Business executives, whether sales or production managers or research men, share the weaknesses and limitations of mankind. Consumers, workers, executives, owners, tend to form habits and resist change. They form opinions as to the best way to achieve results and are loath to change them. We should not be surprised to find that many companies do not change, but continue to use old machinery, and that they do not employ the latest processes. Often we find the scale of operation too small to warrant the lowest cost of production.

The business management of a company producing, for instance, wire wheels for automobiles, is confronted with continuing problems, particularly if it is aiming at high production. These problems must be solved. Decisions must be made. In the continuing problem of getting out production, executives must pay constant attention to the sales volume or expected sales to determine how much and what to produce. They must take the responsibility for seeing that costs are such as to enable the firm to compete at a profit.

If they are to attain both of these objectives, they must consider new and more effective equipment and processes. They must endeavor to improve management and secure improved performance by workers. The pressures to do so at a particular time may be insistent or only very minor. In boom periods when wire wheels are in great demand, profits may be made with relatively less effort. But at other times, the executives in the wire-wheel business may be urged to buy new equipment in order to meet competitive costs and competitive prices; even if the enterprise is making a sufficient profit at the moment, executives must look ahead to see the future necessity of keeping their production processes and their product up to the needs of the market. Nevertheless, these executives may not know or have time to find out about the better ways of producing. Even if they hear of some improvement, they may be skeptical, for their experience in making changes may not have been invariably successful. They may have reasons for maintaining a skeptical attitude.

The manufacturers of the machines needed for welding wire wheels encounter, likewise, the necessity of selling effort. A manufacturer who has developed a more productive machine cannot sit back and depend on an automatic flow of orders to keep him busy. He must go to the manufacturer of wire wheels and demonstrate that through this machine, the wire-wheel manufacturer may secure advantage. Like the manufacturer of wire wheels, a manufacturer of machines stays in business only if he can sell enough machines within limited time periods to warrant continued operation.

In short, the extent to which buying action for welding machines can be successfully developed is dependent in the final analysis upon consumer demand for automobiles with wire wheels. This demand depends in large measure upon the selling by automobile manufacturers and dealers, and in part to the carry-over of previous selling of particular makes and types of cars. Thus demand for wire-wheel welders, for instance, is in turn dependent upon the selling of wire-wheel automobiles by different distributors, upon selling the wire wheels as equipment of other manufacturers, and finally upon the selling of the machines to wire-wheel producers. One might carry the process several steps further and say that the choice between aluminum, steel, and manganese requires selling by such firms as Reynolds, Crucible Steel, and others. Thus in every stage of the producing technology, selling becomes necessary in order to provide buying action, which enables industry to persist. The buying action resulting from this selling at different levels of manufacture and distribution constitutes a motive force in our dynamic economy.

Chapter VII

SELLING IN RELATION TO INNOVATION, INVENTION, AND TECHNOLOGY

RESEARCH, TECHNOLOGY, INNOVATION, ENTERPRISE—these are words often used to characterize our competitive economy, but rarely does one hear in the discussion of such subjects statements that show that the writer or speaker recognizes their relationship to selling. Nor is the contribution of selling to the rate of invention and adoption clearly recognized. In order to give selling its due, it is not necessary to subtract from the great credit due to scientists, engineers, or production men. It is necessary only to recognize that the processes which have enabled us to bring our economy to its present level include selling as an important leadership and energizing factor. We can agree in large part with the editor of a Canadian publication when he writes:[1]

All business progress is the result of invention and discovery. The scientist in his laboratory, the traveler on his voyages, and the inventor at his workbench—these have played a vital part in developing our industrial civilization.

During the past half century science has drawn a never-ending succession of gasps from humanity. It has been told that it is wonderful, marvellous, and unbelievable. Inventors have followed

---

[1] From *Monthly Letter*, Royal Bank of Canada, Montreal, November, 1954.

hard upon the heels of the scientists, so that no sooner is a novel principle uncovered than it is embodied in capsules, gears, or gadgets for popular consumption.

Lest overweening pride should seize us, however, it is well to look back over the life of mankind as Dr. Julius E. Lips does in his book, *The Origin of Things*. Primitive people in all parts of the world showed their inventiveness to so good effect that Dr. Lips needs nearly 500 pages to tell what they did. Today's and tomorrow's inventions are built upon inventions that stretch in a long line from the first tool-using creatures.

No one will deny the profound effect of science, invention, and discovery upon society. What we call civilization could never have come into being had we not been capable of proceeding from old to new things, and eager to make the change.

The position of selling in relation to innovation and advancing technology can be briefly summarized:

1) The extent of that application of existing machines and processes, whether in industry or agriculture, will depend upon the extent of the potential demand and the degree to which that potential demand can be converted into actual buying actions within relatively restricted time periods.

2) The research necessary for new consumer products, for new devices and equipment, for new industrial materials, and other products, can be carried on in industry only if there is reasonable chance that the results of the research will develop new and usable products, or lower costs or improvements of older products. It is clear that industrial scientific research must be paid for and is limited by sales income, actual and expected.

3) New products can be developed and produced in low-cost, large-scale quantities only because it is expected that they can be sold to produce income when needed to keep the firm alive and flourishing. The inventor of a new machine or the man who starts a new trading enterprise finds he must secure income in order to survive. He must produce and sell or must resell what he buys, not just sometime in the vague future but promptly enough to enable him to meet payrolls and buy the necessary materials and supplies. Of course the inventor may secure his income by the sale of his invention to others, who then must solve the problems of practical application and sales.

4) Large amounts of more basic research are carried on by

certain large companies. Such basic research or even pure scientific research is carried on because both on the basis of experience and of careful examination and judgment of particular proposals, executives have been led to believe that expenditures for research "pay." But no research pays unless, sooner or later, it leads to production or improved products that can be sold to create income. That income can be realized in some other ways, such as the licensing of patents and sale of rights to manufacturers, but for most companies these are of minor importance as compared to the income potentially realizable from sales.

The larger the company, the wider the range of products in a field, the greater the chances that basic research will be rewarding in this practical manner. A company such as General Electric can experiment with man-made lightening because what it learns can be applied to the design of power lines, power transformers, generators, motors, and many other products in the electrical field. Du Pont can carry on basic research in almost any chemical field because the results can probably be embodied in one or many of the wide range of products the company now sells. Not that all such research projects pay off. Far from it; but the opportunities for development of salable products or for the production of salable products are important enough to warrant the outlays, even though such application may take a considerable time to develop.

5) New products are developed and produced for the public primarily because someone believed that people wanted them or would come to want them within a "reasonable" time. Many an inventor or producer has learned that even for desirable products, people will not come to want them automatically even when shown. Wishful thinking of inventors and producers has frequently to give way to the realization that selling in simple or complex form is the only solution, the only way to survival. Whether the product be a new grinding machine, a new electric razor, a new automobile, fabric, or prepared food, someone, and particularly the producer, must provide the first impetus to buying action.

In short, in our economy, selling determines the extent and rate of adoption of new consumer products and the rapidity with

which development of new workers takes place and new processes are applied. Thus it determines the speed at which the
results of innovation, research, and technical advances are
brought into use for the benefit of all.

An assumption on the part of some economists, of some scientists, engineers, and inventors that selling is unnecessary has been
disproved too frequently to require much attention. But it may
illustrate the point to cite several examples of the selling requirement, drawn from various sources. My colleague, Professor
E. Raymond Corey, relates the experience of Alcoa in its effort
to sell primary aluminum windows (not storm windows):[2]

In 1929, as a first step in promoting the use of aluminum in
primary windows, Alcoa representatives called on three major manufacturers of steel windows. Two of the companies indicated no
interest in the project. The third company was interested to the
extent of accepting an order to make aluminum windows, from
extrusions which Alcoa supplied, for a building that Alcoa was
erecting in Cleveland. The job completed, this manufacturer expressed a willingness to accept any other orders that Alcoa's salesmen might obtain, but he would not actively promote aluminum
windows through his own salesforce.

From 1929 on, Alcoa representatives concentrated on calling on
industrial architects in an effort to create a demand for aluminum
windows at the end-user level. In these calls, Alcoa sales personnel
particularly emphasized the fact that, in contrast to steel or wood
windows, aluminum windows required little or no maintenance.
This program was pursued steadily during the depression even
though very little building was being done. With the start of the
Federal Government's program for financing public buildings, however, the work that had been done with architects began to bear
fruit. Aluminum windows were specified by architects on plans
for post offices, court houses, hospitals, schools, and other public
buildings.

A few small steel window manufacturers did begin to make and
sell aluminum windows shortly after World War II. Two are of
particular interest. Both concerns, although small, were old, established firms. These two companies offered to supply architects
with either aluminum or steel windows, without necessarily rec-
ommending one over the other. One of the companies made windows of the same dimensions in each metal and then put sales em-

---

[2] E. Raymond Corey, *The Development of Markets for New Materials*
(Boston: Division of Research, Harvard University, 1956), pp. 36–38.

phasis on interesting architects in specifying windows by brand name even though a decision might not be made until the building was nearly under construction with regard to the choice between aluminum or steel windows. This sales program was highly successful.

· · · · · ·

In the years immediately following the war Alcoa engineers did a considerable amount of work with a number of small concerns which wanted to get into this business. Although there were only a relatively few aluminum window manufacturers in the United States in 1946, there were 158 companies in the field by the end of 1953. It is interesting, however, that none of the three largest steel window manufacturers took steps to enter the aluminum window market until 1952. In 1952 one of these three concerns acquired a manufacturer of aluminum windows. Another of the three companies made the decision in 1952 to sell aluminum windows, but by the end of 1953 it had not been decided whether this company would buy aluminum windows from another manufacturer for sale under its brand name, or actually manufacture its own aluminum windows.

Thus, although Alcoa's original efforts to develop fabricator-customers were directed at the large steel window manufacturers, it was the small steel window manufacturers which undertook to make and sell aluminum windows. . . .

Or another example in the consumer products field, namely Owens-Corning's experience in the Fiberglas-reinforced plastic luggage field:

Owens-Corning did not itself manufacture and sell FRP end products. These products were made by the company's Fiberglas customers. Owens-Corning, however, gave these customers as much help as possible on problems of processing FRP materials, seeking new markets, and promoting their products. In addition, Owens-Corning encouraged custom molders to make proper use of the Fiberglas name in order to help them build their own end-product markets. The discussion which follows [describes efforts] to promote the sale of FRP luggage made by [one] of Owens-Corning's customers.

Boyce & Dyer, Inc.[3] Owens-Corning's first work in the FRP luggage field was done with Boyce & Dyer, Inc., a luggage manufacturing concern, having its plant and offices in Portland, Oregon. This company had been in the luggage business for many years, and before the war it did a substantial volume of business

---

[3] Fictitious name. Corey, *op. cit.*, pp. 70–72.

in making low-priced luggage for special retail promotional sales. During World War II Boyce & Dyer had contracted with the United States Government to make aerial camera cases out of a resin-glass material, and this work had been outstandingly successful. The cases were designed to be leakproof and to withstand high impact without damage.

In 1947 Mr. Dyer, the president of the company, undertook the development of FRP luggage as a means of strengthening his civilian business. The product was improperly designed and was on the market for only a short time after it had been introduced in 1949. With the start of the Korean War Mr. Dyer withdrew this luggage from the market and discontinued this development because of the urgency of his military business.

In the summer of 1953 Mr. Dyer had again become interested in this project and had redesigned his case. His samples were prepared in time to enter them in the National Luggage and Leather Goods Show in New York in August 1953. The line included five sizes and seven different colors. The outside shells of the luggage were made of Fiberglas-reinforced plastic, while edging and hinges were constructed of extruded aluminum parts. The inside of the case was lined with decorative vinyl plastic. The Boyce & Dyer luggage sold in the "luxury" price range of $40 to $80. In the last four months of 1953 Boyce & Dyer sold over 10,000 pieces of this luggage.

In spite of the success of the product in late 1953 there was some question regarding the design of this luggage line. In making a case that would have exceptionally high impact resistance, the company had made the walls quite thick, and the case weighed slightly more than a piece of leather luggage of a comparable capacity. In designing the case, therefore, full advantage had not been taken of the natural lightness and the high strength-weight ratio of Fiberglas-reinforced plastic.

Another question concerned the price range in which this manufacturer had chosen to sell. While the public appeal of the name Fiberglas and the pleasing "jackstraws" surface pattern of FRP material were elements that could command a premium in the luggage market, Owens-Corning personnel wondered whether selling in a lower price range might not broaden the market considerably and increase the luggage manufacturer's profits.

If this was to be done, however, it would probably be necessary for the company to broaden its distribution. As of 1953 Boyce & Dyer luggage was being sold direct to retail buyers throughout the country by four salesmen, three of whom were located in California and one in Minnesota. All orders were shipped from a warehouse adjacent to the plant in Portland. Mr. Dyer's philosophy, however, had been that he would rather concentrate his sales expense on large outlays for national advertising than on the costs of a large sales force and warehousing program. He would build his advertising partly around an unprecedented guarantee that Boyce & Dyer luggage would not break. Mr. Dyer was willing to invest as much as $100,000 annually—and perhaps more—in advertising.

Following his success in 1953 he had faced the 1954 season with the anticipation of achieving a substantial increase in sales. He had therefore approached Owens-Corning with the proposal that the two companies undertake a joint national advertising program. Mr. Dyer pointed out that he had purchased a large amount of Fiberglas materials in the past year, and that if Owens-Corning reinvested part of its profits in this business in national advertising, the company could substantially increase its sales to him in 1954. Since Boyce & Dyer, Inc., was the only company making FRP luggage at that time, there would be no problem of having to give advertising support to other companies. Furthermore, this application was a good one and it could be materially advanced by a strong promotional program.

Examples could be multiplied if space permitted, but while we need not go so far as to agree fully with an eminent British engineer, we can recognize much truth in what he says, in speaking of the crucial problem of movement and transport:[4]

These truths are so simple and fundamental that one wonders why they are presented or why there is any need for . . . men to encourage and stimulate a thing so necessary to all the people. It is not simple, it is very difficult, because the human being is naturally lazy; he is not only impervious to ideas, but will also oppose anything new, and, to sum up, he doesn't care whether his standards of living are improved. If it were not for the shred of ambition or pride with which most of us are possessed, we would all be hoboes. And it is this shred of ambition upon which you as enterprisers and stimulators play. It is this constant pressure upon the mass millions by business leaders which prevents the standard of living—such an artificial thing it is—from slipping backward and downward. No one will ever know the amount of energy expended in switching people from coal oil lamps to 22,000,000 homes with electricity. No one will ever know the energy expended in bringing about that thing which today seems to be our very second nature, individual transportation in the form of the automobile.

---

[4] From an address by Merle Thorpe, editor, *Nation's Business,* before the Traffic Clubs of America, New York, April 20, 1952.

TECHNOLOGICAL ADVANCE

In the American economy we have set up as one goal the reduction of taxing and fatiguing work to a minimum and an increase of leisure and strength with which the worker may enjoy the highest living standards that can be attained. The conflict between desire for more goods and services and the desire for less work with more time to enjoy and benefit from higher standards is resolved through greater productivity of labor and management. Through technological advance, this greater production can be achieved because advances in the management of men, in the application of materials, in the utilization of machines, have enabled labor to contribute more in terms of output in goods and services. Only if labor is continuously made more productive both by its own effort and competence and with the co-operation of management and owners can high and rising standards of living be supported.

Back of technological progress, and often directing it, are businessmen whose decisions advance or retard technological progress. Business administration decides whether research departments shall be set up; it decides their scope, magnitude, and limits of freedom. To secure tangible results within a reasonable period is usually required of the administrator by the owners. He must therefore try to direct the expenditures for research into potentially profitable channels. He must have the imagination to look beyond the current year and to realize that his own imagination is limited. He must, when over-all operations warrant it, engage in far-reaching, fundamental research, e.g., in development of atomic power for peacetime use long before practical, competitive applications become feasible. But pervading all deliberations is belief in selling.

Business executives at top level make the decisions to replace expensive equipment before it is worn out, to gain advantage in manufacture with newer machines. Business executives decide to buy computers, controls, and other devices for application of automatic production processes because they believe that thereby the enterprise for which they are responsible can best achieve stability, growth, and earning power through income derived from selling its output.

It has been pointed out earlier that our economy furnishes manifold instances and conspicuous examples of increases in production accompanied by a lowering of the amount of labor involved; and in Chapter VI, the record was cited to show that productivity and total production have increased but hours per worker have decreased. The conclusion is drawn, not only by the Department of Labor but by students generally, that goods and services have been produced more rapidly, that working hours have been shortened, and that people have more time to enjoy goods and services than at any earlier period in history.

To this development, selling has made a vital contribution and must continue to do so effectively, although that fact has not been understood by people generally. The contribution is in part an indirect but vital one of energizing the whole process of technological research and advancement, of bringing about greater productivity and furnishing incentive for innovation and enterprise. Selling works through the expansion of buying action and of consumption as well as through its actual and potential influence on future buying action.

Technological progress as viewed by the business executive assumes varied forms. He may distinguish first those minor changes in processes or machines which enable the same or better products to be turned out with less effort. Here as in more important changes, ideas and suggestions may come from many sources. Workers if motivated and rewarded, as in successful suggestion systems in both larger and smaller companies, have been a fruitful source. Suggestions may come from executives, from owners, from salesmen or customers or suppliers, from expert consultants and laymen. Many companies employ an inside staff devoted to product development or process development. Competitive products furnish a powerful pressure toward change and improvement. For instance, one company that had devised a certain type of electrical switch licensed a small competitor to use the essential principles. However, this small competitor improved upon the switch and upon the process of manufacturing so that not only did he produce a better switch but sold it at a lower price. The large company, owning the basic patents, was thereupon motivated to improve its own switch and its own methods so as again to become competitive. The spur of competitive effort toward improved products was direct and real.

Secondly, there are those major changes in process and product which involve major changes in personnel, equipment, and methods of performing tasks and may involve major investment. The objective may be to secure lower costs and profits or to keep up with a changing market. A large business-machines company found it necessary a few years ago to undertake to throw overboard the older model and redesign its typewriter in order to make it again a leader in its field. Over the years many small improvements had been made; but it finally became necessary to take the time (four years) and funds (in millions) to do a complete redesign job. The major change is likely to involve scientists, inventors, and engineers; but it always involves risk that must be assumed and decisions that must be made by executives. The risks involved are, first, that the change will not be successful in accomplishing the purpose; but a major risk, sometimes the principal one, is that sufficient sales will not be made either as the result of lower prices or the result of change in product to enable the company to continue manufacture without loss or make a profit that will enable it to carry on further improvement.

Technological advances thus provide the basis for continued production and greater productivity. New equipment and new processes are discovered and applied so that goods may be made more cheaply or products or services developed better to serve the needs and wants of the public. Furthermore, productivity is increased by better management, which enables equipment, material, and human resources to be used more effectively. The result is greater total production with less effort.

Development of Advances in Technology, Innovation, Invention and Discovery

The scientist in his laboratory, the inventor who embodies scientific principle in new or better products or processes for the betterment of mankind, have played an important part in the development of our industrial civilization. Invention and discovery are, of course, by no means new; what is new in modern society and particularly in the United States is the greatly accelerated rate of invention and discovery during the past half century.[5]

Invention and discovery are no longer left solely to chance or luck. Industry has learned that inventions and discoveries can be enormously speeded up by direct action with the result that many, although by no means all, discoveries and inventions emerge from research departments of business enterprise or research groups supported by business enterprise. Historically, it has sometimes seemed that invention was the result of accident, although at other times it was declared to be solely a response to the needs of the times. Necessity may be the "mother of invention" but need, coupled with facilities and capital to support research, thought, and experiment brings results much more rapidly. Because business can no longer trust to the slow process of accidental response to the needs of the times, we must anticipate wants and needs that are barely emerging. Business endeavors, therefore, to improve goods and discover and develop new products so that they will be ready when the people are ready to accept them. Since inventions, improvement and refinement of product, production means and processes, still require substantial time, sometimes measured in months or years (as contrasted, however, with the generations required in former days), the process of developing a new and unproved product from a workable idea to a useful article for sale may involve a very substantial expenditure. One electric company recently spent $5,000,000 over a period of five years in redesigning a single line of general purpose electric motors. The whole purpose of the development was to embody in the new motors the increased technical knowledge that had been acquired since the previous revision of the line and to develop a new line that would embody as far as possible the qualities believed desirable.

Creative ideas, which furnish the basis for improvement in products or in methods, are more likely to come from research than from any vague consciousness of need. Whether the in-

[5] See *Innovation*, a philosophic analysis of the processes of invention and innovation by H. G. Barnett (New York: McGraw-Hill Book Co., Inc. 1953).

ventions have come from university laboratories or industry, there can be no doubt that in few, if any, cases does a brilliant new product or process spring full-blown into existence. The human mind does not work that way. New ideas are not born in a vacuum. They have ancestry and they may give birth to new ideas.

Furthermore, scientists and inventors know as well as do businessmen that the mortality of new ideas is high. In a recent volume on chemical development,[6] the statement is made that:

The experience of 20 large companies concerned with successful new product development was as follows:
540 possibilities in the idea stage were considered at the research level;
442 of these were subsequently eliminated during the new product conference;
98 were then selected for preliminary laboratory investigation;
8 appeared sufficiently promising to warrant further development;
7 were dropped as unsalable or unprofitable as determined at the semiworks stage; and only
1 survived and was placed in regular production.

Psychologically, a new idea is the recombination of previous impressions and ideas stored in the mind. A new idea builds on old. Where technological advances and materials produce new processes, the new idea must be built on previous ideas and impressions already present in the minds of those who are working to make this advance. It is significant that the greatest inventors and discoverers are generally those whose familiarity with the field has been the greatest.

One needs only to turn to the recent history of atomic development to realize the truth of this assertion. The release of atomic power for world use was a task assigned to the greatest scientists of the world, most of whom had spent years, even a lifetime, in making and experimenting with such problems. The result of the research was that atomic energy development was hastened many years by the pressure of the war situation. If

---

[6] H. M. Corley, *Successful Commerical Chemical Development* (New York: John Wiley & Sons, Inc., 1955). Quoted in *Technology and Your New Products*, by Alan A. Smith (Small Business Management Series, No. 19) (Washington, D.C.: Small Business Administration, 1956).

one examines this effort as an example in discovery and invention under the pressure of necessity, one sees that there were several elements that have a bearing upon our examination of technical advance:

1) Competent scientists who were familiar with what had been done in the field and who had already collected a vast fund of impressions and ideas were enlisted.

2) They were backed by men in government and elsewhere who had the courage and vision to assume the risks and make the commitments necessary to furnish a solid basis for carrying on the work of finding answers to atomic energy problems.

3) The provision of equipment, materials, and other research made it possible to have ideas and hypotheses discussed among men with varying accumulations of background and to have these hypotheses and ideas tested both physically and in prior discussions among scientists.

4) The relatively rapid success of the research effort was due in no small measure to the courage, wisdom, and patience of administrators who endeavored to fuse the efforts of individual scientists into a team effort, both to increase the assurance of success and to speed up the development of ideas and discoveries and inventions needed to secure the end result.

5) Finally, there was the motivation of those who took part in the work itself. Under the pressure of war, the motivation was very powerful to participate in what promised to be a most important development if successful. There can be no doubt that the willingness of the scientists and their staffs to go much beyond the call of duty speeded up this development. The creative urge, plus facilities, plus incentive, brought results in years that might otherwise have required decades.

If improvement and innovation are to come in industry as rapidly as desirable for sound advances in standards of living, we must have competent persons to formulate ideas and carry them through to a final development in terms of producer or consumer products. Furthermore, development is hastened if the provision of the necessary equipment and materials is made possible. Either co-operatively or within a single firm or through research institutions, the necessary technological development must be forthcoming. Incentive must be provided for owners, managers, or others to take the inescapable risks. The managers of small business enterprise likewise need to be alert to technological development. As the National Resources Planning Board points out:[7]

The small enterprise has the option of carrying on whatever sort of research it can afford, of developing its own technique, of training its own technicians and experts, of acquiring new knowledge by hiring trained engineers, or by participating in professional-society activities, by paying for the services of consultants or scientists, by financing specific research projects through technical institutions, or by buying outright new technical developments or inventions from individuals or other companies.

New Products

If we attempt to analyze search and research for technological advance in products, production, and distribution, we discover quickly essential similarities in the steps required. Goals and objectives must be set. At times research may be required to find the goals to be set for research projects. Exploration into unknown fields, the securing of answers to preliminary questions, even finding out what questions to ask, all require a high order of creativeness. Once the objectives or goals are set, at least in preliminary fashion, it becomes possible to think about, choose, and devise methods of research and of securing the pertinent data and collating and interpreting it. Finally, and sometimes most important for innovation, is the application of this knowledge or fundamental discovery to the design of finished products or to the improvement of processes or management.

From a practical point of view, a manufacturer finds out what to make in a number of ways. One of these is to study existing products, asking himself and his associates questions as to how a better product can be made or how a new product might be devised that would perform the same needed service. The going concern may look upon complaints and reports of

[7] National Resources Planning Board, *Research—A National Resource* (1940), Section II, p. 79.

difficulties from users as the beginning of ideas for product improvement.

Secondly, a manufacturer may, after study, simply imitate competitive products or adopt outstanding features. In some areas of industry, this is the principal technique. It is an essential one, for instance, in the garment trades, in which styles and other changes in men's and women's wear are adopted from originators for reproduction in products for mass distribution at low prices. Imitation has been a successful method in many industries for the reason that it becomes possible by imitation to choose for study and improvement those products which have already shown a degree of market acceptance. Thus the risk is reduced, although the reward of ingenuity and innovation may likewise be reduced.

A third method of determining what to make is derived from studying data as to the needs of people or specific groups. The various research methods have been used to secure data on needs, even to secure ideas as to the way in which those needs may be met by specific products. The automobile industry, the home-appliance industry, have made much use of this technique, but in no case have they used this technique exclusively. Somewhat similar to scientific study, although perhaps dependent more upon characteristics and brilliance of certain individuals, is the plan of applying the imagination to the results of new discoveries, to develop hypotheses relating to practical application.

The need for selling to secure the introduction of new consumer products, however, has frequently been stressed, as has the common need for aggressive selling in order to secure buying actions and income within the reduced number of months or years permitted by financial and other limitations of the enterprise. Even in the pharmaceutical field in which new, often remarkable, products needed in the field are introduced, the record shows that while some initial sale and consumption may take place without special effort, the widespread use of beneficial discoveries by the public is achieved only by selling effort. Besides publicity in general and medical journals and paid advertising, the major ethical drug companies operate extensive field organizations. A large consulting organization in a study of the industry estimated that each of seven large manufacturers employed over 600 field sales representatives in selling to drug-stores and drug wholesalers, and in calling upon physicians. Several others traveled over 100 representatives.[8]

Not so familiar is the need to persuade business and industrial executives and owners to buy goods and services that will contribute either to making new or better products, or to rendering better service, or to lowering costs. The alert and progressive management is on the lookout for such improvement, but executives find it difficult to keep informed of all applicable or potentially applicable changes in equipment or materials. Some changes may involve very large risk. If present operations are profitable, the pressure not to take such risks is greater than if conditions compel making some type of change. Selling affects these decisions. Take the case of a company considering setting up an automatic production line. If it would be the first in its field to do so, questions would emerge as to the possibility of selling the entire output, or of selling the output at a rate that would permit steady production.

It is extremely likely that the companies selling electronic and other controls essential for automation would be soliciting both prospective users and those consultants who might have been hired to install the new process.

That industrial equipment manufacturers make it a practice to employ sales forces, sales engineers, and specialists to sell to prospective users and their advisors, is commonly known. Such sales organizations vary from one or a few men selling the output of a small machine shop, to several thousand. One large manufacturer employs 1,500 sales representatives, with an equal number of industrial and equipment specialists, in order to sell supplies, components, and equipment, varying from a small coil spring to a complete multimillion-dollar plant.

The need for selling to industrial buyers will continue in spite of the assertion of some purchasing officers that they will take the initiative and buy, that like government "they buy"—they do not need and do not want "to be sold" or persuaded to buy. Such buyers frequently do take the initiative in much of their buying. But nevertheless, they generally rely to a con-

[8] Arthur D. Little Co., *The Technology Behind Investment* (1952).

siderable extent upon the efforts of the seller to inform, to explain, to sell. The use of technical catalogues, technical advertising, and technical specialists, all parts of the producer's effort, is very common, even by those who are in a position to devote much and expert attention to buying. The range of products used by many industrial firms and by middlemen is so wide that it is uneconomical to take full initiative in every instance. Nevertheless, good selling will adapt its plans and its methods to such situations to the extent needed. Parenthetically, it may be remarked that emotional factors play a part in industrial buying, though a smaller one than in the buying of the ultimate consumer.

While personal selling is by all measures the most important form of effort to secure buying action in the field of industrial goods and services, advertising in its various forms plays an important part. Trade and technical publications, general magazines and newspapers, are used as well as much direct advertising in the form of catalogues, data books, and circulars. While only suggestive of the scope of such advertising, a single issue of a well-known newspaper read by many leading businessmen contained fourteen large advertisements of industrial producers. These advertisements, each one-fourth to a full page in size, were part of the selling programs of firms in various fields, selling a variety of products; for instance, pre-engineering electric power substations, dictating machines, cable dump trailers for road building, new type of lighting, electrical drill systems for oil well drilling, air freight transport service, commercial and industrial construction, chemicals for industrial purposes, new type of nylon, new type of electronic tube with special properties, steel for road construction, chemicals from Germany. In addition there were many other smaller space advertisements for industrial products as well as for some types of commercial goods.[9]

CONCLUSIONS

Advancing technology in production and distribution, inventions and discoveries are all aspects of change and innovation.

---

[9] *Wall Street Journal*, New York, November 14, 1956.

The incentives to innovation are of several types. Barnett in his exhaustive study of innovation[10] discusses self-wants and credit wants. One may innovate to satisfy a personal desire. Many have found it desirable to devise some new solution to a problem or difficulty confronting them. The visitor to Jefferson's Monticello is struck by the many ingenious contraptions Jefferson devised for his own comfort.

But much innovation is based upon innovators' desire for credit. While some persons love to invent for the sake of inventing, while desire to improve things is strong in some persons, such desires are stimulated by desire for reward. That reward may be personal gain or ego satisfaction.

Gain or benefit to be derived is probably the strongest motivation to innovation in the fields of goods and services that go to make up a high standard of living. It is not the only motivation, particularly as one approaches more and more closely research in pure science.

The firm that makes expenditures to support research, or that provides the facilities and man power to advance technology and design new products, does so and can do so because it depends upon present and future sales effort for the income to make the enterprise a going business. With the growing complexity of our technology, it becomes more and more difficult for business or research institutions to innovate without greatly increased investment and expenditure.

Innovation, invention, discovery—reflect the creative urge of many people in response to desire for a better life in an atmosphere and a hope that it may be attained. But creativity, to serve its great purpose, requires that the man who has ideas do something about them. The imaginative dreamer may have his place, but the man who does what he thinks should be done, even if it is unsuccessful, is more creative than the man of many ideas who mentally sits on the fence and does nothing.

Basically, our rapid progress in reconciling higher levels of living for all the people with less work to attain them rests upon individual freedom. It stems from the fact that in the free-enter-

---

[10] Barnett, *op. cit.* See also F. W. Taussig, *Inventors and Money Makers* (New York: Macmillan Co., 1915).

prise climate and in the social structure that prevails in the United States, there is greater assurance of obtaining reward for innovation, for technical improvement than ever before in history. Because reward can be made fairly certain for desirable innovation through selling, more people are enabled to search for beneficial improvement. More people are spending time and effort seeking to discover something new. The chance of reward for innovation that serves a real and recognized need has been rendered much greater because that advance can be brought to the attention of enough people who will benefit by it. They can be persuaded to buy the product in needed volume soon enough to assure continued existence and service for the project or enterprise.

Chapter VIII

ECONOMIC AND SOCIAL
EVALUATION OF SELLING:
I. CONTRIBUTIONS AND COSTS

The need of an over-all evaluation of selling from the economic and social points of view is emphasized by the paradoxes of our present system. The previous analysis has shown that selling makes positive contributions to welfare; but in practice, weaknesses, abuses, and wastes have developed. It has been asserted that selling makes a vital contribution to high and rising standards of living, but it has also been pointed out that selling is not accorded the respect its great contributions should bring. However, up to this point no effort has been made to summarize the positive contributions of selling, to analyze and assess the weaknesses and abuses of selling and advertising, or to appraise the actual effects in order to arrive at a balanced judgment. This task requires both objectivity and a willingness to look at what may be bad in selling as well as what is good. Furthermore, it requires an indication of the standards to be set up as a basis for judging whether or not selling effort is socially beneficial or socially detrimental. Perspective and a sense of proportion must be sought if the evaluation is to be useful.

Selling effort as well as any other effort should be appraised on the basis of its objectives, its methods, and its results. It has to be studied in its setting in the United States, within the existing political and social environment. While the conclusions may have much broader application than to the United States and Canada alone, no special effort has been made to extend the study to other areas. Some comparisons have been drawn with other countries and with other political systems, but largely for purposes of illustration and contrast. Furthermore, the economic and social evaluation of selling must be based primarily upon aspects of economic and social welfare as applied to the people as a whole, not as applied to limited or favored groups. The economic accomplishment in the United States has been the attainment of high levels of living for the great majority of our people, not for a relatively limited favored class.

In our evaluation, we are dealing also with the several common forms of persuasive effort to sell goods and services—neither with personal selling effort alone nor with advertising alone. While advertising has encountered a greater volume of adverse criticism, personal selling has not escaped feeling the sting of well-merited criticisms, the barbs of ridicule, and the smarting of unjustified accusation. The latter has often been based not upon malice but upon ignorance or mere annoyance, for while almost every person comes in contact with advertising, the average person comes in contact only with a limited portion of the field of personal selling. It has been declared that many persons looked upon Willy Loman, the central character in Arthur Miller's *Death of a Salesman*, as typifying the salesman and his work, rather than as a weakling who happened to get a selling job and who failed to mature in a changing world.

The weaknesses and abuses of personal selling are largely the same as those which occur in advertising; and the criticisms and objections to advertising are similar to those which are encountered in personal selling. Serious writers who have devoted attention to advertising have occasionally inserted a footnote to say that similar criticisms applied to personal selling and other sales promotional efforts.

Advertising in the free countries and especially in the United States can and does reach every man, woman, and child old enough to see, hear, or read. Therefore, if in daily newspapers, radio, and television, advertising and selling persuasion is willy-nilly brought to the attention of the critic, he will judge it by his own standards, feelings, emotions, and reason. Advertising has thus become the prime target for adverse criticism of selling; it was pointed out earlier that in spite of this fact personal selling and other selling effort cost the American public more than twice as much as advertising.

Advertising persuasion by its very nature is standardized and repetitive as between different prospective buyers, whether the run be a few dozen direct-mail cards or many million as in a single advertisement appearing in *Life, Saturday Evening Post,* and other magazines with large circulation. Thus the layman cannot escape the pervasiveness of advertising. When he hears that it costs thousands of dollars for one page of advertising, or that a television program may cost $25,000, $50,000, or even $100,000 or more for a single hour, the lump sum creates an additional impression of high cost and waste. One businessman in the advertising field refused finally to give lump figures to any lay group. He would point out that it cost ¼ cent per package to reach prospective buyers, a very low figure both in relation to the price of that package and the need for selling effort. Nevertheless, for general evaluation, total figures are desirable; and would be most useful if satisfactory measures of results could be developed.

Personal selling, on the other hand, can be individual and adjusted to the personality, preferences, and prejudices of the prospective buyer insofar as they are known. If the salesman is competent, he can adjust his effort during the actual contact. The consequence of this is that salesmen, by and large, have caused less annoyance and have attracted less attention from the critics. The relatively small amount of critical comment on personal selling is explained also in part by the fact that the public generally has little understanding of the extent of personal selling and usually has little chance to observe it as a whole. It sees clerks in retail stores and often criticizes the store that does not have enough salesclerks to pay prompt attention to the incoming customer. He knows clerks are not highly paid but not that such personal services are among the largest expenses of store operation.

Both in public schools and in universities and colleges, selling and advertising have frequently been either ignored or adversely criticized. Therefore, when a brash salesman comes to the door, or a retail clerk seems to be incompetent or less courteous than the buyer thinks he should be, or especially when a buyer encounters an advertisement in bad taste or one which in some way is irritating to him, he is very ready to condemn. The average person, and even persons who should assume the responsibility for more penetrating thought, fail to understand the place of selling in the functioning of our complicated economic institutions. The displeasure or annoyance they feel may be the result of an abuse of selling comparable to abuses in other forms of leadership, or it may be the outgrowth of a personal or individual objection not shared by others. If, however, an intelligent layman endeavors to obtain a balanced point of view on selling, he finds it extremely difficult to get literature, or instruction, or other help that will be convincing.

EVALUATION OF SELLING LEADERSHIP—
BASES AND OBJECTIVES

Any social evaluation of selling must consider and endeavor to answer the question as to whether the abuses and costs outweigh any positive benefits. It must distinguish between those criticisms which deal with actual wastes and abuses that can and should be corrected, and those alleged wastes and abuses which are essentially inseparable from democratic processes in any area of leadership, whether business or government. It must be recognized further that criticisms of selling based upon ideas involving material change in our general economic structure, extensive economic planning by government officials or by extreme socialistic or totalitarian government controls, require separate consideration, which is reserved for a later chapter.

Much of the criticism of selling has come from those who believe that selling in various ways has caused neglect of other essential portions of good living. If progress in political, social, and cultural areas has lagged, it is conceivable that it could be because leadership in those fields has lagged in relation to selling leadership. Nevertheless the criticism must be considered.

However, no examination of the abuses and weaknesses of selling itself would be complete without examination of the inherent correctives that exist to restrict the extent of abuses of selling and to remedy weaknesses. The positive effects and the limitations of enlightened selfishness, the types and nature of co-operative action of business itself to reduce abuses, and other corrective forces exercising influence toward ethical and socially approved forms of selling effort must all be included. Lastly, some appraisal of the part played by trade and business organizations and by government should not be overlooked.

The immediate objectives of selling leadership are to sell more goods and services; that is, to influence prospective buyers to take buying action. The broad basic objective is high and rising standards of living for all the people. It has been argued in detail that the totality of reactions brought about by this influence adds up to higher consumption and to higher actual levels of living. If the leadership is effective in bringing about the buying action, it sets in motion the chain of events, actions, and decisions that finally bring about greater productivity on the part of the people. It follows logically that the same groups that work to enjoy high and rising standards must provide for the necessary production of the goods and services.

The objective and result of securing greater buying action does not necessarily add up to better living, any more than the results of political leadership necessarily add up to better government. In a democracy of free economic choice, people make bad choices of their own volition, just as bad or misguided leaders may influence them to make bad choices. Objectives that may initially be considered bad or badly chosen can be appraised sometimes only after experience, because they may, on balance, prove to be neither antisocial nor bad when attained. In the case of selling effort, progress in levels of living for which selling can take much credit has actually been attained with much realized good and great potentials for further good. In spite of the adverse opinions of critics in each generation, the masses of people rather than the critics may be right.[1]

The desirability of widespread and widely enjoyed high economic levels of living will generally be approved as a goal of selling effort. But they will be approved by every right-thinking person without losing sight of the accepted fact that these are not the only goals of human endeavor. One of the merits of our economic system, however, has been that in operation it has actually enhanced the opportunity for a broader and more rewarding way of life. No longer do long hours of work, no longer does exhausting strenuous work take away all zest for recreational, intellectual, or cultural pursuits. Nevertheless, the need for other forms of effective social leadership to stimulate people to make more productive use of the new leisure has emerged as a great challenge to our people and especially to leaders in noneconomic areas.

The objectives of selling effort are, on the whole, in the public interest. They are socially beneficial. The objectives of some sellers, nevertheless, may be wasteful or antisocial, selfish at the expense of social welfare. As in any economic form of leadership, there are some leaders whose objectives are not in the interests of those whom they influence. It is one of the facts of our economic life that selling leaders whose objectives are essentially antisocial do not ordinarily last long, nor do their operations bulk large in total.

Positive Economic Contributions of Selling and Advertising

The positive contributions of the persuasive leadership we call selling have been analyzed in detail in previous chapters. Consequently, only a brief summarization will be appropriate at this point. Adverse criticism of selling persuasion needs to be read with a clear understanding of the positive contributions in order that negative aspects be brought into focus. Thereby one

---

[1] An interesting and careful examination of historians' opinions on the level of living during the early days of the rise of industrial capitalism is to be found in Professor T. S. Ashton's essays on the subject in F. A. Hayek, *Capitalism and the Historians* (Chicago: University of Chicago Press, 1954). He shows how both historical and contemporary opinion were apparently developed without knowledge of the real facts of improvement.

is not so likely to be misled, as many writers have been, into forgetting positive functions of selling and emphasizing mainly or exclusively certain unfavorable aspects and criticisms, which, whether valid or invalid, fallacious or sound, should be judged with due regard to their relative importance.

Early analysis has presented selling as an essential, pervasive form of leadership toward progress in the economic sphere of human activity.

1) It has been shown that people benefit by selling in the first instance because selling persuades them to buy the goods and services that go to make high material levels of living. Furthermore, it has been shown that these buying actions start a complex chain of reactions that lead people to produce the goods and services required for those levels with proportionately decreasing amounts of human labor.

Selling causes consumers to buy more and obtain more satisfaction than they would without the exercise of that form of persuasive leadership. Without stimulation and intensification, the desire for goods and services that make up high levels of living is not strong enough to bring about the buying actions that in quantity, uniformity, and timing are such as to enable a highly productive technology either to operate or to develop rapidly. Thereby the worker's productivity is enhanced to a point where he can produce and support a high standard of living.

2) By securing buying actions conforming to the requirements of an advanced and advancing industrial system, society is benefited through greater and more rapid rise in the standard of living than would be possible without it or possible under any other type of leadership.

It is on selling that competitive activity is focused. The producer endeavors to offer a better product or a lower price in order to induce the consumer or other buyer to take action. Competitors do likewise. Each tries to persuade the prospective buyer to purchase his product, by pointing out the special features of his product or his price or service. This competition is a powerful spur to improvement because less and less can the weak producer seek refuge in ill-informed and ill-supplied markets.

What the manufacturer does to plan better products or to offer better prices, or to give better service succeeds or fails in the market place at the point where he tries to sell his proposition—the product plus other elements of his offer—to the prospective buyer. Out of such competition and its grueling tests, greater production has been obtained—by shorter, not by longer hours of labor, because selling enabled incentives to be given to those who have invented, discovered, and applied new processes, new machines, better management, to the job of producing and distributing what the consumer needs and wants.

3) Selling has helped consumers buy wisely. Since most selling is applied to repeat sales, it is to the interest of the seller to sell those things which will create goodwill and a desire to make further purchases from the seller. Furthermore, selling also requires that the seller make it easy for the buyer to buy. Emphasis upon the positive and helpful aspects of selling requires that one give due credit for honest effort to the vast majority of business firms, retailers, wholesalers, manufacturers, and other producers, who try to buy or furnish what will be wanted by consumers or other buyers. Retailers generally do what they can to buy what the community will want; they grow and prosper in a competitive environment only if they do so. Mail-order house catalogues have often been pointed to as models of informative selling. Likewise, other middlemen who sell to more or less experienced buyers offer expert help to customers. The selling by industrial distributors to factories and machine shops is characterized by much selling help in finding products, components, supplies, and equipment suitable for production needs. Manufacturers' selling representatives in the business-machines field are trained to give competent technical advice and service in fields about which buyers know little. One could multiply examples of sellers' helpfulness.

Everyone knows, however, that there is much selling that tends to create wants but that does not help the consumer to buy wisely. It is asserted that certain selling practices may have the result of causing people to buy too much or of buying the wrong things. These and other criticisms are taken up in the following chapter. It is apparent that critics, however, and particularly those who write in the field of consumer economics, lay much stress upon weaknesses and abuses, and perhaps too little stress upon the inherent helpful characteristics of competitive selling.

4) Society has benefited from new products, from the establishment of new enterprises, from the application of advanced technologies, and from the continued availability of known desirable products. None of these can develop except very slowly and haltingly unless the demand is sufficient and unless that demand can be converted into buying action within time periods limited by the requirements for continued existence. In a free-enterprise society, securing buying decisions within appropriate time periods can be accomplished only by the application of selling persuasion. In any other form of society in which government planning or allotment are predominant, there has been no demonstration of progress in any area comparable to that shown by free enterprise. Furthermore, as will be discussed later, predominant buyer initiative does not and cannot produce innovation, new products, and better production, as rapidly or as fully as free enterprise with selling persuasion.

5) Selling has enabled people to enjoy freedom of choice while securing the advantages of large-scale production and advanced technology and skilled management. All of these require volume of sales and volume of buying actions, which do not develop automatically. Persuasion must be carried on by each seller to have buyers place orders within the critical time periods required for survival and profit. Inevitably some of this leadership fails. Unless products are considered desirable, people will not generally buy; but just as surely, unless people know about products and feel strongly that they will benefit from purchase, they will also not buy.

Consumer freedom of choice within high living standards is the accomplishment of free enterprise. It is the evidence of economic freedom. One of its results is the spread of incentive, the arousing of initiative to action in attaining the desired elements of economic welfare. The consumer exercises the power of approval or disapproval. He awards success to some and withholds it from other businessmen depending on the way they serve.

6) Successful selling effort, by increasing the volume of buying-selling transactions, increases the volume of production and provides employment and the basis for greater productivity through the application of technical advance. During the depression years of the thirties, the National Federation of Sales Executives, endeavoring to combat unemployment, gave wide currency to the slogan "Sales Mean Jobs." From Adam Smith on, it has been accepted that division of labor and the use of power and machines have been limited by the extent of the market. But by market, one can only mean the quantities of goods that can be sold and therefore can be put into production. In the present-day economic structure, what can be sold, both from the viewpoint of producer as a whole and from that of the private firm, determines the rate of production and the rate of employment.

Other societies claim to furnish full employment, but it is employment in which the workers' choice of jobs and choice of satisfactions to be derived from those jobs are severely limited. At the worst it is slavery; it subordinates the individual to the state. To paraphrase, it is "government of the state, by the state, and for the state." It is employment at the price of liberty in return for low living standards.

7) Selling, though aimed primarily at economic progress in terms of higher standards of living, contributes in various ways to progress in other areas of human interest. Selling contributes to cultural progress both directly and indirectly. Directly, selling has enhanced interest in the arts in an effective way, sometimes as a philanthropic gesture, but mainly in other ways more directly in line with its objectives and its functioning. The expansion of amateur interest in arts and crafts has been an important measure fostered by advertising and selling effort. In part through the selling effort of those who produce and distribute radio sets, phonograph records, and musical instruments and in part through the programs, orchestras, and musical groups supported by those who sell, the taste of the masses appears to have improved. There has been an enormous increase in those

interested in the graphic arts. Amateur painting and photography have found new enthusiasts by the tens of thousands, until exhibitions, displays, and art-club meetings, are matters of everyday occurrence in any large city, as well as in many smaller places.

In discussions with educators in various fields and particularly with those interested in the arts, one finds some who when called upon to appraise our progress in cultural development have no hesitation in asserting that progress in these directions has been more rapid and widespread for people generally than at any time in our previous history; indeed, one noted authority claimed that at no time in history had so many people risen so rapidly in appreciation of the arts as in our own country in the past half century.

There are those also who see in our economy and especially in selling quite a different picture. They still point to Europe as the center of culture, usually blithely ignoring the narrow, privileged circles to which their concepts of culture are confined. It is interesting, therefore, to come across the judgment of a trained and impartial observer who wrote several articles for his European newspaper while in the United States. Upon his return from the visit of several months in connection with the "International Seminar" he had an opportunity to attend at Harvard University, Mr. Eric Mettler, the *Neue Zürcher Zeitung* correspondent in London, concluded a series of articles with the following summary. Mr. Mettler had come across much evidence of a certain anti-Americanism in vogue in Europe and reports his contrasting impressions in his article entitled "Impressions of America."[2]

One often hears it said among European intellectuals that the Americans, while exceedingly successful in technological and economic respects, really have no culture. But when these same critics want to put something really stirring, something truly creative on their stages, they are forced to have recourse to the pieces of Thornton Wilder, Tennessee Williams and Arthur Miller. And when they wish to name some leading modern novelists, they point to Hemingway, Faulkner and Steinbeck. The existen-

---

[2] Published in the *Swiss Review of World Affairs*, November, 1956, Zurich, Switzerland. By permission.

tialist adolescent lounging in Paris' St.-Germain-des-Prés and criticizing all things American hardly realizes that the tight pants he wears as a sign of his unfettered individuality are an imitation of the traditional "blue jeans" of the American cowboy.

Many Europeans take great pride in a cultural heritage toward which they have hardly made a contribution themselves. They quote the classics of antiquity and the Renaissance, but do not create any such works themselves any more. Does the half-starved helot of southern Italy or the British white-collar worker watching his commercialized TV program embody a higher stage of civilization than the American average citizen who, at the end of a well-paid five-day week, adds another piece to the house he is building for himself, reads Tolstoy—if perhaps in an abbreviated version—and tries some Beethoven on his record player? Even if the Americans had not written a single book until now and never produced any other work of art, the mere deed of settling and industrializing their huge country and at the same time establishing the most powerful democracy on earth would constitute a rare feat of cultural and historical magnitude. The finer arts are not as a rule developed by pioneer generations. First comes the log cabin on the raw frontier, then a burst of skyscraper vitality, and only then follows the beautiful architecture of which some can be seen today in New England and California. In some of the Boston suburbs this writer became acquainted with, ugly houses are a rarity. Of which residential section of any European city can the same be said?

Europeans who have lived in the United States for a brief period only sometimes complain that they feel like exiles in a barbaric land. Such feelings are familiar to this writer from his trips to the borders of the Arabian desert or to distant Slav countries. In America, quite on the contrary, he experienced a sensation of exhiliration, of gratitude for the fact that courageous people from ancient Europe—for the civilization of which Jacob Burckhardt was willing to die—have populated this continent and transplanted some of their old world to this virgin soil. The tree-studded city of Washington pleases by its generous harmony, a soothing reflection of 18th century graciousness. The first President's country house on the shores of the Potomac radiates a charming simplicity. It was by the principles of moderation that the fathers of the American constitution embarked upon their great venture. Why should their successors have lost, or never possessed, that *mesure de l'homme?* Traveling through the Middle West this writer, to be sure, felt concerned over the unrealistic isolationist tendency of these people, but he also felt gratified at being treated by them like a relative. These farmers of Scandinavian and Alemannic origin have by no means turned their backs upon the old world once for all. They go to Europe for their vacations and send their sons and daughters to study in European universities.

At Harvard a young American invited us to contribute a chapter to a book to be published under the title "What's wrong with the United States?" We declined without hesitation. There is enough self-criticism in progress in the United States already, we feel, a self-criticism compared to which many a European satire on America looks like mere superficial snobbery. The intense desire of so many American intellectuals for greater maturity, deeper experience and true culture is surely a healthy sign. All the outstanding Americans we met were fundamentally humble, reverent men, deeply convinced that pragmatism and technology must not be allowed to take control. They also see the dangerous aspects of that propensity to conform to uniform standards, which is so necessary in a people of immigrants, but in the long run must be superseded by free individual development. As for the mania of many critics at home and abroad, finally, to seek for the germs of decay behind every material achievement, one might do well to remember that each and every civilization has taken its toll of victims. The pyramids of ancient Egypt were built by armies of slaves, and masses of poor proletarians helped build Queen Victoria's empire—not to speak of the horrible price still being paid for the industrialization of Russia. By comparison, the tribute of Americans landing on psychiatrists' couches or succumbing to premature heart attacks appears surprisingly modest. Puritanism would not be such a powerful motor of human achievement if it did not also produce some maladjustments.

Soon the anxious question on this writer's mind, as he traveled throughout the United States, no longer was whether the Americans have any culture, but whether they are willing and capable of carrying, for an indefinite time, the burden of world-political tasks that has fallen upon them. A visit to Arlington Cemetery reminded us of Rome's Via Appia. Just like the old Romans the Americans are building many of their cemeteries directly on the road without any fences around them. Are they, with their system of extreme separation of powers, adequately equipped to assume, on behalf of the Western world, an imperial responsibility on the pattern of ancient Rome? This question, it seems to us, can be answered in the affirmative, provided the White House is occupied by a strong Chief Executive endowed with farsightedness and imagination—a leader, a statesman. If, on the other hand, the head of the Government in Washington were to conduct himself more as a constitutional monarch than as a Chief Executive, we would feel some serious concern to be called for, indeed.

A recent item in *Time*[3] magazine contains a pertinent report along somewhat similar lines, taken from the London *Times*, whose influential editor Sir William Haley reported apropos of Mr. Mettler's last point:

It is easy to be superior about American brashness and naïvety, to be scournful of material progress as a purpose; to picture a whole continent slowly being moulded to the ideals of Hollywood [he wrote]. These things are only the surface froth that gets whipped about by the winds of publicity. Underneath there is the great solid sea of an American nation as simple in its aspirations, as traditional in its virtues, as conscious of its high destiny as any there has ever been in the old world.

Continuing, Sir William then paid the respects of the sensitive traveler to the breathtaking scope of U.S. farming, the "defiant pinnacles" of its cities, the eagerness of its university students, and concluded:

Here is a people rather baffled, but a people resolved to know; a people faced, as it seems to them, with a whole globe needing to be set to rights, but determined, either with or without it, to get things done.

Of all nations, its history has a higher proportion of greatness than of baseness; of all peoples its motives are the least suspect. Its errors have been, and are, many. Its instincts have been, and are, magnificently right. We see the small debits from day to day. Let us look rather at the huge credit through the years. Amidst all the dangers that beset us, we can be thankful that it is to this dynamic, humorous, impatient, impulsive, generous people there has passed the leadership of the world.

But the greatest contribution of selling beyond that of increasing material welfare is that which results from its energization of the whole productive machine. The enormous increase in productivity of human labor, which selling has made possible within a period historically very short, has brought surcease from exhausting work and has furnished the opportunity, the leisure, the strength for cultural, intellectual, and other pursuits essential to balanced living.

Selling obviously does not furnish the complete leadership toward balanced living. That leadership must come from blend-

---

[3] December 10, 1956, pp. 20–21.

ing the various types of leadership influence that emanate from the different sectors of our social and personal environment. Which leadership will be strong and influential, and which will exert insufficient influence to secure balance, poses problems of basic social concern. Positive, pervasive, and effective leadership is needed in all sectors to assure a balance that accords to economic welfare its rightful place in the scheme of things. One cannot assume, however, that it is necessary to forego high living standards in order to arrive at a "good life."

Finally, it needs but to be mentioned that the advances in productivity and production are required not only for a rapidly increasing rising standard of living for an existing population but also for future populations. The increased rate of population growth in the United States, which has made estimates of growth of only twenty years ago look highly unrealistic, presents an increased challenge to maintain our present high standards and raise them for a rapidly growing population. The maintenance of employment at high levels even with shortened hours depends upon sales, upon purchase action that will bring into consumption the full output of more and more productive human effort. This challenge presents the further difficult problem—by no means a new one—of sharing the results of higher productivity and production in such a way as to elevate the level of living for all the people. Concurrently, sufficient incentive must be retained for those who manage and those who furnish capital to maintain and improve existing production under existing technology, while going beyond that to develop new products, new processes, and new machines. The need for incentive to venture should not be overlooked in the struggle of men to share the benefits of ventures already undertaken successfully, if society as a whole is to benefit. Obviously if ventures are unsuccessful, as many are, there is nothing to share.

The recital of the economic and social contributions of selling and advertising effort does not constitute an appraisal, for objective observers will want to take into account abuses, negative factors, and causes. Not a few critics either explicitly or by implication give the impression that these adverse factors outweigh the positive contributions. While the extreme view is certainly fallacious, the undoubted existence of abuses and wastes requires that any investigator look into them with an open mind and without prejudice. Good selling leadership must work toward the elimination of abuse and the reduction of wastes. But an understanding of the nature and basis of adverse criticism is essential.

CRITICISMS OF SELLING

The criticisms of selling effort, including in that term personal selling, advertising, and other forms of persuasive effort to induce buying action, are both economic and social. The line is not always clearly drawn, because economists have almost always ignored the selling function and have only incidentally criticized advertising and selling on economic grounds from the standpoint of social welfare; occasionally they have criticized selling on the basis of its cultural influence, waste, and the like. However, the principal criticisms can be classified into two groups, one of which is primarily economic in character, the other primarily social and cultural. In the first group are the following:

1. Selling activities are unnecessary, or if they are necessary, they are excessive in amount.
2. Selling effort costs too much.
3. Competitive selling is wasteful and uneconomic.

Other technical criticisms such as the relation of advertising and selling to imperfect competition and monopoly, the effect upon cyclical fluctuations, are dealt with in Chapter XII, "Selling and Economic Theory."

Other criticisms cover a wider range. Principal among these are:

4. Selling influences people to buy too much. People buy more than they can afford. It leads to self-indulgence. Selling creates wants which cannot be satisfied and thus leads to frustration, discontent, and dissatisfaction.
5. Selling influences people to buy the wrong things. Goods that do not fit needs. People are induced to buy things that do not possess individuality. It tends to spread bad taste and lowers tastes instead of elevating them.

6. Selling influences people to buy the right things for the wrong reasons. Emotional appeals are used. Appeals are made to lower desires rather than higher.
7. Selling causes people to buy harmful goods. Goods that are injurious, physically or mentally.
8. Selling effort is often untruthful and insincere. Fraud, sharp practice, and deceit are common.
9. Selling effort itself is often cheap, vulgar, and in bad taste.
10. Selling causes people to be too materialistic. It causes them to accord unwarranted importance to material things.

These groups include most of the criticisms of selling that appear in the public press and in the writings of economists, sociologists, and students of consumer economics. Some of the most severe critiques have appeared in the business press. But as remarked elsewhere, the most significant indicator is the absence of opinion or the meager and inadequate attention devoted to selling by those who essay to write upon the functioning of the American economy and to pass critical judgment upon it.

The adverse criticisms of selling and the abuses of the leadership function include not only those based upon actual abuses and failures of social leadership but also those based on the divergence between the desires and the ethical and social standards of the critics and the realities of democratic living. Some judgments are obviously derived from observation of a limited but not necessarily typical portion of the functioning of selling and advertising. Whatever the basis, the various criticisms deserve careful examination and study. It is with the economic criticisms that the remainder of this chapter is concerned. Social and cultural criticisms are dealt with in Chapters IX and X.

Selling Activities Are Alleged Excessive in Amount, Even Unnecessary

The precise phrasing of the criticisms of those who assert that selling is excessive in amount ranges from those who believe that selling is entirely unnecessary to those who believe that some selling is necessary but that it is used in excessive amounts with social waste and higher-than-necessary costs to consumers. A quotation will illustrate.[4]

---

[4] Kenneth Boulding, *Economic Analysis* (New York: Harper & Bros., 1948), pp. 594–95.

The "wastes" of competition are also characteristic mainly of imperfect competition. Perhaps the most important of these wastes from a social point of view is that involved in competitive advertising. There is a case for a certain amount of advertising, such as the purely informative advertising which is descriptive of the qualities and prices of commodities. This is a form of consumer education which is necessary if consumers are to make intelligent choices; in fact, it makes competition more nearly perfect. This virtuous advertising, however, does not bulk very large in the total. Most advertising, unfortunately, is devoted to an attempt to build up in the minds of the consumer irrational preferences for certain brands of goods. All the arts of psychology—particularly the art of association—are used to persuade consumers that they should buy Bumpo rather than Bango. Look through the pages of any magazine or newspaper, or listen to any program on the radio, and see how much space or time is devoted to an accurate description of the properties and prices of goods; the amount is surprisingly little.

This "competitive" advertising is a clear social waste. The only possible case for it is that it may increase the velocity of circulation of money and thus avoid some unemployment. There are, however, cheaper and more dignified ways of increasing employment. Apart from this, competitive advertising does not result in the creation of wealth, for the consumer would spend his money in any case, advertising or no advertising, and he would probably spend it more wisely if there were no competitive—only informative—advertising.

But other economists do not go so far; C. Lowell Harriss[5], Sumner Slichter, and others do not see selling as "all black." However, the concept of "perfect" competition is useful only in studying a static society—not in arriving at conclusions concerning a dynamic economy.

The economists' frequent omission of discussion of selling is perhaps more significant than the limited discussions of a few. Galbraith takes the point of view in *American Capitalism*[6] that much selling effort is of a competitive type, which is a waste but a waste associated with the opulence of our society. His argument is a peculiar mixture, which does not go far enough beyond personal annoyance and emotional attitudes. Like many

---

[5] C. Lowell Harriss, *The American Economy: Principles, Practices, and Policies* (rev. ed.; Homewood, Ill.: Richard D. Irwin, Inc., 1956), p. 551.

[6] John K. Galbraith, *American Capitalism* (Boston: Houghton Mifflin Co., 1952), chap. viii.

others, Galbraith tends to use conspicuous examples of cigarette and liquor advertising as typical of selling effort. He might have pointed to cosmetics, soap, and other conspicuous advertising frequently singled out for adverse criticism, which would add up to as much as 5 per cent of advertising, or less than 1 per cent of total selling effort. That something beyond simple informational selling is necessary is not indicated in his discussion.

The criticisms of selling in this area seem, therefore, to be of three types. There are, first, those criticisms which expressly or implicitly assert that selling is really unnecessary; that a good product will sell without selling leadership and effort. The corollary is, of course, that selling effort is a waste of man power and resources. Some of these critics apparently believe that production creates its own demand; others that selling is a purely private acquisitive activity not really necessary for the enterprise itself. The former criticism, which stems from earlier economic theory, especially the "law of markets" of Jean Baptiste Say is dealt with later. Another form of the criticism is illustrated in an extreme manner by the strictures of Jordan, a retired professor of philosophy in *Business be Damned*.[7]

It is quite evident that such criticism is wholly unrealistic, in its effort to separate industry, which presumably the author admires, and business. It fails to recognize the need of stimulating demand for the products of industry. It blandly assumes that all products which in his philosophic wisdom are considered worth selling will require no selling effort, informational or otherwise.

Such criticisms which amount to a denial of the necessity of the selling function are basically aimed at free competitive enterprise; for the continuance of free enterprise on any substantial scale is dependent upon selling. Although such authors do not say so, they must either favor the alternative of predominant buyer initiative which has nowhere been tried and which examination shows to be essentially unworkable, or some form of

---

[7] Elijah Jordan, *Business be Damned* (New York: Henry Schuman, 1952), pp. 26-257. In condemning all business and selling, Professor Jordan apparently looks nostalgically back to premachine days, and holds to "romantic" ideas concerning the condition of the common people which have been shown by research to be false. Cf. Hayek, *op. cit.*

government allotment, socialistic or communistic in character.

The second group of criticisms takes the point of view that while some selling is necessary, the actual amounts of advertising and selling effort are excessive. Critics give the impression that businessmen deliberately use more selling effort than is needed to get results, or that executives should be content with less selling effort than is believed necessary to reach the market effectively. In point of fact, the determination of the amount and range of selling leadership needed to dispose of the products of a particular producing organization is a problem of baffling complexity in any but the simplest and smallest enterprises. It involves complex facets of human behavior. Changes in demand, in supply, in competition affecting consumer buying action are not scientifically predictable as applied to specific firms.

The decisions executives have to make with respect to advertising and selling are decisions that must be based upon inadequate information. For in seeking to influence human behavior, we quickly encounter the limits of our knowledge of the ways and means of accomplishing particular results. Therefore, it may well be that excessive amounts of selling effort and advertising are employed in particular cases. It may also just as well be true that not enough selling effort is carried on by other firms from whose goods or services society could benefit in increased measure. It has been shown that society has benefited by the steadily increased selling effort through the past century. It is at least conceivable that wider and wiser use of selling and advertising might have brought even more rapid progress.

The implication in some criticisms of selling that businessmen know precisely what to do and how to do it at minimum cost in selling is flattering but misleading. It is not warranted by the facts. The effectiveness of particular types and forms of selling persuasion cannot be predicted in most situations with any degree of assurance. Past experience may help, but in a dynamic economy it is not a trustworthy guide to future human behavior when applied to the particular problem of particular sellers.

No seller uses more selling effort than he thinks may be

needed to reach his objective. If he puts in less effort than needed, he fails to dispose of the product and services he has on hand. Commonly, this brings loss, sometimes disaster. If the seller hires too many salesmen, or employs too much advertising, he wastes his substance and reduces profit. Since the ability of the enterprise to stay in business depends upon buying action, upon selling, to bring income that will enable him to recover costs and yield a profit, he may well be conservative in making sure of getting the necessary volume even at the extra cost of effort that, in hindsight, proved to be excessive.

To sum up, the conclusion is inescapable that the amount of selling effort a particular firm uses in its effort to make sales is not excessive in view of the risks involved, the importance of securing results, and the lack of detailed knowledge and ability to predict results. Any layman who undertakes to find out the probable effectiveness of a program of selling effort in advance of the advertising and personal selling will soon discover that even if he uses all the guides and research data he can lay his hands on, and employs all the intelligence and common sense he possesses, he can arrive at no accurate forecast, although he can reduce the probabilities of error. For as in any other leadership, the reactions of individuals are the resultant of a multiplicity of influences. A particular program's results in terms of buying action are affected by many factors over which sellers have no control. Both too little and too much are wasteful, but the measures of what constitutes too little or too much are only partially developed. The safety margins that must be included in plans must be wider because knowledge of what the selling task will require is affected by factors over which the seller has no control, such as actions of competitors and changes in the attitudes of buyers.

Selling Costs Too Much

That selling costs too much is asserted by critics and admitted by businessmen. A businessman believes that selling costs too much because he hopes and believes there must be improved ways of getting buying action. Selling, therefore, should be improved so that it costs less. However, the critics are not always clear whether they mean that selling costs too much because we do not know enough to do a more effective job or because business spends more than needed for the results desired.

Does selling leadership to secure buying action cost too much in terms of public welfare? In a study of distributive costs of some years ago, The Twentieth Century Fund, after an exhaustive search, was willing to estimate that 59 cents of every dollar went into distribution (not selling) expenses; but they were unwilling to make any radical suggestion for improvement, although they pointed out some areas in which greater effectiveness might be secured. It might have found similar inefficiencies in production, for there is an all-too-common assumption that all production is as efficient as our technology and management skills will permit. In fact, while production has made great strides in the application of new technical advances, those advances have been made in part as the result of selling persuasion. Production is more efficient today because of selling persuasion applied to owners, managers, scientists, and technicians. But to assume that all production is as efficient as technical advance will permit is as unrealistic as to assume that all distribution is inefficient. It is obvious that selling costs more than it would if all firms made full use of the best knowledge we have as related to selling effort.

Selling and advertising with all their weaknesses and faults are wide open to public scrutiny. In production and other areas of business management, the public has little chance to examine and appraise. Consequently, the public learns of the conspicuous successes and advances through advertisement, publicity, and other sources. But the weaknesses of production, the inefficiencies in other areas are in many companies not so likely to be published. Featherbedding by labor, incompetence in management, antiquated and inefficient equipment are not observed except by those who are unlikely to advertise their existence.

The estimates of selling costs as a part of marketing are large, very large, representing over one third of total marketing costs. For this the American consumer pays; and by paying this, he is enabled to have a higher real income than anyone else on earth. We pay for selling because we believe it benefits us, and yet we want selling to cost as little as possible consistent with perform-ance. We want to pay what is necessary to secure freedom of choice and give incentive to innovation, new enterprise, and new products. In short, we are not unwilling to pay the price necessary for economic democracy, but we are not willing to pay more than is necessary.

The consumer pays billions of dollars to be persuaded to buy. Theoretically, the consumer would pay less for products if there were no selling effort, but only provided certain conditions were met. In reverse, they constitute the justification for more selling effort.

Selling effort would be unnecessary, first, if enough people would buy enough products of the various types offered so that enterprises that made an effort to serve the public well, could continue in business on a sufficient scale to provide eco-nomical production at competitive costs, and have a margin with which to carry on research, provide for depreciation of ma-chinery, and provide the incentive required and necessary to maintain a constructive active interest. Businessmen generally do not believe that this condition would be met, and an unbiased observation of the facts does not show that the businessmen are wrong in their belief. The assumptions of economics that people buy these products without selling effort is discussed at various points, but it does not correspond to the facts of human be-havior.

Second, the cost of selling effort could be devoted to lower prices or more products if people would buy new products put up for sale within appropriate time limits, ranging from a few weeks to a few years, so that smaller or larger enterprise could secure an income enabling it to continue in business. There is no evidence that people will, of their own volition and on their own initiative, buy most new products in volume. In fact, firms introducing many of those products which now constitute im-portant elements of our high standards of living in the United States have earlier found survival difficult, even with active and aggressive selling effort.

Third, from another point of view the consumer could pay less for products and reduce costs provided people would tell producers what they wanted at a time when the producer was compelled to take action to arrange for the production of the new product. This means that people should tell producers what they want from a few weeks to several years in advance of their needs. That people will do this, particularly that the ultimate consumer will do this, is clearly the wildest type of illusion.

Finally, if the consumer wishes not to pay for selling costs, he would have to pay for buying efforts. He would have to join with others in bringing about acceptance of uniform ideas as to wants so that the advances in productive technology could be utilized. There is no evidence in historical record that buyers on any scale have ever been able to get together to agree to take a specific uniform product that they asked producers to manufacture. Nor is there any evidence that ultimate consumers band together on any scale to encourage and finance technological advance. Industrial and commercial buyers may on occasion initiate, but few, very few, industrial concerns can depend upon buyer initiative alone.

One should probably ignore the naïveté of those who support the statement that selling costs too much by pointing to the increased portion of the final consumer price represented by distribution cost. The rise of the proportion of consumer prices represented by distribution costs is a well-known fact, but it has led to much naïve and fallacious argument. It has been assumed that because of this rise, selling has become less effective and selling has taken too large a part of the consumer dollar.

The first fallacy involved in the general argument is the assumption that at some earlier period the relations between selling and manufacturing were in a more desirable relationship. That has never been proved and obviously could not be proved. In fact, such evidence as exists from the standards of living available to the masses clearly tends to support the conclusion that these earlier relations were undesirable.

Secondly, there is the fallacy that low absolute or relative costs of one factor alone are in the interests of the consumer, irrespective of the effect of that low cost on other factors entering into price. This attitude denies the point of view that the real consumer interest is in what he has to pay for the total product, for the satisfactions or utilities he buys. His interest in production costs or in marketing or selling costs is in their effect upon his total buying price, not in their absolute levels or their relation to each other, or to total costs.

The third fallacy that production costs and selling costs are independent of each other is implicit in many of the criticisms. To the extent that selling affects the quantity sold, it affects the quantity manufactured. Certainly quantity is one of the determinants of the extent of the division of labor, the application of machinery and skilled management, and the development of research. Thus a firm in an industry that operates under conditions of decreasing cost will be vitally affected by the success or failure of its selling and advertising effort.[8]

The cost of selling effort can be reduced by curtailing errors and mistakes in planning and in the execution of the planning itself. Research in products to obtain those more fitted to market needs reduces the difficulty but does not eliminate the need for some selling effort. The application of valid studies of market behavior may help the executive to make correct decisions and reduce waste. The studied approach to influencing people to take buying action contains possibilities of reducing waste, even though the study of human behavior is one whose scope and difficulty can be recognized by any thinking person. Too precise knowledge would have harmful potentials in the hands of a minority of unscrupulous sellers, but it would be even more dangerous to public welfare in the hands of unscrupulous leaders in political, religious, and educational fields. One can conclude that while we may need to lessen the cost of selling by more knowledge of human behavior and better application of that knowledge, we must accept as part of the price of democratic freedom of enterprise, the risks that mistakes will be made and that actual costs will exceed some vague ideal cost, which ignores important aspects of human behavior.

Competitive Selling Is Wasteful and Uneconomic

Those economists who discuss selling and advertising make much of the argument that competitive selling is wasteful be-

---

[8] In an article entitled "Does Distribution Cost Enough?" Paul Mazur defends the thesis that greater expenditure to improve marketing and distribution would be of benefit to the public. See *Fortune*, Vol. XXXVI, No. 5 (November, 1947).

cause it tends to cancel out.[9] Firm A sends out salesmen, advertises, and secures business. Competitor B feels it must follow in order to maintain or regain its market position. After both of them have carried on in this way, they find themselves in the same relative position as before. Only selling costs have risen. The argument that competitive advertising is wasteful is thus plausible and possesses certain limited validity; but further analysis shows that much more is involved:

1) It must be recognized that to some extent total demand is increased so that the competitive firms, even though they maintain the same relative position, are selling and producing more. Depending upon the stage of market development, more or less of that selling effort may have to be devoted to creating what a colleague calls "primary" rather than "selective" demand.[10] The initial difficult, slow stages of introduction of new products are followed by increasing acceptance of product, so that selling effort required per unit is reduced. Eventually, competitive conditions become more difficult and pressure increases to produce new or substantially improved products in order to maintain or improve market position.

2) It has been shown that selling effort is required to maintain demand at high levels. Without such effort, several forces are at work to cause decline. The first is the constant shifting in the personnel of those groups which buy. Both the shifting of age groups and the shifting of those with the capacity or authority to buy bring about many changes in the course of a year. One authority has termed the consumer market a "procession" rather than a constant group. Again, consumer demand for particular products tends to deteriorate if desire is not maintained. While education, environment, and social pressure exercise much influence on the maintenance of standards, they do not exert sufficiently powerful influence to raise standards or to reach all the prospective or actual buyers. The cessation of selling effort leads to decline in purchase action, not merely the transfer to other sellers. Necessary buying action in connection with new

---

[9] For instance, see P. A. Samuelson, *Economics* (2nd ed.; New York: McGraw-Hill Book Co., 1951), p. 214; or, Harriss, *op. cit.*, p. 529.

[10] Neil H. Borden, *Advertising: Text and Cases* (Homewood, Ill.: Richard D. Irwin, Inc., 1953), pp. 20–21.

products does not take place automatically, any more than does action toward progress take place automatically in any other field. Without selling leadership, levels of living tend to deteriorate just as governments deteriorate without pervasive and continuous leadership effort. History seems to tell us that while the forces of habit and environment are strong, they are not enough by themselves to bring progress.

3) Thus, both selling to increase total demand and selling developed to increase the share of a particular seller create the intensity of desire needed to motivate production and productivity and to give an impetus to those activities which increase productivity and leisure.

4) Finally, the freedom to compete is freedom to try to sell as well as freedom to enter into business enterprise and freedom to operate in such a way as to produce goods or services. It is not sufficient merely to produce and price a product. What the producer has to offer must be brought to the attention of those who are prospective buyers because only in exceptional cases will prospective buyers take the initiative. When several competitors each try to sell, each realizing that only through selling can his effort to produce wanted products be paid for in values that enable his enterprise to continue, the rivalry may appear to involve a waste of expense; but it is the cost of competition as compared to the costs of alternative economic organizations.

Leadership in other fields does not give us much of a clue as to the lines along which alleged wastes can be reduced. Political leadership, competition for office, in democratic governments involve rivalry for position and power. There is much talk of waste in government and much talk of wastes in political effort, which often we shrug off as a part of the price of democratic freedom. Alternatives in totalitarian governments conceivably might be less costly in terms of economic goods, although experience has not so indicated; but they are more costly if broad human values are considered. That selling involves expenditures that might be termed wastes may be admitted; but even Veblen suggests in his *Theory of Business Enterprise*,[11] in writing

---

[11] T. Veblen, *Theory of Business Enterprise* (New York: G. Scribner's Sons, 1904).

of competitive wastes, that their inducement to production out-weighs their cost. Fifty years later, a world-renowned economist points to the spirit of competition as one of the causes of the economic superiority of the United States and one of the secrets of American prosperity.[12]

Thus, to repeat: Some of the costs of competitive selling are part of the price we pay and must inevitably pay in order to have high standards of living and freedom of choice.

The alternative advanced by some European businessmen, as well as by some social scientists and lay critics, that those who sell or advertise could contribute more productive work by dis-continuing selling and advertising overlooks the fact that unless there is a balance between production and distribution, no pro-duction can long continue. There is perhaps some "automatic" demand for many products. That is, a demand by those who know they want the product and take the initiative to order it in advance and to buy it when finished. But such demand is generally so limited as to make economic production impossible. For that argument assumes that consumers generally and as indi-viduals want high standards of living and would make the effort to obtain them, either as individuals or collectively as organized consumers. Conversely, the argument may assume that sellers or any one whom they might consult would know precisely what the user wants, when he wants it, and in what quantities. Obviously these assumptions are invalid.

In competitive selling as it operates, there are certain im-portant correctives. Products too far removed from actual con-sumer needs or desires generally fail to sell profitably in compe-tition with other products. Products that do meet these needs can, on the contrary, be sold more profitably than those that do not meet needs well. Furthermore, it is to the interest of the manufacturer to use the minimum amount of selling effort to reach particular goals required by technical and other considera-tions. If those goals are dictated by delusions of grandeur, the high costs of minimum selling effort tend to reduce the profits and to cut the seller down to size. Sometimes increased amounts of selling effort lead to lower costs of production, which, on

---

[12] Cf. William E. Rappard, *The Secret of American Prosperity* (New York: Greenberg, 1955), p. 104.

balance, are more favorable to the consumer, at least eventually in competitive selling. Furthermore, in competitive selling, free price competition tends eventually to remove that seller from the market who attempts to cover costs that are excessive in relation to those competitors whose costs are justifiably low. Competitive rivalry generally represents effort to serve an increasingly intelligent public as a means of obtaining profit.

Chapter IX

ECONOMIC AND SOCIAL EVALUATION OF SELLING: II. WEAKNESSES AND ABUSES

SELLING AS A VOCATION is open to any man, woman, and child in our country. No licenses are ordinarily required, and the work may be attempted by persons of widely divergent backgrounds, ages, education, and standards. Even the youngster who peddles a few Christmas cards to his neighbors in order to buy himself a new pair of skates or a space helmet becomes a seller. At the other extreme is the highly trained professional man or the president or vice-president of a large corporation who seeks to sell a large and complex installation. Only in limited fields does the law sometimes impose special requirements upon those who enter selling, for instance in the pharmaceutical, financial investment, and insurance fields. Entrance of an individual into selling is primarily restricted only by his desires, and the willingness of others to hire him for the purpose if he does not want to act on his own.

The consequence of the freedom of access to selling careers is that all kinds of people try selling and many types find jobs. Some prove competent; others incompetent. Some are skillful and informed; others are ill-informed or even ignorant. To some, honesty is not the best policy. Some prefer to follow ethical lines of conduct and eschew practices of doubtful nature. Others skirt the fringes of the illegal and the unethical, in a cynical attitude of "getting away with" what they can. Precisely how much selling is the dishonest, fraudulent, unethical type, no one is in a position to say. That divergences from acceptable conduct are news is perhaps an acknowledgment of the fact that most of the billions of business transactions in selling and buying are carried on in a spirit of honesty and good faith as between buyer and seller.

Selling is basically communication intended to bring about specific types of human action. The possibilities of failure to communicate are always present. Incompetent though well-meaning selling leaders are all too common, and their performance is inefficient and unsatisfactory. Some of this is ascribable to management and direction. The unethical or "just within the law" behavior of salesmen and the undesirable character of advertising may reflect the character of management. In appraising some of the weaknesses and abuses of selling and advertising, we are constrained to recognize that here, as in other aspects of living, freedom to sell is necessarily bought at a price of some misuse of liberty, as previous analyses have shown, and as subsequent discussions in this chapter bring out.

FURTHER CRITICISMS OF SELLING

*Selling Influences People to Buy Too Much; Causes
Self-Indulgence; Leads to Dissatisfaction, Discontent,
and Frustration*

The argument that selling causes people to buy too much is to be distinguished from the argument that selling causes people to buy the wrong things. It is not always clear whether critics are asserting that people buy too many products in relation to their purchasing power or whether they are asserting that buying too many products leads to self-indulgence, which is undesirable from some points of view. Both assertions have been made expressly or by implication.

Selling influences are undoubtedly powerful and on the whole effective. Selling sometimes induces people to buy goods that, in the opinion of others or, on sober second thoughts, in their own opinion, they should not have bought. Selling is accused of encouraging extravagance, of causing people to buy more than they can afford. Brought out to support such criticisms are the examples of families obligated to pay each month for purchases on the installment plan more than the total income of the family. Instances of alleged bad personal financial management can be found in many communities, the responsibility resting, possibly in part, upon sellers and their selling and credit practices, and in part upon the individuals. In fact, throughout history, one can read of debt slavery and overspending. Selling did not originate it nor would the discontinuance of selling eliminate it.

Criticisms usually boil down to assertions that a family with limited income has been extravagant in buying an automobile, a television set, or a new suite of furniture for the daughter's bedroom—or something else the critic does not agree with.

The recent rapid rise in the volume of installment debt has in some quarters been viewed with alarm, although careful students of our financial structure do not evince any apprehension. The installment plan does make it easier for the consumer to buy many types of satisfactions that otherwise would be unobtainable. The recently announced fact that more than 50 per cent of American families own their own homes, the all-time high in automobile ownership, and the widespread ownership of electrical appliances is a tribute to the effectiveness of the enormous amount of selling effort expended to persuade people to buy these commodities.

What is subject to censure is the limited—although too large—amount of sharp practice and deceit that characterizes the business practices of certain installment sellers. While generally within the law, they tend to prey upon ignorance by charging excessive prices for goods and excessive rates for credit. Gradually, here, too, the competition of commercial banks and of installment terms offered by reputable sellers has tended to curb abuses.

The bases for asserting that people buy too much often appear to be the personal standards of the critics themselves; adverse criticism stems from some departure from those personal standards. Implied in the criticism is often the direct and complete allocation of responsibility to the seller alone and a total denial of responsibility to the buyer. An appraisal of this argument is not easy because quantitative facts are not available, either to those who advance the criticism or those who seek to evaluate it. If credit losses were the criterion, there would be little to censure. On the whole credit losses are relatively small. Nevertheless, abuses of pressure and intimidation occur in collection procedure, although ordinarily the penalty for nonpayment is limited financial loss. That the desire for goods and services is a powerful force toward greater production and that in general, selling persuasion brings about the transformation of wishes for better living into actual levels of living, needs always to be kept in mind when viewing fallible human judgments and varied motivations in perspective.

The valuations placed by consumers upon goods and services vary widely. A family that spends freely on food and clothing may regard as extravagant another family in the same income class that spends money for an automobile; but that is not tantamount to valid adverse criticism of those who sold the automobile nor is it proof that the family that purchased it had been unwise. Who is to judge whether the family that is induced to buy high-fidelity phonograph and classical records has been adversely influenced if it has to skimp on other expenditures?

On the other hand, if the purchase causes failure to provide proper nourishment for one's self or one's family or adequate clothing and shelter conforming to minimum standards of health and decency, it is to be deplored, whether the causes are the ignorance of the consumer or seller, or the seller's sharp practices. In our economy it is highly unlikely that the kinds of purchases that deprive people of subsistence essentials will bulk very large in total. The proportion of our income receivers who might be so affected has steadily declined. Nevertheless, consumer education should help further to reduce extremely unwise consumer purchasing.

The common tendency to set up our own personal standards and apply them in our judgment of others is pernicious and misleading. When a charwoman purchases a television receiver, is it sensible or objective to claim that the purchase is unwarranted extravagance and that she has been harmed by selling? Under some conditions, probably it is bad judgment on her part to be so influenced; possibly culpable selling influence is involved. It was commonly observed that when television was first introduced, aerials appeared over the poorer sections of the city before they appeared over the residences of the well-to-do. The conclusion that this represents either bad judgment or wasteful expenditure of income is obviously superficial. On the whole, such purchase represented an expansion of satisfactions beyond those previously enjoyed.

Such criticisms are basically criticisms of the wisdom of the buying actions of consumers. It is alleged first that consumers are sold undesirable things they usually cannot afford because of the size of income, thereby implying some alleged "suitable" expenditure pattern for such persons. Most incomes permit a good deal more than the necessary minimum for food, clothing, and shelter, and the basic requirements for diet and health. It is to these that consumer freedom of choice applies with particular force and becomes of particular importance. It is here that persuasion begins to be more necessary and more effective. In a society in which there is fairly free movement from one level to another, the choices that consumers in various income classes make are to a much greater extent dependent upon ideas as to what will give the consumer satisfaction than upon any fixed consumption pattern. It should be considered a matter of independent choice as to whether with increased income the family chooses to spend what it has in terms of optional income in additional family pleasure, or in the purchase of other desirable consumer goods, or to save in one of several ways or to invest in real estate.

The self-indulgence argument is one that asserts that either society would be better off with less economic goods, or that some substantial portions of the population would be better off without so much in the way of goods and services. An alternative form of the argument is that less economic goods and services would contribute to higher intellectual, moral, or other aspects of living and that some individuals at least might benefit by having less material goods.

To assert that society would be better off is equivalent to asserting that all our people have more than they need or want of this world's goods. We know that for most people this is simply not true. There are still individuals and families who are compelled to endure substandard levels of living. But there are many more who, while enjoying minimum or better standards, are desirous of better material living standards, better housing, better clothing and food, and more enjoyment of noneconomic satisfactions. There are undoubtedly individuals whose share of goods and services is more than is needed by a wide margin and whose consumption habits are far from being in the public interest. Selfishness, vulgar display, degrading consumption, are no novelty in world history. Social groups in Rome, Greece, and Egypt, and in more modern times in India, United States, and South America, have achieved notoriety through self-indulgence and dissipation. The leveling influences of recent decades and the demands of people to improve their lot are reducing the opportunity for the rich to afford or display such self-indulgence.

The world's basic efforts at betterment of conditions are more largely aimed at higher standards of living than at any other single goal. The effort of our foreign aid program under Point Four, the European Cooperation Administration and other programs, are intended to establish the basis for higher standards of living for the peoples concerned. The objective of high standards has been agreed to be a worthy one, and the only opponents are those who have rather ill-defined philosophic objections to high standards in their effects upon other sectors of our living. Eventually, therefore, the argument becomes a philosophical one. Those who claim self-indulgence as the result of selling are by inference asking for more emphasis upon other aspects of living and less upon material things. Implicit is the assumption that one cannot have both and that very high material levels of living and high achievement in other fields are incompatible.

As argued in an earlier chapter, there is little to prove that higher intellectual, moral, and political standards thrive in poverty or that high levels of living are inconsistent with them. The phenomenon of mass achievement and enjoyment of high standards of living is so new that its possibilities are largely unexplored. We know contrariwise that poverty has fostered communistic sympathy with its negation of democratic liberties and the rights of individuals to work out their own destinies. That many individuals have been self-indulgent and have not developed strength of character, which struggle and effort tend to develop, can readily be granted. And it can as readily be conceded that we must achieve balanced living in a new climate, not one of adversity, but under conditions that one writer has called the "golden age." Nevertheless, one still does not know whether millions of people, all the people of a large population, enjoying a high standard of material welfare, will fail to develop finally a better-balanced high level of living than the world has ever previously achieved. Personally, I have faith that we shall learn gradually to steer clear of harmful self-indulgence and be able eventually to reach a high new balance of the desirable elements of a good life.

Lastly, let us examine the argument that sellers intensify desires that cannot be satisfied and therefore lead to discontent and frustration. The seller may, of course, arouse desires to the point that a balance between these desires and the ability to satisfy them cannot immediately or eventually be established for the individual. But the proportion of satisfactions actually secured in relation to need and comfort is increased by the very processes that strong desire and buying action set in motion. Von Mises writes in abstract terms:[1]

We call contentment or satisfaction that state of a human being which does not and cannot result in any action. Acting man is eager to substitute a more satisfactory state of affairs for a less satisfactory. His mind imagines conditions which suit him better, and his action aims at bringing about this desired state. The incen-

---

[1] Ludwig von Mises, *Human Action* (New Haven: Yale University Press, 1949), p. 13.

tive that impels a man to act is always some uneasiness.* A man perfectly content with the state of his affairs would have no incentive to change things. He would have neither wishes nor desires; he would be perfectly happy. He would not act; he would simply live free from care.

But it must be recognized that desires at times may expand rapidly, and more rapidly than the ability to satisfy those expanded desires. Even here, standards of living must be judged by absolute standards as well as relative standards, and not merely by the relation of the comforts and luxuries that persons enjoy in relation to their desires. Economists and other social scientists have often asserted that the wants of human beings are limitless. It is the contention of this volume that the wants which are important from the standpoint of achieving high standards of living are those that lead to production and productivity. These are limited but expansible. Much of the "wanting" about which economists write is the vague general sort that leads to no action and to no production to satisfy those wants.

The disparity between desire and actual attainment of satisfaction may, of course, lead to dissatisfaction and discontent. Is that bad? It can be argued that a healthy dissatisfaction is one that leads to efforts to improve standards of living, just as it leads to improving standards of government or of ethical or religious conduct. Discontent of certain types is to be desired and fostered rather than deprecated. Such desires, often strengthened by parents' desires to have high standards of living for their children, is a motivating force in our highly productive society. Men work consistently and regularly to provide the things they want for themselves and family. Workers will carry their utilization of our productive technology much beyond minimum requirements for food, clothing, and shelter because those desires exist, and have been expanding beyond vague wishful thinking. Most desires for goods and services in a high-level economy are the results of environment and education, plus persuasive and selling effort on the part of selling leaders. Much evidence can

---

* Cf. Locke, *An Essay Concerning Human Understanding*, ed., Fraser (Oxford, 1894), I, 331–333; Leibniz, *Nouveaux essais sur l'entendement humain*, ed., Flammarion, p. 119.

be cited that the rapid improvement of standards of living has occurred where selling effort has been plentiful and aggressive, and that rapid improvement has not taken place where such aggressive selling has been absent. Studies in European and other countries lead one to believe that the lack of intensified desire and contentment with low, stratified standards of living are in large measure responsible for slow improvement in level of living for the masses of the people. Vague desires appear to incline many people toward other forms of protest, not toward the effective measure of increasing production and productivity.

Selling Influences People to Buy the Wrong Things

Critics say that selling influences people to buy wrong things because the goods themselves fail to give the expected satisfactions. No alert observer could fail to observe that not all purchases buyers make are in the immediate interest of the consumer himself. While there are limited checks to prevent widespread occurrence, these are not completely effective.

The consumer may be induced to buy goods or services that for various reasons fail to give the satisfaction expected. The products may fail to give satisfaction because of faulty manufacture, because the design has not been sufficiently tested, or because unforeseen rough handling or unexpected use may have caused failures of design that did not emerge in the ordinary effort to produce and test the product. It is an accepted fact that faulty products may be brought on the market, even though the vast resources of testing laboratories have been utilized and the care of executives has been extended to a point that would seem to be much beyond any reasonable requirement. Sometimes the anxiety of the entrepreneur to put products on the market in order to recover the cost of development income quickly, because his capital is exhausted, tempts executives to place products on the market before they are completely "foolproof." At other times, the fear that competitors will secure a prior hold on the market may cause premature introduction; or wishful thinking in the testing procedure may lead a product to be placed on the market that is at least partially unsatisfactory, although there has been no intention to defraud or harm buyers.

Even in such cases, much effort may have been expended without entire success to make the product satisfactory for consumer use.

The experience of some companies shows that the rectification of such mistakes has cost established companies dearly; and it has harmed or severely damaged small- and medium-sized companies. Even very large companies have been compelled at great cost to recall faulty products or to repair them without charge. The large motorcar companies, the large electric companies, can all admit that such losses have been incurred. One small company making an automobile attachment lost an amount equal to its entire capital within a year of its starting because its executives felt compelled by their ideas of equity and by the desire to have a sound basis for future business to replace every faulty installation, although there had been no misrepresentation.

The consumer may feel that he suffers injury in the purchase of services and products because they fail to come up to his reasonable or even extravagant expectations. Some of these expectations have been based on advertising and selling effort. Here the seller may have been at fault, and the buyer has taken puffing and extravagant statements at face value. In other cases it is the wishful thinking of the consumer and the faultiness of communication to which the dissatisfaction must be charged. The implication that certain cosmetics will make women beautiful is probably nowhere accepted by an intelligent reader, but it may be accepted emotionally by some of the women who buy such products. Some are disillusioned and feel they have suffered injury because of the selling effort. Such disillusionment is more frequent in certain limited fields. The extravagant claims in cosmetics, toothpaste, and a few other fields, have led to much adverse comment and have injured the creditability and effectiveness of much advertising and selling effort. But these industries represent but a small percentage of the total.

Some disappointment at the divergence between realization and expectation is a frequent result of any kind of leadership. These disappointments are not always the result of bad leadership, but they do point to the probability that such disappointments are inevitable in human affairs. Political leaders make compromises or express hopes that cause citizens to believe that prompt improvement will be forthcoming. The difficulties of bringing about changes in habits are known both to leaders and to the informed; but wishful-thinking citizens sometimes forget. They expect the unlikely and even the impossible.

Another criticism emphasizes the failure of selling to serve as an informative guide.[2] It is unrealistic to expect that the seller will, or even that he could be, a completely impartial or objective adviser. In the first place, the seller has endeavored to design, choose, or make those products which he expects his market, that is his list of customers or prospective buyers, to buy in competition with other products. In order to sell them at an acceptable price, he must do the best he can to balance desired characteristics with cost. These desired characteristics are not theoretical ideas of durability, style, or beauty; they are actual qualities that appear to be wanted in the next few months if effort is made to sell them. He must make, then sell what he produces. He cannot be impartial, for his business depends on selling what he can produce, not something else. But his own integrity and long-run interest influences him to seek out those customers who will be benefited and not misled if they buy his product. The point is illustrated by an episode from the investment-banking field when a young man graduating from a school of business in the thirties was offered a position to sell bonds. He was discussing the opening with an adviser when he exclaimed: "I don't like the idea of persuading widows and orphans to buy risky securities they really shouldn't buy!" His adviser assured him that he did not hold with such practices either. But he added, "Perhaps you don't know that the best security salesman works to build up a varied list of customers so that when a certain type of common stock is to be sold, he knows investors who want that type of risk and are well able to assume it. When gilt-edge bonds are to be distributed, he has lists of trustees, banks, widows, and others who want security of investment even at the usual lower income." It is the practice

---

[2] Warren C. Waite and Ralph Cassady, *The Consumer and the Economic Order* (2nd ed.; New York: McGraw-Hill Book Co., 1949), p. 112.

of good selling to select for solicitation customers and prospective buyers who can benefit from purchase of particular products.

Character, added to intelligent self-interest, goes far in making sellers better guides to buyers. In the industrial field, the advice given by technical sales specialists will often be relied upon implicitly by buyers, knowing from experience that these sales representatives are fully dependable. Many a salesman who sells to retail stores has, by constantly dependable selling leadership, won the privilege of writing the customers' orders for as much goods as the salesman thinks are needed. I have questioned various groups of salesmen and found that more than half the salesmen of many concerns have attained to such privileges. Testimony from salesmen of wholesale concerns is very similar. Here, clearly, intelligent self-interest, coupled with self-respect, makes the sellers good buying advisers. Nevertheless, at the retail-consumer level many a seller is not reliable. In types of retail selling where repeat sales are not expected, long-run self-interest is less effective as a corrective and more dependence must be placed on character of the seller. In any occupation where entrance is free to all comers, there is bound to be as much poor leadership at each level of responsibility as will reflect the ethical standards of the people who elect by their actions to retain and promote the leaders. The sifting process that goes on in the progress of aspiring leaders from level to level does not completely screen out bad leaders in selling. But it should be remarked that neither does the screening process do this in any other hiring activity.

The seller is and must be biased in favor of his own production. He will recognize needs for which his products are clearly not suitable, and ones which cannot be satisfied with his product. He does not expect to sell every customer or buyer; but he hopes to sell a sufficient proportion of them to make a profit. He knows that his knowledge of what the customer or prospective buyer wants is limited. But he also knows that the buyer himself is often not clear as to what he wants. Therefore, persuasion to take what the producer has designed in advance is likely to be necessary to the seller if buying action is to result.

In most cases, this gives satisfaction to the buyer. But mistakes will be made, and bad guesses will cause buyers to make bad purchases.

Selling persuasion tends more often to lead to more buying of wrong things if the seller is ignorant or unethical, or both, and if the buyer is ignorant of his own interest and unable to judge the product. The majority of sellers know their products, although too often the salespersons in retail stores do not know enough to be good advisers. The range of knowledge of product extends from the sales specialist's comprehensive knowledge of a complex technical product to the indifference and ignorance of some temporary retail salesclerks in a large store during the Christmas rush. The knowledge required to be a good buying adviser includes knowledge of individual buyer's needs; sellers frequently know more than the buyer himself as to what an individual buyer needs, particularly in narrow, specialized fields in which the buyer has little experience.

Too often, therefore, critics judge selling on the basis of poor advice and persuasion by ignorant or unethical sellers who are dealing with highly uninformed consumers. They forget the large and growing informed group of consumers. They neglect to consider expert industrial and commercial buyers whose volume of purchases is as great as that of the ultimate consumer group. They forget that even among the uninformed, the influence of good sellers and of education, and the tendency to reject unsatisfactory products and to avoid sellers who have misled, are partial correctives. Furthermore, any one who has observed the complaint and return desks in any large retail store realizes that consumers claim and get adjustments, many beyond those required by principles of fairness and justice. The customer is not always right. But store failures and mistakes that result in returns and adjustments are very costly to the seller.

Nevertheless, there is too much inefficient and too much misleading selling at the retail level, even though the great bulk of retail trade is done on an ethical basis with full regard for public interest. It is the abuses that make news, not the everyday transactions marked by decency, restraint, and mutual regard of buyer and seller.

Two different aspects of the accusation that selling causes people to buy wrong things relate to the effect of selling in creating uniformity of demand as compared to individuality. Coupled with this is the accusation that the effect of selling and advertising is toward the "cheap and nasty," not toward objects that in the words of one critic "ought to be such as can serve as a model or example for all objects of its kind." It is declared that the uniformity of demand is, and can be, attained only at a low level. Good taste is therefore discouraged. To this argument it is pertinent to reply that only by attaining some uniformity of demand, which will enable large-scale production and advances of technology to be used, can higher standards be achieved by higher production and productivity for the masses of the people. The process is dealt with at length in previous chapters.

One of the prime objectives of selling is to bring about sufficient uniformity of demand so that people may have more goods at lower prices. But that that uniformity of design implies necessarily bad products or low levels of taste is fallacious. Selling is a type of persuasion that enables taste to be elevated, not as rapidly as critics might like, but as rapidly as public reaction will permit. In the discussion of the effects of selling over the last half century, one should look at the record. Examination of the level of tastes of products popularly used today, compared to the general level of taste in the products sold even as short a period as twenty-five or fifty years ago, will compel the unbiased student to conclude that there has been marked improvement in taste and in quality of design. Two volumes devoted to the history of Sears, Roebuck & Company show this very clearly. The first by Cohn[3] showed progress up to World War II, but a comparison of goods offered in the catalogues twenty or thirty years ago with those offered in the 1956 catalogue is very revealing indeed as to changes in taste. The second, a scholarly study, by Professor John E. Jeuck,[4]

[3] D. L. Cohn, *Sears, Roebuck & Company* (New York: Simon & Schuster, 1940).

[4] Boris Emmet and J. E. Jeuck, *Catalogues and Counters* (Chicago: University of Chicago Press, 1950).

then of the University of Chicago, confirms this observation. A Boston writer in a feature editorial not long ago emphasized in popular vein some aspects of this problem:[5]

Pearls created by nature's error in the oyster are no less glamorous on the throat of a beautiful woman now than when a Boston banker spent a fortune for 10 to complete a matched string 40 years ago.

Scarcely less becoming, however, are the cultured pearls and the man-made pearl beads which today are in the reach of every woman, whatever her station or circumstances.

And these very pearl beads are symbolic of a widespread and penetrating change in the social and economic life of our country.

Pleaders for special causes—and collections—always are chiding Americans these days for putting out astronomical sums for chewing gums and beads, cigarettes and cosmetics, pills, pop, and other cheap and impermanent "luxuries," and failing to provide like or larger amounts for the good work for which support is being sought.

As censure this seems to fall somewhat flat and as an argument to be unconvincing.

There is no evidence that if pennies did not go for pills and pop they would be applied to research, rescue or the serious drama —any more than were the dollars once spent for real pearls. For we may submit with whatever grace to inescapable taxation, but we still hold it our free man's privilege to throw our money around any way we like, even though at year's end there may be little left to show for it.

Indeed "cheap and impermanent" constitutes an indictment that might be laid against much of the stuff that Americans buy in a year. Yet it is not necessarily a damning indictment, however it may sound when it comes sneeringly from the lips of the connoisseur, self-styled or otherwise. For cheap need not be unuseful, nor impermanent, unlovely.

Grant that one generation's junk is the collector's item in those to come. Leave all the implications of Keynes' theory of high national income and free spending to the economists and bankers to view with favor or alarm. It still is possible for the thinking man on the street to say that he likes it that way.

For one thing he may not care for old things, whatever their quality. For another, he is honest enough to admit that never in the world could he hope to pay the price of goods produced to last a lifetime; and he is independent enough to demand an adequate

---

[5] Frances Burns, Editorial, *Boston Globe*, August 30, 1953. By permission.

and usable substitute. Finally, he may owe his very bread and butter—and jam—to the manufacture of one or another of the mass-produced, cheap and impermanent and easily replaced objects.

Great Grandmamma's wedding gown was made by Worth. The countless tiny stitches of its stiff unweighted satin were put in by the cold fingers of shabby, black-clad Parisian midinettes. Yellowed and mellowed, it is as good now, and as beautiful, as on the day it first was worn. Yet laid away in layers of paper in a great box it has constituted a housekeeping problem for every generation since.

And wedding in a day when Worth is only a name belonging to social antiquity, when few people any longer make tiny stitches, and the feminine figure has changed shape, like as not great-grand-daughter doesn't want to bother with the funny old dress. She'd rather have a creation that, at a fraction of the value of grandma's, will enhance her loveliness in a way that we think the boned and stayed affairs of Victoria's day never did.

She'll wear her own wedding gown, altered a little, to special parties for a year or two. But there is no room in her bright, compact new house for storing something that would not be taken out until her still unborn daughter were planning her wedding, ready to go to the mat over the merits of the latest against the taste of another generation.

The costly and handmade still are to be had, but for one of them now a thousand mass-produced gowns are lovely enough to satisfy the longing of many a woman to be her most beautiful as she walks down the aisle on her wedding day.

And who can say that beauty is only to be found in the rich and opulent as he watches grandmothers and granddaughters alike on the street, in church, at the tennis matches. Their fresh, crisp, well-cut frocks, good shoes, clean gloves, all are mass produced, and all tend so to wipe out social and financial distinctions that you can't tell the boss' daughter from his lowliest filing clerk.

The need for mass production implies merely the need for uniform products in sizable quantity. It does not imply the con-tinuing need for badly designed products. A whole profession of industrial designers has emerged since World War I because manufacturers found that good design in mass-produced goods made them easier to fashion, and easier to sell because consumers could afford them. But producers and designers found occasion-ally to their sorrow that taste in mass-produced goods can be raised only as rapidly as the public is willing to accept them.

Expenditure and income to produce in quantity are in terms of annual or at best relatively short-range plans, not in terms of the rise of taste over generations. There have been many partial or total failures of firms that have attempted to move too far ahead of general acceptance by the public. Failures in the latter twenties of furniture manufacturers who were convinced that people were ready to buy modern furniture emphasized the fact that the success of the Paris Exposition of Decorative Arts of 1925 and the acceptance of modern design by a few high-income groups were not sufficient to support the requirements of mass production. Twenty years later, other furniture manufacturers have found desirable, large markets for modern furniture.

Look where you will. In taste and design, the products now sold in the mass market are generally much superior to those available a generation ago. Though it has been done, it is not consistent to compare the furniture people generally buy today with the masterpieces of master craftsmen of an earlier day, who produced a few products for a few members of a limited privileged class. The comparison should also include the products available and used by the general public of a contemporary period. The individuality of an earlier day was based upon hard labor at costs that were low and yielded only low living levels. Some of the individuality of past times was a type of luxury available only to a wealthy few, who sometimes subsidized the artists. Wealthy patrons assisted struggling artists and designers. Literature likewise was subsidized. But very little is said about the standard of design and the desirability of the arts and products used by the masses of the people. Museum pieces, which cause the sophisticates to exclaim with delight, were the possession of the few. One needs to visit a different kind of museum, one that reflects the living standards of the common people of centuries ago, to realize how low were the standards of living as well as of taste and of design at that time. As to the evaluation of human labor, one must expect that some of the traditional types of works of art, which required enormous expenditures of human labor, will gradually become scarcer and scarcer. It is unlikely that more than relatively few will be produced each year of those types that require unconscionable amounts of hard labor. A Persian hand-woven rug requires enormous amount of hand labor; for example, a certain Oriental rug about 4 feet by 6 feet contains 480 hand-tied knots to the square inch. At a conservative estimate, more than six months of long working days would be required to make that rug; yet the worker probably received less than the equivalent of $50 for half a year's work. This was the human price of individuality and hand work produced for a limited wealthy or aristocratic group in an undeveloped nomadic society.

Today, firms and their designers can point out an increasing proportion of machine-made goods that conform to the canons of good taste. Men and groups of men have been commissioned to develop products the intrinsic and artistic merits of which are in tune with the growing cultural appreciation of beauty in line, form, and color. And tastes have been so improved that these products can be sold at prices ordinary people, wage earners, can pay. The human costs of good design have been enormously reduced.

Whether our democratic society will produce geniuses comparable to the outstanding creative artists of past generations or not remains to be learned.[6] However, in terms of scientific discovery and in terms of the potential for human welfare, no previous generation has a comparable record. It is likely that improvement in material welfare in which selling plays so large a part will continue to be accomplished by improvement in taste by people generally, no matter how the "taste makers"[7] may fulminate against some current products.

Selling Influences People to Buy the Right Thing for the Wrong Reasons

Those who advance this criticism assert that even though the products themselves may be beneficial and give satisfaction, selling induces people to buy them for the wrong reasons. The argument may be directed at either the use of emotional appeals to get buying actions or at certain types of appeals believed to be bad. A number of those critics assert that advertising and

---

[6] Cf. Chapter VIII, p. 172.

[7] Russell Lynes, *The Tastemakers* (New York: Harper & Bros., 1954).

selling are useful when they convey information but harmful when they seek to persuade by emotional appeals. The implication appears to be that appeals to the emotions are necessarily bad, while action based upon information is to be considered reasonable action and is good. In the light of the previous arguments, the conclusion is obvious that this criticism is superficial and unsound because it ignores the fundamentals of human behavior. Human behavior is only in part, perhaps in smaller part, ruled by reason. Emotions constitute a powerful, sometimes all-powerful, governor of behavior. No leader in any walk of life can ignore emotional behavior and emotional influences if he seeks to influence any sizable number of people to take action. In our economy, consumers must buy goods and services. They must make choices in buying as they must make choices in other activities. These choices are made partly from habit, partly on the basis of reasoned or emotional reactions to needs, wants, and situations.

The seller's desire to dispose of his goods may be much stronger than the buyer's desire to acquire a particular seller's goods, because the seller's continuance in his job depends on selling while the buyer's future may not at all depend on a particular seller. It may not depend on buying from any seller. He is free to choose between sellers and products. Furthermore, selling exists in part because buyer's desires have been shown to require intensification.

Information about products is frequently, if not usually, insufficient to induce buying action, certainly insufficient to bring about buying action in the amounts and types required for high levels of living. The facts about products are themselves not so important as what those facts mean in terms of expectations and buyer satisfactions. As soon as we bring in the concept of satisfactions to buyers and try to inform buyers as to the satisfactions they may expect from the product, we generally find ourselves, of necessity, dealing with emotional satisfactions, particularly when we are selling goods that are not intended merely to satisfy simple, fundamental requirements of food, clothing, and shelter. It should not require demonstration that the buyer makes his purchase when he feels that the satisfactions, whether emotional or reasoned, that he receives will outweigh the value of the money he has to give up in exchange. The facts may not at all convey what he really wants to know. He has to decide whether he will get satisfaction that he wants if he buys the product. A home economist has figured out that the food absolutely necessary to sustain life for one year for one person could be purchased for substantially less than $100; but neither she nor anyone else wants to forego the satisfactions that come from superior foods. It is taken for granted that our minimum standards for housing go much beyond the minimum requirement of shelter. So even for the fundamental satisfactions we cannot get away from nonrational influences.

Therefore, the use of emotional appeals becomes necessary if communication to buyers in terms of their desires is to be established and wants intensified to the point of starting the wants-purchase-production-productivity chain reaction. Nevertheless, emotional appeals may be used both in the public interest and against it. Reason may be used both in the interest of consumers and contrary to this interest. The course of common sense is not to condemn emotional appeals as such but to condemn their misuse and to avoid the assumption that any use is misuse.

Objection has been raised to the use of certain types of emotional appeals as harmful, base, or unworthy. Some of these objections are at least partially valid, although some merely represent the personal annoyance of the critic. For criticisms of advertising and selling have stemmed not only from objective consideration but also from personal prejudices. Many a critic considers himself "above" being influenced by emotional appeals. Furthermore, he believes that it is not right that he should be subjected to such emotional appeals. He prides himself that he can make his own buying decisions on the basis of fact. Therefore he says: "Give me the facts and I will make my own decision." He may or may not recognize that the furnishing of facts in understandable form is a part of such selling. He may or may not recognize that under some conditions, even this may mislead, but it will probably not persuade even if the product is precisely suited to the buyer's real needs.

If we exclude harmful goods and goods that do not reasonably give satisfactions that could be expected, we can confine our discussion to that selling which causes people to buy the "right" goods for the wrong reasons because of emotional appeals. Here the appeals usually singled out for denunciation are self-indulgence, social emulation, appeals for social exclusiveness, fear of social disapproval, fear of accident, or fear of sickness. The self-indulgence argument has been dealt with above.

In much selling and in more advertising, some ultimate consumer products are sold on the basis of appeal to the desires for social distinction, exclusiveness, or snobbishness. These appear to be sometimes powerful appeals. Some of the firms that use such appeals know that they have at best a limited market because of the prices or nature of what they offer. Other sellers whose goods have wide potential markets may use such appeals to differentiate their products from others, even though people know that any one with limited funds may buy them. Some persons buy illusions, and possibly they may secure desired satisfactions from such illusions. What such selling does to buyers, however, is the basic question. Does it harm them? Would such consumers get more satisfaction by alternative expenditures? Frankly, we do not know. Unless one wishes to substitute his own valuations, there is at least as good an argument for the negative as for the affirmative.

Is the desire to be exclusive, to be different, or to achieve social distinction necessarily bad? Is the desire to achieve superiority in any area necessarily bad? There is no doubt that the desire to be superior can be in some ways a powerful force for good, just as that effort may lead to "phony" efforts to be superior. Here we get again into the field of human motivation and into one's philosophy of life. Long before selling became important, the incentive of this desire was powerful, although limited to relatively small numbers of people because the mass of the people had little hope or desire to rise above age-old patterns of living. The significance of the wide use of social emulation, superiority, even snob appeal, is not that they are the highest appeals, but (1) that they are directed at all the people, which, of course, assumes a large measure of social fluidity, and (2) that desires may be created that may have important economic and social repercussions, desires that contribute to that type of discontent which causes some people to rise in the social scale and do so on the basis of sound human values. The desire to possess a fine, possibly distinctive, home or automobile leads those who cannot buy now to plan for eventual buying action to realize their desires, just as the desire for a college education for children is created not only by environment but by the desire to enable the children, at least, to rise in the social scale. Consequently, when one considers the use of all aspects of such appeals, one cannot quite so confidently condemn them in wholesale fashion, although one may condemn particular fraudulent or deceitful selling or bad taste as judged by generally accepted standards.

Broadly, the purpose of selling leadership is to influence people to buy. It has been demonstrated that while reason moves some people, more people are moved to act by emotional appeals or by combinations of emotion and reason. The men who purchase for large corporations pride themselves that they buy rationally, but emotional reactions in which loyalty, dependability, and personalities play a part influence buying decisions that vary widely from firm to firm and from buyer to buyer. The influence of emotional appeals and buying action is important, although it varies from complete and dominating influence on some ultimate consumers to those situations in which competitive purchasing officers apparently accord them small place.

Strike out emotional appeals in any leadership and it loses much of its effectiveness, perhaps so much as to make it valueless. Certainly in selling, appeals to emotional desires have the same possibilities for good or evil as in other fields of human activity. Therefore, if the goal of high and rising standards of living is to be attained we cannot neglect those appeals which, by themselves or in combination with reason, bring desired action. We can condemn and even outlaw harmful use of such appeals. As reformers we have a right to criticize and to do what we can to attain our goals. We do not have the right under the guise of objective scientific examination to condemn indiscriminately the appeal to emotions in selling.

Chapter X

ECONOMIC AND SOCIAL EVALUATION OF SELLING: III. ABUSES AND CORRECTIVES

ꗩꗩ

STATISTICAL VERIFICATION of the frequency and importance of selling and advertising abuses is manifestly impossible to find, since no private or governmental agency could afford the staff, time, and costs of continuing and carrying on widespread observation and study. Relatively few cases are brought before judicial or administrative bodies for review when alleged infractions of law are involved. That many more instances occur than are presented is accepted as one of the facts of life. But the conclusion that such practices are characteristic of business in general does not follow any more than it follows that murder or burglary are characteristic of a people's way of life because so many people are brought to court. One cannot generalize for the group upon the basis of a relatively few exceptional cases.

Only a small percentage of the staggering total of billions of buyer-seller transactions[1] can truthfully be said to involve

---

[1] As an example of the large number of transactions, the 535 department stores (representing 342 firms) reporting for 1955 to the Harvard Bureau of Business Research totaled $4,695,709,000 in sales and an average transaction size of $4.90. Thus, this relatively small sector of our economy accounted for over 950,000,000 transactions.

A recent report placed total annual retail sales in the U.S. at $190 bil-

abuses or be contrary to public welfare. But it is these that give rise to adverse criticism, which often is extended in scope much beyond any conclusion warranted by available evidence. Dissatisfied customers have a real and powerful adverse influence on a seller's welfare. If he possesses even limited foresight, he will be impelled by his own self-interest (if by nothing else) to treat buyers decently. But the limits of this self-interest are apparent in certain situations.

CONTINUATION OF CRITICISMS OF SELLING
Selling Causes People to Buy Harmful Goods

Selling and advertising are frequently criticized on the ground of influencing people to purchase harmful goods and of being guilty of misleading and fraudulent practice. The general criticism takes various forms. It is declared that selling and advertising bring about the purchase of goods that are harmful such as drugs, tobacco, injurious cosmetics, and the like. It is alleged that products and services are misrepresented, either directly or by inference to an extent harmful to the public.[2] Others go so far as to say that sellers cheat the public and steal from it, that they use slippery slogans and make false claims and use other devices for defrauding buyers. It is claimed by some that advertising and selling persuade the public to buying ac-

---

lion. If one were to apply the same transaction size, the total would be nearly 40 billion transactions. It can be argued that this figure is so conservative as to be misleading; nevertheless, the total is staggering.

[2] For example, "The consumer's health as well as his pocketbook is at stake. When Upton Sinclair published the novel *The Jungle*, showing what conditions were like in the Chicago stockyards early in this century, many people stopped eating meat. Against the heavy opposition of business interests, Congress passed pure food and drug acts, but an American is still free to poison himself with hair dyes and to go to an early grave as the result of taking patent medicines and being his own doctor. The Federal Trade Commission prosecutes corporations indulging in extreme forms of misrepresentation in advertising, with the result that greater reliance is placed upon innuendo than upon direct statement. (For example, the label on a famous women's compound now says: 'This preparation is recommended for those ailments to which it is adapted.')" See P. A. Samuelson, *Economics* (2nd ed.; New York: McGraw-Hill Book Co., Inc., 1951), p. 214.

The interested reader may be referred to the somewhat partisan views expressed in A. Kallet and F. J. Schlink, *One Hundred Million Guinea Pigs* (New York: Vanguard Press, 1933), and Stuart Chase and F. J. Schlink, *Your Money's Worth* (New York: Macmillan Co., 1927).

tion by craftiness, deceit, guile, and chicanery. In other words, it is alleged that sharp practice and shyster, even criminal, behavior prevail in selling and advertising.

Such statements constitute not merely criticisms. If true of any large proportion, they would constitute a devastating indictment of selling and advertising. Typical of the extreme indictments relating to harmful goods are those that appear in such publications as *Your Money's Worth, One Hundred Million Guinea Pigs,* and many articles in *Consumers Research* and Consumers Union publications.

The use of selling to bring really harmful goods into consumption must be condemned without argument. Nor can one deny that some persons, some firms have actually sold harmful goods, sometimes apparently within the law, but more often outside the law. The "dope" pusher, the distributors of tickets for gambling rackets, deserve all the indictments, all the scorn and contempt that have been heaped upon them. But not so simple is the problem of passing judgment on goods that give satisfactions to consumers but which in more than limited use, or in misuse, may be harmful. And among these are some in which highly injurious habits may be formed. Properly used, some products have beneficent effects. Improperly used they may harm or even kill, as for instance, the barbiturates. Here sellers, medical men, consumers, and the public must all assume responsibility for minimizing misuse if we are to be able to enjoy the good such products have to offer. Also difficult to appraise is the selling of products the consumption of which enjoys a good deal of social approval, even though wide differences of opinion prevail as to the degree of harm that comes from moderate indulgence. For alcoholic liquors and tobacco, as an example, there seems to be nearly unanimous opinion as to the harmful effects of "excessive" use but again, wide divergence of opinion as to what "excessive" means. Since health authorities also disagree, businessmen in these fields find themselves in a quandary—a situation that tends to discourage some men of high principle from entering such industries. This conceivably could have the effect of lowering standards to the minima of legal requirement.

The broad assertion can confidently be made that the overwhelming proportion of business enterprise does not sell harmful goods or indulge in fraudulent practice. Entirely aside from the moral considerations involved, the smooth operation of business enterprise, whether manufacturing, wholesale, or retail, requires that satisfactory goods be sold. Selling harmful goods is the way to business disaster. Even the inadvertent sale of a small lot of defective goods, which may have proved harmful to some persons, gets wide currency and may have devastating effects on sales and earnings, even endangering the existence of a firm. Business in general depends on repeat sales for profit, not initial sales. The sale of positively harmful goods has also led to damage suits, which no less endanger a firm's continuance in business.

The problem of the sale of harmful goods is obviously limited to a narrow range of enterprises and generally to new or small firms. The opportunity undoubtedly exists for careless and unscrupulous firms to profit by selling harmful goods. The record shows that such firms cease operations quickly, although the individuals operating them may try again. The seller is culpable whether he has been careless in testing the product before sale or has callously ignored the possibilities of harm to users. The carelessness in critical fields and the ignoring of harmful effects cannot be too strongly condemned. Although instances are relatively few in number and small in size, we cannot ignore them.

More difficult to judge is the position of the firm that after careful research wants to make a product, takes all reasonable precaution to develop and test it, and then learns upon distribution to the public that the product injures some people. One of the episodes in the distribution of the Salk vaccine is a case in point.

Selling and Advertising Are Untruthful and Insincere

Those who criticize selling and advertising as untruthful make such statements as the following:

"Most selling is untruthful; it is insincere."
"Exaggeration is characteristic of advertising and selling effort."

"It is misleading and undesirable."

"Much advertising copy is hysterically scarehead, misleading."

"Salesmen and advertisements tend to phony arguments and presentations."

"Advertising and sales persons make untruthful assertions."

The extent to which selling is untruthful and insincere is difficult to determine, just as it is difficult to measure truth and sincerity in any broad human activity. That untruth appears we know; that it is more common in some industries and some groups is also generally apparent. But how large a proportion of selling is carried on with substantial untruth and lack of sincerity cannot be measured. It is easy for adverse critics to find instances of abuse. To the objective thinker, they seem not to bulk very large in the perspective of the total number and size of buying and selling transactions.[3] Most selling transactions are carried on in good faith between parties, each of whom benefits by the transactions.

The objective critic who seeks a supportable balanced point of view looks at the instances of abuse and is duly, but not over, impressed by examples cited. He realizes that untruths and insincerity are found in any form of leadership and seeks to assess the good and the bad and arrive at a conclusion. The history of advertising shows clearly that untruth and insincerity in advertising and selling have decreased over the past half century. It will be observed also that in this field of selling toward which

---

[3] Professor David McCord Wright, among those who have perceived the similarity of selling leadership and political leadership, writes: "One of the most widespread criticisms of the modern economic market is that capitalistic advertising is not always truthful. Who, however, could maintain that political speeches are always truthful? Again, products, it is said, are often 'sold' to the public rather than spontaneously demanded by it. Is this not often true of political programs? Next people will say that certain capitalist businessmen have special influence over the market. But do not certain political leaders have special influence over the political market? Finally some people object that they are forced to choose among the alternatives presented to them and cannot simply have anything that they wish. They are, in other words, forced, to a considerable extent, to choose among the goods actually in the stores; and unique or unusual tastes may have to go unsatisfied. But also in political life are not most of us obliged to choose among the candidates presented to us in a given campaign rather than 'running our own man'?" David McCord Wright, *Capitalism* (New York: McGraw-Hill Book Co., Inc., 1951), p. 47.

most criticism is directed, the sellers and other advertising interests have done much to correct and improve standards.

But most important in the objective critic's mind will be the fact that most selling is done not on a one-time "hit-and-run" basis but on the basis of repeat transactions between the same buyers and sellers. Sellers hope by their selling and their products to make customers, to create a willingness to buy again. Thus untruthful selling and advertising practices tend to set corrective influences in motion because people cease buying. The cost of selling new prospects is so much higher than selling to established customers that failure faces the firm that does not make customers in many areas of business and industry. Goods sold in most retail stores are sold to people who are accustomed to repeat purchase but are free not to do so. A large portion of industrial goods is likewise purchased from suppliers with whom buyers have had previous dealings. Untruthfulness, insincerity, usually bring their own reward.

Nevertheless, a characteristic of some advertising and selling, classed by certain critics as untruthful or insincere, requires separate analysis. This is the practice of exaggeration, of making or implying inflated claims and "puffing" one's wares. It may or may not involve insincerity or untruth. In considering this common characteristic, whether the result of genuine enthusiasm on the part of the seller, or known exaggeration, several factors need to be borne in mind.

1) Precisely what the truth about many products is may be difficult or impossible to determine. For one reason or another, the purpose and way in which a product may be employed in a particular purchase may not be known.

2) The desires and needs of people who buy vary so widely that one purchaser might feel virtues of a particular item underestimated and the faults negligible, while another might believe that virtues had been exaggerated and faults glossed over.

3) As has been pointed out elsewhere, many products are compromises between quality and cost factors required by the fact that if many people are to be influenced to buy and to be able to buy, prices must be within reach. These prices may not permit the workmanship and the care required for the highest

quality, even though the essential characteristics required to give consumer satisfaction are retained. The consumer's desire for incompatible characteristics in a product requires compromise from the standpoint of the manufacturer, and consequently the statements made as to quality may appear to be exaggerated.

4) The interest and efforts of sellers to devise products that will sell and repeat frequently lead them to an understandable lack of objectivity. These men are induced by competition and self-interest to try to get products superior to those of competitors or lower in price. Their efforts may in their own thinking be successful; in the opinions of others, these efforts may not be. If such a seller presents his products in terms of his own perhaps wishful thinking, exaggeration is likely to creep into his sales solicitation.

Here again, we encounter difficulties of communication because what is intended by the seller may not be so understood by the prospective buyer. Of course, there is also to be taken into account the fact that in competition, some of this exaggeration is self-defeating. Some advertising and selling practices assert or imply absurdly great benefits. Cosmetics, and some patent medicines of the older days, are guilty of this. Even though the products are not harmful, they tend to mislead some people. Not every car or every refrigerator can be "best." Each may have some desirable features, sometimes at the expense of less desirable requirements. The public has learned this and therefore tends to discount such claims as well as other types of exaggeration. Some exaggeration is expected and not considered undesirable. The enthusiasm of the seller at any level leads to exaggeration, which may stem from sincere belief or cynical effort to influence buyers; but obviously, there is a point beyond which that exaggeration should not be discounted and become culpable. It often becomes a matter of judgment as to where the line is to be drawn.

Businessmen generally are opposed to misrepresentation and do not ordinarily cause goods and services they sell to be represented in any misleading or fraudulent fashion. The principal restraints on businessmen are the compulsions that derive from character and the desire to do the right and decent thing; but also the supplementary influence of enlightened selfishness is especially powerful.[4] Fraud, misrepresentation, and sharp practice do not pay off in the great bulk of business transactions. It does not stand to reason that where there is freedom of choice, the buyer will repeat purchases from defrauding or misrepresenting sellers. With all its faults and with all the limitations of its knowledge, the consumer public is not stupid. No able businessman operates on that assumption. The restraints provided by our laws deter many of the minority of our businessmen whose personal standards would not otherwise compel them to act in accordance with public welfare. The Statute of Frauds and many specific enactments deal with socially obnoxious practices. However, clever and unscrupulous men tend to find loopholes in selling regulations as they find loopholes in other laws.

Selling Is Often Cheap and Vulgar and in Bad Taste

Critics assert that advertising and selling methods themselves are cheap, tawdry, and vulgar. Much in advertising is alleged to be sordid and spurious. Therefore, selling and advertising, so the critics say, tend to lower taste rather than to elevate taste. It is true that on occasion advertising and selling must plead guilty to charges of vulgarity and cheapness.

Sometimes, not often, advertising or personal selling in clearly bad taste has been effective in terms of the narrow interest of the single seller. There is considerable force, however, in the argument that bad taste in advertising affects the general influence and creditability to such an extent as to decrease the general effectiveness of selling effort. Thus the apparent effectiveness of some selling and advertising in bad taste, even though it does not immediately boomerang to the injury of the particular seller, is even in opinion of advertisers themselves, more than offset by the general detrimental effect on selling leadership.[5]

---

[4] C. B. Larrabee, "Thunder on the Right: Special Report on the Growing Criticisms of Advertising," *Printers' Ink*. See weekly issues from March 7 through June 13, 1952.

[5] *Ibid.*

But what constitutes bad taste is a controversial question. Much selling effort must be adjusted to the level of individuals and groups to be influenced. If this taste is low and mediocre, the advertiser or salesman does not dare get too far ahead lest he fail to influence enough people to keep his business alive. In this respect also, leadership in other fields fails if it is too far ahead of the followers. On the other hand, leadership that is behind in its thinking ceases to have influence except by force or tradition.

The criterion set up for judging taste may be the sophisticated, trained taste that has been the possession of only a small minority during our history. If articulate, these sophisticates may exert influence to elevate standards by their writings and creative efforts and their criticisms. Since the objective of selling is to reach all the people, the effort must take the realities of the market situation into account. To that extent, the possibility of improving taste and developing cultural activities is increased; but the validity of the adverse criticism is greatest when the level of selling leadership is lower than required to secure socially desirable buying action.

Some advertising is certainly in bad taste, but an improving taste is exerting its influence.[6] When a television program recently used copy that tended to overemphasize the alleged deprivation of the child whose family did not own a TV set, public protest was so prompt and vehement that the manufacturer quickly changed the script. However, the alleged existing examples of bad taste, even though less than sometimes asserted, are not easy to eliminate so long as public tastes move slowly. Nor is the practice of appealing to lowest tastes to be condoned, no matter how it is done. Here the self-interest and self-respect of sellers must exert a healthy influence to cover the gap left by legal prohibitions and by lack of particular pressures by society. It is significant that advertising associations have for many years endeavored to establish a code that would raise the level of advertising effort. In personal selling effort,

---

[6] A comparison of 1956 advertising of many important newspapers or magazines with the advertising of a half century ago clearly shows much progress in taste.

there is usually no need to find a common denominator for the whole of a heterogenous market. Sales representatives may be specialized so as to be able to approach different types and levels of buyers. The choice of sales personnel and the adaptation by sales representatives to the particular customer tends to reduce the amount of abuse and the annoyance to others.

To some critics, a particularly annoying feature of advertising is that it involves excessive and banal repetition. Such criticism is in large part based upon personal tastes. It assumes that entirely aside from the cultural level and entirely aside from the good or bad taste of the advertisement, its repetition in various forms and various media amounts to banality, lack of taste, and to offense and annoyance to the public. While many personal salesmen use the same or very similar techniques, even to using the same words and phrases in their contacts with customers, the similarity of the statements made by salesmen to different prospective buyers is, of course, much less obtrusive than the phrase or slogan, suggestions, or arguments that appear on billboards, in news magazines, and on radio, and television.

The reasons for such repetition are sound and fundamental. Constant repetition has an impact on the mass of a population which may and often does offset the annoyance to the few. For good or evil, the technique of repetition of simple messages is used in politics, in religious teaching and preaching, and in other aspects of life where some men attempt to influence others. Selling differs only in the degree to which that repetition may be brought to the attention of the individual by mass media of communication.

The use and effectiveness of repetition in selling is based upon several factors:

1) Since many products are demanding the attention of the prospective buyer, a single message may make little impression or may be totally ignored.

2) Repeated messages tend to reinforce each other so that more than proportional impact may be gained from repetition. There may be a limit to effectiveness, but it is indefinite;

perhaps repetitions may be excessive, but too little precise information is available on the point.

3) It must be remembered that new prospective buyers are constantly entering the market. Each year new families are created, and new persons become buyers of products that heretofore held no interest for them.

4) The use of mass media may and does frequently require for effectiveness in covering a market excess duplication from which the seller cannot escape if he would. Duplication of messages beyond the point the seller would choose cannot be avoided, because of the overlapping of readership and listenership. The readers of newspapers and of general and specialized magazines, the listeners to radio and followers of television programs, together with the readers of technical and business magazines, and those who see billboards and posters, are not clearly separated groups. Neither are they identical groups. As has been shown by other studies, there is a great deal of overlapping; but such studies also show that readers of *Atlantic Monthly*, for instance, are not generally readers of *True Stories*. In turn, the latter's readers usually do not read *Factory Management and Maintenance*. The housewife who listens to morning radio programs while doing her housework does not usually see the *Farm Journal*.

Consequently, the executive who is trying to reach a broad market finds no single publication that covers precisely the groups he wants to reach. He is compelled to make the choice between duplication, which may involve annoyance to some with apparent waste, or risk failure to reach select portions of his market. Some executives decide one way; some another. As a rule, the evidence supports repetition; but of course that evidence usually does not prove that repetition has not been carried beyond the peak of effectiveness.

That repetition and aggressiveness in selling will annoy and offend some people, just as aggressiveness and repetition in other fields annoy or offend some people, is to be expected. Here we are not dealing with unethical practice, unless applied to harmful or fraudulent products, but rather with a technique

234 · SELLING IN OUR ECONOMY

of leadership that frequently, but not always, has on balance proved effective; and in the hands of good leaders with selling objectives consistent with public welfare it is to be accepted as necessary and sufficiently beneficial to offset the annoyance to the few. This is, however, not to exclude the possibility of a repetition of certain messages so annoying and offensive as to go beyond the limits both of good taste and reasonable consideration for the minority of the public.

Selling and Materialism

Both in its objectives and in its effects, selling effort as applied to economic goods and services is directed toward the material aspects of living. This is obvious; but what is not so obvious is that selling energizes the whole economic process of production so that more material welfare may be acquired at less cost and so that greater opportunity is given for development of a well-rounded life.

It has been already asserted and should be repeated that material welfare is not the sole aim and end of living; that intellectual, spiritual, and other sectors of human living have full rights to a place in any scheme of a good life. What that place is and what the place of material welfare should be are today matters of controversy as they have been for much of recorded history. Even the earlier Greek philosophers were divided among themselves on this point. The philosophies of the Athenians and the Epicureans were in the direction of high standards of living. The philosophy of the Spartans and the Stoics tended to play down the desirability of high material standards. But none of them enjoyed a high standard of living as we know it today.

However—and this needs repeated emphasis—writers, philosophers, and thinkers of past centuries and ages have very largely been members of the privileged classes or persons subsidized by those classes. They enjoyed relatively high standards of living either as members of the aristocracy or as their hangers-on or subsidized workers. Aristotle came of well-to-do forebears, had powerful sponsors, and was himself wealthy. Plato's concern as well as Aristotle's was with ruling aristocratic privileged groups. The work to support such groups was to be done by slaves, peasant workers, free men, and others; but there was little concern for their standard of living. The concept of comfort and even luxury for the many was absent from their philosophies, just as it was absent from the thinking of the medieval Schoolmen and other church philosophers.

The basic question is not, "Are high and rising standards undesirable as a goal of selling leadership?" That statement of the question seems to find support in some of the strictures of the clergy and some of the statements of social reformers. Rather the question should be phrased as to the best balance among types of leadership. What is the best balance among the various activities and interests of individuals and of a people?

Gross material luxury enjoyed by limited groups has been more persistent under conditions in which earlier forms of leadership have been dominant than in the democratic economy of the United States. In countries in which church leadership is dominant, such limited groups have persisted alongside impoverished masses. Likewise, under certain forms of political leadership, totalitarian and despotic governments have at times given lip service to democracy, but there has been little accomplishment in the direction of high and rising welfare of the people. Only in democratic society has selling leadership been able to show its power for good.

One may ask, therefore, whether at the present conjuncture of affairs our failure to secure a better balance is due, as a recent diatribe puts it, to high-pressure selling and advertising or is it the very effectiveness and influence of selling that in its results shows up so much more favorably than leadership in other areas. One can daily find instances of inept, even vicious, political leadership. It does not require much searching to find ineptness and occasional vicious religious leadership. There has been much controversy over educational leadership. Granted that intangible values are the most difficult to "sell," granted that leadership that calls for high ethical conduct, whether in government or private affairs or in business, requires a very high order of ability, there is still much question as to whether the solution is the reduction of the amount and effectiveness of selling leadership or the improvement of leadership in other areas so as to secure the desirable balance. Furthermore, it is the leadership of the rank and file that is important, the singleness of purpose and the skill of millions of leaders who determine the final outcome, whether in terms of high standards of living, a high spiritual plane, or high civic performance.

What selling in our economic system does is to give the people generally the opportunity to develop. That we have made the fullest use of such opportunity is greatly to be doubted. The accomplishment of higher standards of living with less work has occurred in so short a period that a social, spiritual, and intellectual development to match is hardly to be expected. We have experienced an "explosive" change, a revolution in our living of such a magnitude that there is no historical parallel. It is true that we have not found the balanced life; but it is also true that that failure presents a challenge not only to selling to correct its abuses but even more to other forms of leadership. Evidence that business has made contributions not only to material advancement but also to intellectual and cultural pursuits is cited elsewhere.

Progress in economic welfare in the United States has been the accomplishment of free men; men who were free to venture, to sell what they made; men who were free to succeed or fail in providing what they thought consumers wanted; men who were free to devise new processes, to venture new support for more productive machines because they could persuade other free men to buy them; because they did not have to wait for the slowly moving processes of buyer initiative to bring the buying action and the income required for survival of free enterprise.

Above all, in this development, which goes beyond material things, is there not a deeper significance? Is there not a regard for the individual, a regard for human life? A more widespread "reverence for life," to use Albert Schweitzer's phrase, beyond anything which society had previously developed? That we have the opportunity for more rapid progress toward balanced living must be conceded and that opportunity has come in no small measure from the contribution of selling.

INTERNAL AND EXTERNAL CORRECTIVES

At a great many points in the discussion of selling weaknesses and abuses, it has been emphasized that in our economic system the consumer is protected in various ways. Nevertheless, it would be misleading and false to assert that this protection is complete. The buyer is not protected completely against his own bad judgment or against the bad judgment or worse on the part of sellers. The buyer is not protected completely against misrepresentation or fraud; he is not completely protected against being influenced into purchases that "reasonable" people would think foolish or even into purchases that are positively harmful. It has also been pointed out that these abuses are relatively infrequent and limited to few types of industry. Furthermore, it has been emphasized that if one tries to pass judgment on the whole range of buying-selling transactions in retail, wholesale, manufacturing, institutional operations, one cannot escape the conclusion that selling and business in general are marked by customary probity,[7] rather than by general dishonesty or deceit, although a few choleric and ill-informed writers have asserted the latter.[8]

The protection the public enjoys against detrimental selling is fourfold in nature. First, there is the protection that comes from the essential decency of man, from the general desire not to harm fellow men, and from the character of individual leaders. Obviously such influence is important even if not measurable, although how much importance will be attributed to it depends upon several factors such as the individual's philosophy of life, and the experience, thought, and faith that enter into that philosophy. The contacts I have had personally with many people at various levels of selling, differing levels of responsibility and in widely diverse fields, have given me fully as high an opinion

[7] R. J. Watkins, *Toward Enlarging the Sphere of Freedom* (Berkeley: University of California, 1951).

[8] Elijah Jordan, *Business be Damned* (New York: Henry Schuman, 1952).

of them as of any other large and representative group in any major vocation.[9]

Secondly, the next important protection and by all odds the most pervasive is that of intelligent self-interest, because it operates to protect the buying public against possible harm from those who, through misplaced enthusiasm or bad judgment, are not serving the public. Even those who are willing to disregard consumer interest may find that their own selfish interests lie in the direction of serving the consumer well. Since most buying and selling transactions are repeat transactions, types in which the buyer repeats a purchase, it is to the interest of the seller so to conduct his selling that his actions will be satisfactory to the buyer.

Another form of this check on bad and wasteful selling is the high cost of bad selling. It has been pointed out that if firms in many industries could not expect repeat business at lower costs than the costs of initial sales, failure would be inevitable. Most sellers, therefore, attempt to develop products of such value that having been persuaded to buy those products the first time, the customer is disposed to buy them a second time and repeat subsequently. The check is important because it is precisely the point at which the profit motive operates.

Third, group attitudes and group actions of sellers themselves, considering both their long-run interest and their desires to act uprightly, have caused considerable progress to be made in setting up and securing acceptance for codes of advertising and selling conduct. A recent series of articles in a leading publication devoted to advertising and other articles and studies extending over a long period of time are some indications of the lively interest in improvement. A code of practice proposed many years ago and revised since World War II was that published by *Printers' Ink*. This has been taken as a pattern for

---

[9] Dr. Ralph J. Watkins in the Barbara Weinstock Lecture, 1951, at the University of California, Berkeley, on the "Morals of Trade" asserts that the net work of contractual relationships (in the American business enterprise system) with suppliers and customers both written and unwritten, is predominantly characterized by commercial probity. *Dun's Review*, September, 1951, pp. 3–5.

relations regulating advertising practice in a number of states.[10]

The divergences between the code and actual practice are evident to any interested observer. But those divergences have lessened over the years, both because of public pressure, particularly through legislation, and because of the self-policing actions of business itself. In both selling and advertising, the

[10] The *Printers' Ink* Platform of Advertising Principles reads as follows:

Desiring to preserve and enhance the values in advertising to the benefit of the public and business alike;

Recognizing that advertising has played a dynamic role in the growth, development and expansion of commerce and industry in the United States;

Convinced that organizations now in the field of advertising can by joint endeavor preserve, elevate and make fully effective adequate standards for the conduct of advertising;

Reaffirming the principles that have already been advocated by farseeing leaders in advertising;

Determined to eliminate abuses in advertising that tear down its acceptance by the public and its value to American business;

We affirm the principles set forth below as essential to the welfare of the public and all those engaged in advertising:

I

We believe that the primary function of advertising is to inform the public of the attributes of goods and services and to induce their purchase. We deplore the use of advertising primarily as an instrument to disparage a competitive product or service or to attack the truthfulness of competitive claims. Such abuse of advertising tends to destroy believability in all advertising claims and to cause grave damage to the American system of private competitive enterprise.

II

We believe that the sponsor of the advertising message has an especial responsibility for the content of that message. We deplore claims of fact that cannot be verified by objective tests. Anyone using the advertising message to mislead, confuse or deceive the public is acting irresponsibly and to the detriment not only of his own advertising but of all advertising.

III

We believe that advertising is a social force for the public good, and we support advertising that contributes to the general welfare of the public. We deplore advertising that does not adhere to generally accepted standards of good taste and morality.

IV

We believe that all those engaged in advertising should work together in the public interest and in their own interest to advance these advertising principles. We shall therefore lend our best efforts to further every movement designed to preserve, elevate and implement these standards.

Better Business bureaus of all major cities exert a salutary influence upon those who would depart from the paths of decency and respect for consumers' interests.

The work of educational institutions, especially of home economics teaching in schools and colleges, the work of certain government bodies, e.g., the Bureau of Agricultural Economics, and extension work by state and other universities have helped to make more intelligent and discriminating consumers. The women's magazines and the consumer organizations have also contributed much to consumer education, in spite of the fact that both groups would find difficulty in proving that they were free of bias.

Finally, legal measures embodied both in legislative and administrative law have helped to limit and even to check some types of bad selling. The sale of clearly harmful goods has been legally prohibited. The sale of detrimental habit-forming products has been brought under close control. Fraudulent misrepresentation is under the ban of the law. Nevertheless, abuses continue in the twilight zone between clearly harmful and illegal practices and definitely beneficial and legal practices. The progress of business and public opinion has tended to bring more of the probably harmful practices under restriction and control. Much remains to be done, however, to clarify precisely how the public interest will be best served.

Discussions of all these types of protective influences and devices in any detail must be reserved for another study. One is constrained to conclude that all of these are powerful helps to the buying public as well as to honorable sellers. That they are not so adequate as they should be and will be is obvious; but they help to reduce abuses to a point that enables selling to show on balance its great contribution to public welfare.

SUMMARY AND CONCLUSION

More attention has been devoted in this and the previous chapter to adverse criticisms than to selling's positive contributions to our society. A balanced evaluation of economic and social contributions of selling should include also the argument in many other chapters.

Reflection upon the criticisms leveled at selling leads one to conclude that a portion of the criticism is not directed at selling alone but rather against competition in our economy and against free competitive enterprise and private profit as motivation. Clearly in some cases, the intention is largely to influence improvements in our economic structure and its functioning. In others, the aim is to substitute some other form of economic organization within a capitalistic structure; or they may go so far as to substitute as an alternative some form of socialistic or communistic organization. It is with these alternatives to selling in a free, dynamic economy that we shall be concerned in the next chapter. And certain criticisms relating to monopolistic pricing are examined in Chapter XII.

Other criticism is leveled at actually harmful practices, at human failure, fraud, and deceit in selling. No intelligent citizen supports these. They should be eliminated, preferably by business itself or, if necessary, by law to restrain those who are not restrained by their own personal standards, by long-run self-interest, by self-respect, or any other motivation to ethical conduct.

Quite different are those alleged abuses and criticisms which take their departure from the standards of taste and behavior that the critics want to set up for others, not for themselves. The tendency of some persons to decree conduct for other persons is a dangerous one, which needs careful scrutiny if the fundamental values of democracy are to be preserved. Freedom of choice, fluidity of society, are endangered by efforts of persons to impose their will, their tastes, and their standards upon others. There is a common assumption among self-styled sophisticates that what they set up as desirable ways of life should be the way of others.

Selling is finally criticized because its objectives diverge from the objectives of those who do not believe in high material standards or high levels of living. Here are fundamental differences in basic philosophy. The criticisms that emerge are not criticisms of selling as such, but criticisms of high material stand-ards of living, which selling tends to bring about.

Finally, there are the criticisms of selling based on the failure of selling leadership to attain ideals of altruism not yet reached by any other form of human leadership. Discriminating and constructive criticisms aimed at improvement should be wel-comed. Criticism which by inference singles out all selling leader-ship for condemnation has been all too common, and does a real disservice to the buyers, sellers, and the public generally.

Chapter XI

ALTERNATIVES TO SELLING LEADERSHIP

ONE MAY ARGUE that leadership is needed to influence people to consume and produce goods and services in such a manner as to achieve a high standard of living, but in itself that does not constitute acceptance of the proposition that *selling* leadership is essential in our economy. We must still examine the argument that other sources of leadership would be superior to, and more effective than, selling. The attitudes of some social groups and the opinions of some economists imply that there are more desirable alternatives. It is with these alternatives that this chapter is concerned. It is proposed that we examine the principal alternatives in order to arrive at judgments as to their relative social and economic values in attaining the objectives that have been set up for selling effort.

The alternatives to selling leadership are broadly two in number. First, predominant leadership by buyers; that is, by ultimate consumers and other buyers, producers, or middlemen set up in response to buyer leadership. Second, leadership by government or governmentally constituted organizations, including allotment or at least far-reaching governmental control over what is to be produced and how much, as well as over the distribution of products and services.

Our present economic system is predominantly based on seller initiative in producing and distributing goods. The seller is subject to manifold influences of demand, competition, and costs, previously discussed; but it is his decision that finally determines what is offered for sale, and what his asking price shall be. He operates in ways that have been described to secure buying action, but success is not assured. Furthermore, freedom of choice among buyers prevails, and that choice may make sellers prosperous or may cause their failure.

However, leadership is not exclusively by sellers. Some leadership and initiative are exercised by buyers in various sectors of our economy. Large retailers, manufacturers, government bodies, co-operative groups of consumers, farmers' organizations, voluntary groups of retailers and wholesalers, all display some initiative in buying and in influencing production and prices. Buyers of some department stores suggest new products for which they think a market exists. Certain retailers have been noted for the innovations in merchandise types and designs that have been included in their lines and offered to the public. Purchasing officers and production executives and workers in manufacturing and other companies not infrequently ask for products to fill specific needs or suggest products for their own needs, which may later be incorporated in the sellers' line. The list of specific instances would be a long one; but nevertheless it would not in amount affect the central fact that producers and traders must generally take the initiative in disposing of what they produce or have bought for resale.

Thus the first alternative to selling would theoretically be exclusive or predominant buyer initiative This extreme alternative, even though within the framework of free enterprise, would find few supporters; but particular aspects of buyer initiative such as consumers' co-operatives have won ardent supporters, who sometimes imply that society would be better off with a complete system of buyer leadership and initiative.

The growth of large-scale specialized production units and the growing lack of self-sufficiency among consuming units, whether ultimate consumers or industrial buyers, have necessarily required an increase in the effort needed to bring consumers and producers together. Satisfaction of consumer needs and wants by specialized producers requires exchange, whether that exchange be effected by the volition of buyers and sellers in a competitive economy or by allotment processes in a controlled economy. In the competitive economy with which we are concerned, it becomes obvious that either the buyer must come to the seller or the seller must go to the buyer or they must share, in equal or unequal portions, the burden of coming together in a market. Otherwise the seller cannot sell that which he must sell if he is to secure a return for his labor and management and for the outlays that he has made for the labor and material furnished by others; nor will the consumer be satisfied.

Historically, both seller and buyer have taken the initiative at various times. In medieval and early modern times it would appear that the seller and the trader took the initiative in bringing imported products to the various fairs and markets. For products made within a nation's borders, particularly products of the craftsmen's guilds, there were definite limitations to the extent to which the craftsmen might go in carrying on selling activities in various localities. Guild rules, as late as the eighteenth century, to a considerable extent compelled the buyer to take the initiative. The growth of the domestic or "putting-out" system by which selling came into the hands of merchants and more enterprising craftsmen indicates the beginning of a period in which the seller more largely took the initiative. However, ordinarily a producer under the putting-out system took no initiative, having shifted the burden of selling to the trader or trader craftsman. It has been argued that it was the reluctance of the producer to take the initiative in selling that caused the rise of the domestic system of production.

With the increase in the quantity of production that resulted from the introduction of machinery and power during the Industrial Revolution, the problem with which manufacturers were confronted in disposing of their products became one of major consequence. The selling task of converting potential markets into active buying markets was, in certain industries, shifted to selling agents, selling houses. This did not mean that buyers took the initiative, but rather that producers, feeling themselves unwilling or incompetent to take the initiative, shifted the necessary selling function to agent traders, who themselves undertook to bring the products to the attention of buyers, whether middlemen or consumers.

Since the Industrial Revolution the seller in the United States has, by and large, taken the initiative in effecting exchange transactions, although there are many circumstances where the initiative is not taken solely or even primarily by sellers. The seller with large quantities of goods on hand as a result of efficient means of production, or with large capacity to produce things, is compelled by his own interest to seek out those members of the buying public who wish to buy such goods. The self-interest of a manufacturer in endeavoring to sell the production of which he is capable is considerably stronger than the interest of the buyer, who may in many cases find it possible to secure such products from a variety of sources and who may at times find substitutes for particular products. To the manufacturer of a specialized product, there is no alternative other than sale at a price—preferably at a price that covers his costs and yields a profit. Continued failure to sell at such a price ordinarily leads to disaster. Contrariwise, failure to buy from one source is not usually disastrous for the buyer.

The growth of expert buying organizations in large-scale manufacturing and distributive enterprises and in institutional consumers has been marked by growth in initiative among such buyers. Nevertheless, the student cannot fail to be impressed by the fact that the buying process in distributive organizations handling consumer goods is still largely a process of selection among the offerings of sellers who have taken the initiative of bringing their wares to the attention of these buyers. Likewise, in industrial purchasing one gains the impression that, except among a small minority of competent and well-supported purchasing departments, the principal role of the buyers is selection among the offerings brought to the buyer by the initiative of sellers. The principal work of most purchasing agents is to make selections using all the aids that the seller furnishes in the way of salesmen, servicemen, correspondence, catalogues, and other sales literature in an effort to go beyond the offerings made by personal solicitation. Passive sellers may occasionally be sought out, but it is the exception rather than the rule that a seller may rely solely upon the initiative of buyers.[1]

PREDOMINANT SELLER INITIATIVE

Whether buyers take the initiative or sellers assume the responsibility, the functions that must be performed by individuals or groups are very similar. This is a striking statement and needs some elaboration before it will be accepted. First, let us take another look at the functions of the seller. In any selling process, it becomes necessary for the selling organization to perform a number of tasks. They are not definite, and they are not taken up in the same order in each case. Each of them may be stressed or minimized, depending upon conditions. Furthermore, many organizations will neglect one or more of them; but that may merely emphasize that the selling function is not well performed and may explain some of the difficulties encountered by selling organizations. However, it is useful to focus attention somewhat more sharply on the elements of the persuasive process of selling so that we can compare them with the elements in the buying process.

1) Before selling persuasion is undertaken by any firm, whether middleman, industrial or institutional seller, manufacturer, or other producer, decisions have to be made as to the goods or services to be provided for sale. These decisions must generally take into account more or less dependable information as to the needs and wants of the buyers to whom they expect to sell. Such information may in some cases be little better than hunch or guess based on limited observation or collateral experience. It may, however, be based on pertinent past experience or on more or less elaborate studies of market demand. Decisions have also to be made as to the ways and means of physical distribution, as to the types of distributors, and as to the prices to be asked.

2) Selling transactions in a free economy are not impersonal.

---

[1] Cf. H. R. Tosdal, "The Advertising and Selling Process," *Annals of the American Academy of Political and Social Science*, May, 1940.

They take place between specific sellers and buyers, although advertising may be directed to classes of buyers rather than to individuals who are solicited personally. It is necessary to take such information as is available to sellers relating to buyers' needs, their desires, their buying practices and behavior, and plan the performance of the selling task. The prospective buyers that some firms must consider are very numerous; thousands of contacts may have to be made both personally and through other selling media. One medium-sized company solicits business from 20,000 retailers upon whom its salesmen call once a month. Another company of similar size calls upon 800 customers once every quarter, selling equipment to "franchised" distributors. Nevertheless, in each case the salesman needs to know the customers and prospective buyers individually, to call upon them, see them, and persuade them as individuals. To the extent that the sellers can get advance information to do an intelligent selling job, they reduce costs; but at some point they must endeavor to secure that information. They must learn the needs and wants of buyers if sales are to be made and buyers are to be well served.

3) Many types of work need to be done in order to see that these contacts are made with buyers. It is necessary to plan the solicitation of buyers in general and of specialized classes as well as particular buyers if the selling persuasion is to be successfully performed at a cost which will not be destructive of the seller's capital. Research, planning, organizing, execution, and control are all involved.

4) With information and with the plans made on the basis of this information, the seller must then, either by personal selling, by advertising, by correspondence, or by other means, singly or in combination, solicit buyers to buy. The object of this solicitation is to secure consent of the buyer to buy, to consummate selling transactions, to secure buying action. The means used are any or all of those discussed in previous chapters. In the solicitation, the attention of the prospective buyer must be secured and an offer made to him in convincing terms, if the products fit his needs and desires.

5) And finally, goods must be delivered and payment secured

therefore. In many a firm it becomes necessary to provide services and perform duties that will increase the satisfaction of the buyer, both to carry out promises made prior to sale and to enhance the willingness of the buyer to make repeat purchases from the same vendor.

PREDOMINANT BUYER INITIATIVE

Now let us examine the processes required for buying. The factual statement that in the United States the largest share in initiating the transfer of manufactured and semimanufactured goods is taken by the sellers requires no defense. But the question as to whether public interest would be better served by placing the burden of initiative upon buyers immediately precipitates the questioner into the controversial ring. Would the gradual replacement of seller initiative by buyer initiative more fully contribute to public well-being? The selling enterprise consists of several hundred thousand manufacturing concerns and several million trade and service enterprises. The buying group consists of all these plus many more millions of ultimate consumers purchasing as individuals or families and likewise as governmental bodies, institutions, or other groupings. Granting the necessity of bringing consumer and producer together, we are confronted, therefore, with the problem of determining the relative costs of the alternatives: (1) sellers taking full initiative, going to buyers at their homes or places of business for solicitation and delivery; (2) buyers assuming full initiative; (3) the burden of making connections shared, either as in the present system where sellers predominantly take the initiative, or in a proposed system in which buyers predominate.[2]

Brief examination of buying processes under conditions of predominant buyer initiative may be brought out of the realm

[2] Buying in retail establishments is treated in Delbert J. Duncan and Charles F. Phillips, *Retailing: Principles and Methods* (4th ed.; Homewood, Ill.: Richard D. Irwin, Inc., 1955), chaps. ix, x, xi; buying in wholesale establishments in Theodore N. Beckman and Nathanael H. Engle, *Wholesaling* (rev. ed.; New York: Ronald Press Co., 1949). Industrial purchasing is the subject of the volume by Howard T. Lewis, Professor Emeritus, Harvard University, *Procurement: Principles and Cases* (rev. ed.; Homewood, Ill.: Richard D. Irwin, Inc., 1952).

of pure speculation by observing the practices of most expert and aggressive buyers of large businesses, such as chain stores and manufacturing enterprises. The elements of the buying process parallel the elements of the selling process mentioned above. It does no violence to facts to suggest a similar list. After determination of general types of goods needed and purchase price limitations, the buyer must:

1. Secure information about sellers and suppliers in general, as well as about individual prospective sources from which satisfactory purchases may be made;
2. Plan purchases by classes of goods, by sources, and perhaps from particular sellers;
3. Establish contact by mail or person or otherwise with sources of supply;
4. Secure attention of the source or supplier and negotiate the purchase;
5. After the order has been filled, received, and paid for, it still is necessary for buyers to handle their relationships with suppliers so as to become a satisfactory and desirable customer from the standpoint of the seller, if delivery and other service is to be secured during periods of greater demand.

Obviously, the completeness with which the list of functions is performed by particular buyers will depend upon the importance of the buying function and the competence with which that function is discharged in the particular situation. In the well-managed purchasing department of an institution or industrial enterprise, or in the buying departments of retail stores, all these steps may be represented. For the ultimate consumer, the performance of even a partial process of purchasing from retail stores is frequently faultily and carelessly done.

If generally similar functions need to be performed, whether the processes are initiated and carried through by buyers or by sellers, the problem of determining social advantage of alternatives is simplified. Little attention, however, needs to be devoted to the two alternatives of complete assumption of responsibility by either buyers or sellers. Under no conceivable efficient arrangement of work would it be possible to have either buyers or sellers take the initiative exclusively without denying the premise upon which this volume is based, namely, that of free private enterprise.

The problem involved is therefore the extent to which the public welfare is served by having initiative taken primarily by the seller as compared to initiative taken primarily by the buyer. Were buyers to assume the responsibility, it is clear at once that at present there are more buying persons or organizations to make the contacts, and that many of these will be duplicating on a small or large scale the work of others situated in the same areas. In the absence of extensive additional organization of consumers, with the possible accompaniment of restricted consumer freedom, the minimum amount of contact work for predominant buyer initiative would be greater—more human energy and time would be required. Practically, the organization of ultimate consumers for buying has not proceeded very far in the United States up to the present. Such organizations as have been formed have as their major objective largely the more economical provision of goods, the original introduction and present distribution of which are consequences of seller initiative. The introduction of newer and better products appears generally to have been the result of the system of seller initiative with intense seller interest in the successful sale of the individual product as a prerequisite.

It is only upon a limited scale and for the most part for limited ranges of products that ultimate consumers have ever been able to organize to do their buying through co-operative groups. The picture is not yet clear, but it is probable that, taking all things into account, co-operative groups cannot perform all the functions performed by private enterprise more economically. Such data as are available represent operation under relatively favorable circumstances for co-operation.

Critical study of the consumers' co-operative movement tends to support the thesis that the movement started in England as the result of woefully inadequate marketing performance by retailers of the time. It has gradually become identified with the labor movement in Great Britain and some countries on the European continent. In northern Europe, consumers' co-operatives have included also the middle class. The glowing account of certain writers when dealing with the Swedish co-operatives tends to emphasize the success of the movement in fighting prominent combines. These writers do not dig deeply enough to observe that generally the initiative which brings new products and new methods is absent or less active in consumers' co-operative enterprises. And other sources are not so favorably impressed as to rate actual accomplishments very highly.

In the United States, with all their faults our retailers have generally operated in such a manner that co-operative stores have been hard put to it to compete. Only in limited areas, such as Ohio and northern Wisconsin, and in spots where certain European nationals have settled, has the consumer co-operative flourished. In the marketing of farm products, the development has been of major importance; but in purchases of equipment, the growth has been spotty and not of major consequence.

Two sound reasons account for the lack of development of buyer organization and initiative. The first is the relatively smaller incentive for the buyer to buy a particular product from a particular seller than for a particular seller to sell his output. The second is the effective force of competition, sparked by aggressive selling and advertising.

If John Jones thinks that he may want a room air conditioner to give greater comfort for the coming summer heat, he expects to find air conditioners of different capacities, different designs, and at varying prices offered to him. If he behaves as consumers have behaved in this market the past few years, he will wait until the heat arrives. If the season is an especially cool one he puts off buying, in spite of the urging of dealers and the advertising of manufacturers. A few years ago, manufacturers expected a substantial rise of demand because past sales trends clearly pointed in that direction, and conservative production the previous season had proved inadequate. But in this year, cooler weather persisted until August. Consumers chose not to buy at all. Manufacturers and distributors were left with nearly half a million units of excess supply of room air-conditioners, which had to be disposed of in subsequent seasons at substantial reductions and even losses. Here was exercised consumer freedom of choice, whether to buy or not to buy.

What would the situation have been with buyer initiative?

In the first place, who would have sufficient interest to initiate the development and production of room air conditioners? Who would be willing to take the risks and the grief of the uncounted years put into development and marketing of air-conditioner products—for more than a quarter century?

It is clear that for the hundreds and thousands of products that our consumer group chooses and uses, the individual would in a few cases be willing to place orders in advance, wait for delivery, and choose from what the officers of his consumer organization thought an acceptance range of product. Co-operative consumer stores, generally, do not produce what they sell; they buy from firms built up by seller initiative. They may provide for the packaging of some products, the production of some staple products. Co-operatives may buy and operate an oil refinery. But the development of that refinery and all the technical refining and distribution apparatus have been achievements of firms supported and energized by selling persuasion. And the automobile market has developed in the United States only under widespread and intensive selling persuasion.

Without spelling out the details, the conclusion also seems warranted that the building of consumer organizations necessary to provide a higher standard of living for all would be slow and cumbersome. Many characteristics of government organization and bureaucratic ordering of production and distribution would tend to creep in. Some buyer initiative undoubtedly is highly desirable as a check upon and stimulus to the sellers. This is, however, far removed from the proposals of general or predominant buyer responsibility for providing the dynamic forces to production and productivity which selling has shown that it can develop.

ALTERNATIVE OF GOVERNMENT PLANNING AND ALLOTMENT

The second broad class of alternatives to selling leadership involves a fundamental change in social structure. It is the adoption of one form or another of widespread government action to produce and distribute the goods and services required for the people. This means at one extreme the complete elimination of private enterprise, or in interim forms, the socialization of a portion of economic enterprise and extensive planning and regulation of the remainder. It involves socialism or communism in varying degrees in contrast to a free-enterprise system. Broadly, under such a system the initiative in economic activities no longer comes predominantly in peacetime from businessmen.

Economic planning is said to be directly aimed at raising the level of social welfare, although obviously much of economic planning that has been observed has been intended to raise welfare only to the extent necessary in order to help attain or retain power for an aspiring, ambitious ruling group.[3] Government officials decide what goods are to be made and what are to be distributed. They decide who is to have them and under what conditions. They decide when new products are to be produced, when new facilities for production are to be established. They adjust the quantities of goods to be produced to the requirements of government policies or to government expediency and to the interest of specific groups in high government position.

In the Western world, the objective of welfare is broadly accepted. For the state is believed to exist for the individuals who make up that state, rather than individuals existing for the state. Totalitarian and fascist systems hold that the individual exists for purposes of the state; that the masses should be led and should be conditioned to accept leadership from the state, exercising no initiative on their own. In liberal systems, welfare, however we may define it, is generally accepted as the goal of economic activity.

Having in mind the operation of a free-enterprise economy, let us compare the steps that government officials must take in order to provide the consumer with goods in Russia. First, government servants must collect information as to the type of goods needed or wanted. On the basis of statistical calculations, some clerks, even armies of clerks, decide that so many pairs of shoes should be made in certain colors and models. This must

[3] See p. 93.

be done throughout the economy. Government servants will choose the models or styles. They will allot to the existing factories the task of producing such models and styles. These would then be offered through state stores to consumers. The models and styles are not likely to be rejected by consumers for the very good reason of shortage of the supply of shoes. The amount that can be manufactured has in practice been so small relative to the need that allotments will often be exhausted long before needs are satisfied, unless the products themselves are so badly made or badly planned that they are unfit for use. The standard of living has been so low and the purchasing power so small that the great bulk of the Soviet population has not gotten much beyond subsistence level. There are a few persons outside of the limited number of people in the party and certain small favored groups who are at the comfort level and only a handful relatively in the higher comfort and luxury levels where freedom of choice means very much.

Obviously the determination of what can be made, how much productive capacity is available, what is to be put into the product, will be made not primarily upon the basis of prospective consumer choice or welfare but upon the basis of the economic purposes of the governing group. If that governing group is interested in building up heavy industry for purposes of power, war, or defense, then the allotment of materials and the planning of production for consumers must take second place, as it has up to the present in the Soviet Union. As mentioned earlier, it appeared in 1953 that attention would be given to the welfare of the population in greater measure than previously; but with Stalin's death and the change in the Politburo, the promises of greater amounts of consumer goods made initially were pretty much forgotten, or at least subordinated to other state purposes.

When goods are to be made and when they are ready to be delivered, the bases on which they are to be distributed must be determined in any totalitarian society. If goods are insufficient to satisfy all demands, whether pricing or some form of rationing is to be used, it has to be decided whether privileged systems, especially state stores, are to be used for the channeling of distribution in accordance with government purposes. Since no socialistic or communistic society, or any extensive governmental planned society, has ever reached a point where comfort and luxury goods were available in abundance at prices within reach of the ordinary worker, the system has not been tested. A minor incident may be illustrative. The writer asked the head of the Amtorg Corporation, the Soviet buying agency located at that time in New York, who visited the Harvard Business School some twenty-five years ago, how his government expected to solve the problem of consumer choice if and when standards of living were raised above the subsistence level. A rather sudden failure to comprehend English caused Mr. Bogdanov to turn to an interpreter and hold an animated ten-minute conversation in Russian. Then he turned to me and remarked that his government would solve the problem when they came to it—certainly no answer, even if it did constitute an acknowledgment of the existing low standard of living. The persistent low standard of living for the bulk of the population has been noted. The availability of limited luxuries at high state prices for a few select workers and other privileged groups has also been mentioned. In this connection, a brief item in the *New York Times* late in August, 1954, carried headlines, "Cosmetics Sales Pushed in Soviet. Perfumes and Face Creams for Different Purposes being Advertised." The brand names of face creams and night creams, "Manon," "Adolescent," "Red Poppy," "Velvet," "Moscow Lights," "White Nights," "Jubilee," "Magnolia," remind one of French "parfumieres" and of "inspired" American copy writers. One paragraph remarked that the "cosmetics trust has embarked on a new sales drive and a widened advertising campaign," using newspaper and billboard advertising and occasional full-page displays in popular magazines, direct-mail advertising, and four-color handbills for store distribution.

The news raises many points for speculation; but one point is clear: Selling persuasion is to be found in Russia despite earlier communist doctrines of the utter economic waste of selling activity.

Appraisal of Governmental Planning: Allotment Methods

Are government servants more competent, more willing, and more able than those in private enterprise who do the task on a very much smaller scale and on a scale that does not overtax managerial competence? Is the motivation, not of the few at the top but of the many workers in government, manufacturing, or distributive enterprises, as likely to call forth the initiative of those who produce or those who distribute as the methods in free societies, particularly in the United States? In other words, is the desire of some government or an all-powerful ruling-group state as effective as the workers' optimistic desire for goods in a free society and the persuasive leadership of sellers in bringing high levels of living?

Such evidence as one can gather in our own economy and from the thinking of government servants is far from reassuring. All reports of the small advance in levels of living beyond subsistence standards in the Soviet Union does not give one faith in the effectiveness of motivating people by fear,[4] favoritism, and general promises of future consumer benefit. Above all, the situation of centralized government planning by a few persons is a long step toward enslavement of a people and toward the destruction of economic as well as political liberty. The Soviet system continues because the people have allowed themselves to be tricked by promises, intimidated by fears and secret police, driven to indifference to the sort of leadership under which they live. Only by sacrificing popular freedom to an all-powerful state, only by an "iron curtain" that deprives people of the knowledge of progress and welfare in free nations has this been able to develop. Soviet rulers are apparently afraid to let the people know what has been accomplished by free enterprise and selling leadership in the United States. They have also endeavored to reduce such desires as exist for higher standards of living by maligning the standards in the United States as bourgeois and overindulgent. However, the behavior of the Soviet representatives who come to this country, who enjoy great luxury and who, when returning, buy American goods and

---

[4] Bauer, Inkeles, and Kluckhohn, *How the Soviet System Works.* (Cambridge: Harvard University Press, 1956), p. 68: "More than any other modern state, the Soviet Union uses political terror and forced labor as an integral part of its political and economic system, and does so on a vast scale. Political arrests have been a marked feature of the regime from the time of the Revolution."

services to the limit that they can take back with them, seems to indicate that the actual attiude is that welfare is for members of the party and the rulers and that the people generally should not aspire to a high degree of economic welfare, nor should they expect it.

The desire for high levels of living is very strong and the Soviet government has been compelled to recognize it and at least to pay lip service to it. They have been compelled in spite of the austere living of a few leaders to provide opportunities for high levels of living for some party members and high officials and for the so-called intelligentsia. The differences in the incomes and standards of living for various sectors of the economy appear to be as great as in democratic capitalist countries. There is also some ground for believing that the differences have been growing greater in the Soviet, while they have definitely been growing less in the United States. The lip service paid to the economic welfare of the people represents a policy of ignoring that welfare beyond the minimum necessary to prevent what the leaders consider as excessive unrest.

There is further much evidence that the lack of optimistic expectation of higher standards of living has led to failure of production in some areas of the economy, a low rate of production and agriculture, and a slow rate of progress in industry, particularly in the sectors of industry which have to do with consumer goods.[5] Advances in production and productivity are, of course, shrouded in a good deal of mystery, but the bits and pieces of evidence that we secure do not show a rise in levels of living that is by any means comparable to the rise in the United States. And that rise in the United States has been in spite of war and in spite of the billions in foreign aid furnished in smaller part to Russia itself and in larger part to many nations of the world.

OTHER ALTERNATIVES TO SELLING

A somewhat vaguely defined form of planning is implied in the phrase, often repeated during the depression years of the

---

[5] The recently published conclusions of the Harvard Study Group seem to confirm this; the forecasts which they make which have so far been borne out by subsequent events. See Bauer, et al., op. cit., p. 248.

thirties, that society should be organized on a basis of "production for use" rather than "production for profit." Among those who advocated extensive government controls and economic planning, the emergence of surpluses of many commodities, which had to be kept in storage, and the existence of low living standards of sizable sections of our population, led to the easy conclusion that governmental planning which would direct these surpluses to those who needed them was to be preferred to the production-for-profit system under which our economy had developed. The implication was present in certain writings, if not explicitly stated, that production for use was socially desirable and practical while production for profit did not serve public welfare.

Let us examine the argument, which was so plausible as apparently to have influenced policy makers in government and economists in their thinking more than might now be admitted. The production-for-use slogan sounds good, noble, and liberal, particularly to those who desire to escape mundane matters or to those who unknowingly are trying to avoid some of the harsh facts of life.

What is production for profit? What does it involve?

1) It is production directed by business entrepreneurs who are under obligation to cover costs if possible and make a profit. Some succeed, many fail. The figures of business failures bear this out. Therefore, it is not merely production for profit; it is production for profit or loss in which those who attempt to make a profit are taking the risk that instead of making a profit they will suffer loss.

2) Production takes place in advance of demand. The consumer exercising his freedom of choice determines whether the product will be accepted or not. If not, the enterprise is a failure, at least in respect to this particular product. Even if the product is accepted by the public, failure is possible in part or in whole on the basis of bad management, or on the basis of competition of other products or other makers who have done a superior job in satisfying consumer desires. Stubborn facts prove that the production for profit is production for profit or loss. Profit is not assured.

3) Under the system of production for profit or loss, there

are innumerable centers of initiative, innumerable enterprises that must depend upon ingenuity and aggressiveness in producing and selling to secure a sufficient share of the consumer market to warrant their continuance in business. There are many trials to win favor and, of course, there are many errors. There is no method of determining precisely what the consumer will want in advance of offer to him. There are many techniques for reducing the area in which the risks must be taken, techniques for determining within some limits what that consumer is likely to desire; but there is no precise measurement technique that will give without sizable error a final answer. The profit and loss system gives a premium on innovation, particularly innovation that represents a closer approximation to what the consumer wants. But risk of loss is inherent in such production.

4) Businessmen do not work exclusively and many of them not mainly for monetary gains, any more than other groups are motivated exclusively by prospects of pecuniary gain or desire to serve the public. There is pride in a good product, in building a smoothly working organization, in helping men to develop; but no organization in the field of business continues to exist if no profits are made. There can be no regularity of employment if goods cannot be disposed of. There can be no possibility of keeping in the forefront of technological advance if profit is nonexistent. But there is the constant stimulus of private profit to make technological advance.

5) There are many checks so that the amount of profit or loss involved in giving the public what it wants is reduced to small (though not negligible) proportions. In fact, since most business is done on a repeat basis, that is between firms and individuals who have had previous buying and selling relationships, the seller who does not go beyond *caveat emptor* is not likely to build a business that will be profitable and successful in these days. With all the faulty and wavering upward course of business ethics, ethical conduct is more generally the role in business today than is commonly believed by the uninformed layman. Enlightened selfishness goes a great distance in protecting the public against abuses of bad actors in business, but it does not go the whole way. Where character and enlightened selfishness are not enough, a further check may be needed,

namely, the legislative and other rules that society sets down for the conduct of certain types of business affairs.

Now look at "production for use." First, because production for use usually means governmental planning and control by public servants, it implies determination by government servants in one way or another as to what is to be made as well as how it is to be made. Instead of millions of consumers expressing their desire by purchase or refusal to purchase, government employees determine on the basis of statistical estimates what they think consumers want, and adjust production accordingly. Slowly and haltingly, that production will be adjusted on the basis of statistical returns from government-planned projects.

Businessmen, using their own experience, hiring the best brains of the country, have essayed to do this and have found they make many mistakes for which they suffer even to the extent of failure. They know they must take risks; they know that only by taking risks can they realize substantial success, but they also may in taking those risks suffer failure.

Usually, failure on the part of a government service is not punished in civil service—not if intentions are good or good excuses can be found. Only fraud is likely to cause definitive action to get a bungling civil servant out of office quickly. Thus the automatic check of personal responsibility is weak, although again, most government servants will be conscientious, earnest, and honest.

The thinking of governmental servants and officials is usually and perhaps necessarily against "sticking one's neck out"; that is, against making changes, venturing on new courses, introducing new products or processes, or lowering prices, which might involve risks of failure. This is particularly true if the controls used are intended to measure the results of the government enterprise. Thus the offer of new products tends to be reduced and eventually to dry up. Innovation, upon which many hopes of rising levels are based is checked, whether that innovation takes the form of new production or improved methods of distributing established products. The tendency is to pass decisions to superiors, necessarily resulting in delay and inability to make decisions promptly.

Moreover, the net result of production for use resulting in

widespread economic planning like totalitarian planning is that the wisdom of a relatively small number of governmental servants is substituted for the collective wisdom of managers of several millions of enterprises operating independently in the United States.

Perhaps one of the most serious considerations in producing for use, as the term has been interpreted, is that the incentive of desire for products would not be stimulated by selling on a scale that would maintain and improve production and productivity at present high levels. For reasons inherent in the nature of consumer demand and consumer behavior, leadership is necessary to maintain production and productivity. Leadership under private enterprise is difficult to develop and to establish. Under governmental controls such leadership is likely not to be forthcoming, partly because the amount of governmental planning that was done would be aimed in the first place at a wider distribution of existing production and only secondly at greater productivity and a wider distribution of an ever increasing production of economic goods.

Lastly, because production under governmental controls would decline, more compromises would have to be made by consumers. Goods produced according to plans would have to be disposed of until such time as standards of living were reduced to the point of automatic maintenance or until desire of the population for high standards had reached a low equilibrium. Lower standards would result from a reduction in the utilization of productive capacity and a reduction of incentive to higher productivity and higher production.

Production for use as the substitute for profit incentives may, of course, mean to some no more than the idea that the businessman should produce with no thought of profit, that operating under a philosophy would be more fully in the interests of the public. To many businessmen today, the desire to produce good products, to furnish good employment at generous wages takes its place alongside profit making as motivation. But no matter how altruistic the motives of a business leader, his continuance as owner or manager and the continuance of such social services as the enterprise can render depend upon income that covers outlays and hopefully yields a margin that can be used for development and improvement, and yet leaves something for stockholders, so that investors will not refuse to furnish additional needed capital.

CONCLUSION

It is clear from the analysis that selling leadership toward higher economic welfare for the people generally is superior both in theory and in demonstrated performance to the alternatives mentioned. One need not in making that statement overlook the points at which selling leadership needs to be strengthened and the abuses and failures which need to be eliminated insofar as possible. There is no doubt but that in limited areas buyer initiative may make a real contribution. In other limited areas of our economy, such as goods distribution in periods of great shortages under war conditions or the introduction and distribution in limited production of some new essential product in short supply, governmental control may be desirable as a temporary measure. Furthermore, it is certainly true that some sellers have been culpably careless about public interest. But all of these do not invalidate the general conclusion that selling leadership is to be preferred.

Selling leadership is soundly based on the necessity of moving people to take action, of energizing people to act in their own economic interest. It appeals to the whole gamut of human desires and wants, which are or can be intensified by leadership to secure restricted short-range as well as long-range action. Selling and the expectations of selling and securing of income to cover outlays and making a profit lead to action, because the action is, in a high level of economy, the free choice of individuals who want improvements in their living and who can and want to do what is necessary to obtain them. Hopeful expectations warranted by the facts of our economic life release the initiative of owners and managers and other workers with results that can be observed on every hand. Thus, increased production, more skilled management, more productive machinery and processes, flow from the laboratories and testing grounds, from workers and officials, from study and experimentation, because people want to produce and improve, not merely as a means of getting more economic goods but also as a means of reducing the amount of work necessary to get the goods and services they want.

Under this system, and under this system only, consumers can exercise meaningful freedom of choice. Most important of all the system does not subordinate the individual to the arbitrariness or indifference of governmental officials. Consumers govern the economic system by their attitudes and by their buying actions. They are not the recipients of allotments or rations by governing servants acting on orders from other governmental servants who, in turn, consider the interests of the ruling groups, their ambitions and desires as pertinent while consumer interests are distinctly secondary. A society in which governmental planning is pervasive in human experience has become a society based upon force. It is no longer a society in which economic leadership is persuasive leadership.

In short, if we value freedom, if we seek to maintain a state in which men can be free; if we wish to avoid what Hilaire Belloc many years ago termed "a servile state," we must see that our leadership in economic as well as in other fields is persuasive, not dominating leadership based on force or fear. Economic progress appears to be surer and more rapid if based on the free desires of people to produce and buy goods than if production is based upon statism, backed up by propaganda pressure, supplemented by secret police and fears of torture, deportation, or worse.[6]

---

[6] "Another way of stating the Stalinist formula is that maximum productivity can be achieved from a social group if maximum pressure, incentive, or coercion is applied to each of the component parts." Bauer, *et. al.*, *op. cit.*, p. 50.

Chapter XII

SELLING AND ECONOMIC THEORY

WITH FEW EXCEPTIONS professional economists do not recognize selling as an important economic function. Neglect and indifference appear to be characteristic attitudes even among those economists who take the trouble to criticize selling and advertising adversely. The opinions of economists upon selling are evident in the texts and monographs they write, the addresses they deliver, their teachings to students, and in the opinions of students and others whom they influence.

Consequently the large amount of selling effort and the sizable proportion of national income expended for selling persuasion, have escaped critical scrutiny. The fact that the selling function is of major importance, whether viewed from the standpoint of the portion of national income expended, the millions of persons employed, or the results in terms of economic and social welfare, means that selling deserves broad-gauge, constructive study and criticism.

If one examines the history and development of economic doctrines and the nature of the economic environment that has influenced economists, we find a partial but not a full explanation of economic opinions on selling. The neglect of selling by economists stems in part from the fact that they have had insufficient personal contact with much of the selling effort to form a sound basis for judgment. Students of economics have been compelled to secure much of their basic opinion through limited printed sources of information and through limited personal observation. The average economist shares with the average layman direct contact with only a few types of selling effort.

The temptation to judge from one's own observation and to assume that that observation is typical appears to have had its influence. The result has been to emphasize advertising rather than personal selling because it is the most commonly observed form of selling effort and possibly to many the most annoying. Annoyance and assumed bad taste are magnified out of proportion to the total of advertising and even more out of proportion to the total actual expenditure for the various forms of selling effort.

Other factors have influenced opinions. The personal pride of some men in feeling that as individuals they do not want to be subjected to or influenced by selling and advertising may play a part. The illusion that people desire and usually do act rationally is one that has plagued economic science. Furthermore, many persons claiming to be scientific impliedly desire freedom to substitute their own judgments as to what other people should buy with their incomes. It is an easy step to the conclusion that other people can be persuaded to act unwisely by selling effort in the majority of cases, rather than in the minority of cases in which the unwisdom of buyers and the weaknesses and abuses of selling are clearly evident.

Again, selling effort has often been ignored by economists because there has been a broad tendency to exclude from economic study the problem of psychological motivation in the economic field. The subject of economic motivation, vital to the seller, has only in recent periods been considered proper for economic study, and even yet there remains controversy as to the appropriateness of its inclusion in the field of economics. Certainly it adds to the convenience of economists to ignore the facts of economic motivation and to substitute assumptions or models. Nevertheless, if economic motivation is to be studied realistically, selling cannot be ignored.

Selling is dynamic and characteristic of a dynamic economy. It is, in fact, quite different from the static situation and "perfect" competition of some economic theorists.

Economists have been in general agreement since Adam Smith's time as to the importance of the consumer and of consumption, however they may have phrased their statements. Nevertheless, up to recent times economists have been apparently unwilling or unable to consider the practically important place of the consumer in their scientific treatises.[1] Whatever attention earlier English writers accorded to consumption and the consumer was usually in connection with the treatment of production. Adam Smith writes of consumption as being the sole aim and end of production but does not carry his thinking further.[2] It is difficult to find in Mill any treatment of consumption, although the importance of consumer demand is dimly perceived in the half-hearted recognition that consumer demand plays a part in directing the employment of labor and capital.[3]

The reasons for the long neglect of the consumer are not clear, but certain facts serve to explain at least partially the inconsistency between general statements and the proportion of attention devoted to the subject of consumption. In addition to the argument that consumption was beyond the scope of economic science, it is clear that studies of consumer demand were few and exclusive and that data concerning consumer demand were difficult and expensive to get. The fact that the problem was not viewed as a pressing one discouraged the painstaking study required to make progress. Furthermore, the accepted use of general philosophic premises and deductive reasoning as adequate rendered the lack of factual materials less disturbing to earlier economists. The convenience of making broad statements as to consumer and buyer motivation could not be questioned.

---

[1] As Professor Paul T. Homan expresses it, "Professional economic opinion is at present divided as to whether economic science can proceed without the theory of consumption or whether such a theory is an essential prolegomenon to the science without being a part of it or whether it is an essential part of a well-developed descriptive analysis of economic action and motivation." *Encyclopedia of the Social Sciences*, "Consumption," Vol. IV, p. 295.

[2] Adam Smith, *Wealth of Nations* (Everyman's Lib. ed.), Vol. II, bk. iv, chap. viii, p. 155.

[3] J. S. Mill, *Principles of Political Economy*, ed. by W. J. Ashley (London: Longmans, Green, 1909), pp. 79–87.

Economic studies in English-speaking countries were largely dominated by the so-called classical school of economists,[4] and the concern of these economists with demand has commonly been confined to discussions of value and exchange. Mill discussed the idea of utility of commodities, while the Austrian or psychological school developed concurrently in several countries the idea of final or marginal utility. The early acceptance of the conception of the economic man and the careless assumption of the exclusivity of economic motivation tended to delay more realistic study which developed the complexity of human motives and the many-sidedness of consumer demand.[5] Economic treatises which have appeared during the last two decades have paid more attention to the subject of consumption, although much remains to be done. There is, however, no agreement as to the scope and extent of the treatment of consumption appropriate for the balanced exposition of economic principles.

Economic theory has continued, however, to use and probably to be much too content with, theoretical "models" and other abstractions when dealing with consumption and demand. As one consequence of such attitudes the function of selling is likely to be neglected. General economic treatises rarely go beyond the point of discussing certain general characteristics of human wants, such as the extensibility and expansibility of wants, the theory of diminishing utility, the appraisal of present as contrasted with future goods, the relation of demands to social standards, standards of living in relation to wages, and similar topics. Obviously, one cannot expect detailed treatment of any subject in a mere elementary treatise. Nevertheless, the approach that characterizes these treatises is significant because

---

[4] Both in the United States and in England the employment of historical and inductive method was *sub judice* until the close of the nineteenth century. It is notable, however, that in the first decisive treatise of the historical school in Germany, namely, Wilhelm Roscher's *Political Economy*, the subject of consumption was especially treated (cf. Vol. II, translation of J. J. Lalor, Chicago: Callaghan & Co., 1882). In chaps. i and ii of bk. iv, Roscher gives a historical treatment of consumption of goods in general and of luxury goods. It is to be noted that in Germany likewise the first intensive statistical studies of consumption were made under the direction of Friedrich Engels.

[5] Among the criticisms of the economic man see G. B. Dibblee, *The Laws of Supply and Demand* (London: Constable & Co., 1912).

college-trained businessmen today who have studied economic theory have for the most part received formal economic training not exceeding what is contained in any one of a dozen popular texts. Nothing in the businessman's general training in economics fits him for any sort of detailed understanding of the consumer demand that will so vitally affect him.

The assumptions that economists have frequently made concerning demand do not correspond to the observed facts of human behavior. One of the earliest of these assumptions, that of the "economic man," may have been largely superseded in current economic thinking; but the new assumptions made about demand, although nearer to observed facts, are not complete or accurate statements of demand characteristics.

One cannot escape an impression that some of the neglect of selling has been due to the persistence of the feeling among academic men that "trade" is not quite respectable, that buying and selling are "common" and not quite worthy of intellectual effort. The persistence of an attitude that merchants and others who sell were concerned only with their own private gain and were not to be accorded a respectable status in the intellectual or social world, particularly as high a status as certain other groups of people, especially the economists, may partly be responsible. Such attitudes are in part a carry-over from attitudes of continental Europe toward business as reflected in the writings and attitudes of members of privileged classes or their supporters. Furthermore, the dependence of some economists upon British opinion for basic ideas may have contributed to attitudes toward selling which made either indifference or adverse criticism easier than a constructive attitude of re-examination and re-appraisal.[6]

The implications of such characteristic attitudes and the criticisms of those who give limited attention to the function cannot,

---

[6] Prof. von Mises mentions certain other possible causes of adverse attitudes in his analysis of anticapitalistic attitudes of many intellectuals (*The Anti-Capitalist Mentality*, D. Van Nostrand Co., 1956). As psychological causes of the vilification of capitalism, he mentions the urge for economic betterment, the status society of capitalism, the resentment of frustrated ambition, the resentment and anticapitalistic bias of intellectuals and of white-collar workers, and the communism of Broadway and Hollywood.

however, be ignored. The treatment of selling by some economists poses a basic question of judgment as to the economic necessity of selling. Barring the excuse that selling is a psychological, not economic, process, one is forced to conclude that many economists believe it largely unnecessary. It is the thesis of this volume that selling is necessary for the greatest economic welfare in a society based on the free-enterprise system. Furthermore, it is asserted that both in fact and in sound theory, such a society has shown a greater promise of high and rising standards of living than any other form of society. The criticisms of wastefulness and high cost, stressed by some writers, have been dealt with above. Some economists further have questioned selling in relation to concepts of monopoly and competition. Not a few have undertaken to distinguish between good and bad selling, not only on the basis of fraud and sharp practice but on the basis of the types of persuasive effort employed. Some of them have approved informative selling as contrasted with emotional or competitive.

SELLING AND DEMAND

The economic conception of a market has been a limited one in which it was assumed that wants existed or did not exist, that consumer wants were limitless. But the implicit assumption has often been present in economic writings that wants somehow expand automatically with income. Business entrepreneurs would declare that assumption fallacious when they contemplate their expenditures for selling and advertising. But economists looking at over-all statistical measures find much support for the assumption that purchases follow income closely.

What is not fully appreciated is that all of these statistical data as to purchase include payment for an energizing or motivating persuasion to buy; and if one examines closely the operation of selling and its effects, the query may arise as to whether the correspondence of available income and purchases is due in considerable measure to the operation of selling persuasion by buyers, not to any automatic behavior response of buyers to increases in income. If one goes a bit farther in his thinking he may well raise the query as to the nature of the causal connection. Does income bring about higher purchases? It can just as well be maintained that the buying desire and action is the cause of income; for desire for goods induces production and productivity, which brings income and enables purchases to be consummated.

While economists tend no longer to follow in detail the thinking of Lord Keynes, the conception of "propensity to consume" still appears as useful in current texts.[7] Defined by Keynes as the "functional relationship between a given level of income . . . and the expenditures on consumption out of that level of income," pertinent discussions point out the concurrent rise of income and consumption, and that the propensity to consume tends to decrease with increase of income.[8]

Keynes and other economists pay little if any attention to the fact that in the statistical data that they use on consumption, there is included the expenditure for selling, for the dynamic influencing of demand. Since possibly as much as 10 per cent and certainly over 5 per cent of total expenditures for personal consumption is currently spent for this function, the probable effects upon demand deserve attention and examination even in macroeconomic study.

The assumption that income causes demand appears to be implicit in a good deal of economic writing. An examination of the actual behavior of buyers tends to support the proposition that demand brings about income rather than the reverse. Desire intensified to the point of being effective is motivation to productive effort from which consumers must therefore secure income. In fact, income in the long run follows demand. It is the desire for what income will furnish, what income will enable

---

[7] See, for instance, Paul A. Samuelson, *Economics* (2nd ed.; New York: McGraw-Hill Book Co., Inc., 1951), p. 262.

[8] John Maynard Keynes, *General Theory of Employment, Interest and Money* (New York: Harcourt, Brace & Co., 1936), p. 90. See also Arthur F. Burns, *The Frontiers of Economic Knowledge* (National Bureau of Economic Research, No. 57, General Series) (Princeton, N.J.: Princeton University Press, 1954), pp. 152–60. D. Hamberg, *Business Cycles* (New York: Macmillan Co., 1951), pp. 190–91, gives another example of searching for causes of what he terms "the constant upward shifting in the community's conception of a minimum standard of living."

people to buy that develops the incentive to work and produce. The propensity to consume is definitely influenced by selling. We know that demand is expansible; that demand is in part a function of knowledge and persuasion; and that selling effort furnishes both this knowledge and persuasion. We do know that demand for some commodities is elastic, for others inelastic. But precisely how much will be purchased without selling persuasion is not known. Nor is it known how much will be bought with a given amount and quality of selling persuasion.

The need for selling effort in its manifold forms grows out of the economic and social objective of high and rising standards of living and the characteristics of human behavior. Typical of widely held opinion on consumer demand is the following:[9]

The origin of economic problems then lies in the infinity of human wants in contrast to the meagreness of economic goods with which to appease them. This scarcity of economic goods, in turn, is due to the niggardliness or resistance of nature, to man's limited knowledge, and to his own lack of endurance or dislike of work.

Hence there arises a threefold conflict: (1) out of man's struggle with his environment, (2) out of man's competition with his fellow men to secure for himself a greater share in the good things of life, and (3) out of man's internal struggle in his own mind between the penny or the cake and beween luxury or leisure.

The "limitless" wants of consumers include wants in all degrees of intensity of desire. Economically important are only a few classes of wants:

a) Wants for necessaries of life. Action must be taken to secure them if existence is to be maintained.

b) Wants for those comforts and luxuries which are strongly desired because of habit, class status, and environmental influences. Action will likely be taken to purchase them and to secure income with which to procure them.

c) Wants for comforts and luxuries beyond the above. Action to buy or to procure buying power will not be taken unless desire is strong and unless purchasing power is available or can be developed at reasonable cost in relation to the desire.

---

[9] Patterson and Scholz, *Economic Problems of Modern Life* (4th ed.; New York: McGraw-Hill Book Co., Inc., 1948), p. 6.

The term "effective" demand, defined as desire or demand plus purchasing power to make the demand effective, is recognition of the fact that purchasing action requires purchasing power. In a simple economy where most people are not far from subsistence levels, the compulsion to work and comply with the requirements imposed by a production system is very clear. In such economies not infrequently the compulsion was as simple as "work or starve." As levels of living advanced beyond the subsistence stage to comfort or even luxury levels, consumer demands for goods and services become less insistent unless desires are intensified by education, social environment, or selling. Desire for progress in living levels ranges from vague desires to wants that lead consumers to work and save in order to satisfy them. But in this field of economic wants and desires, consumers act no differently than they do in other fields of human activity.

The general vague desires of people for goods and services to improve living standards do not have economic significance until action is taken either to increase production or productivity, or the workers' share of production. Action to increase workers' share may be economic pressure to obtain a larger share of current production, within limits of a sound course. But action may be political as pointed out in an earlier discussion[10] in which case the objective may be the redistribution of previously accumulated production, a process which communist and socialist governments have tried.

Any realistic approach to the study of demand in relation to economic progress must arrive at the conclusion that many people do not want high and rising standards of living with sufficient intensity to enable our economic machine to operate and provide the necessary production volume. Consumers' desires must be strong enough to cause them to buy or plan and work to buy in the future. Leadership to stimulate that desire to the point at which it becomes significant is essential.

Selling leadership that is directed toward buying action is not vague and general but very specific and powerful. It must be so if it is to maintain and develop wants and desires for goods

---

[10] Chapters VI and XI.

and services of such intensity that present buying will take place and the foundation for future buying action established. Selling's energizing force on the economy is exerted through its effect on demand. Modern selling, whether personal selling or advertising or other means are used, includes part or all of the following:

1) A determination of consumer or customer needs, utilizing past experience, current knowledge, and the results of careful and comprehensive scientific analysis if available. The available knowledge as to quantitative and qualitative demand characteristics ranges from near zero in its predictive value to a very high degree of probability.

2) As accurate a selection of goods and services to be offered or as nearly correct decisions to make goods and services to meet those wants and needs is a second step. As pointed out earlier, conflicting demands of buyers frequently compel compromise, but the lack of accumulated detailed knowledge of wants and needs involves risks, which are discussed below.

3) Persuasion of the consumer, middlemen, or other ultimate users employs some or all of the means of communication available. Its immediate objective may be only part of the process of getting buying action, for instance, telling prospective buyers that these goods and services are available and that they do meet the needs of the buyers. For products that are new or completely unknown to prospective buyers, it is easy to visualize the need for selling persuasion. It is needed also for products that are established on the market but are unknown to new buyers. It is needed to renew and expand the desire even of those who have used the products previously. Furthermore, persuasive effort must be exerted to the point that agreement is secured to the transfer or ownership of goods on the one hand and the payment for those goods on the other. This is buying action: the consent to purchase coupled with consent to sell under agreed-upon terms.

4) In the best selling practice, the seller follows up to see that the results promised materialize in use. The purpose is to satisfy the buyer, to make him a repeat customer. The seller knows that even if he is only intelligently selfish, he must build

goodwill for future sales, but many sellers wish to have the personal and additional satisfaction of knowing that the selling work has been beneficial to others.

The observer rarely comes into contact with all these steps because most of the work has been done not only by several but by many persons over longer periods of time. For instance, the marketing research necessary to determine lines of development for new products or modification of old ones may have been started months or even years before the product is offered to consumers. Plans for advertising and selling must likewise be completed much in advance. Preparatory and training work must be done before the consumer or other ultimate buyer comes into contact with the selling effort devoted to specific products. The first step therefore in acquiring the bases for economic appraisal of selling is a realistic knowledge of the continued extent and limitations of our knowledge of consumer demand. For the starting point for planning either product or selling activities is that demand. Since the decisions that producers must make in order to plan and operate production machines and processes have to be concrete and detailed, vague abstractions about consumer demand do not suffice.

Although with varied objectives, universities, governmental bodies, and other research organizations of various types have joined in the research and study of consumer demand.[11] Research upon characteristics of demand has been spotty, superficial, and sporadic, particularly when viewed in light of the vast area to be covered. Buyers' behavior, comprising both behavior as consumers and other behavior that affects consumption, comprises a very large section of human behavior. No one would deny that we still have much to learn and that we add new knowledge year by year in these fields relatively slowly. Since a separate chapter is devoted to demand in relation to selling, it is unnecessary to repeat the more detailed discussions of the nature and limitations of sellers' knowledge of demand. Generally, the entrepreneur has been able to obtain little help in making decisions from economists' discussions of demand.

Economic discussions of demand may deal with preference

[11] See Chapter III.

ratings, indifference ratings, marginal utility, or other aspects that relate to the intensity of desire or demand. Economists assert or assume that such differences exist, as indeed they do; but they do not discuss how they are to be determined and measured in such detail as to assist in making business decisions, or how they can be determined by the seller except by the process of offering products for sale and purchase. Thus the seller is expected to take risks using information about demand that is ordinarily faulty or incomplete. A monopolist who produced graphite electrodes for industrial electric furnaces would know every electric-furnace customer and on the basis of rate of operation could compute consumption of graphic electrodes. But even in such a situation, risks would have to be incurred in forecasting business conditions and in forecasting the demand for electro-steel as compared to steel made by other processes. Obviously, both as to the quality and types of products and services needed, the executive is expected to plan and produce products in advance of demand. Furthermore, the time factor involved in production and physical distribution alone is given scant attention, even though within those time periods shifts and changes in demand may occur.

SELLING, PRODUCTION AND PRODUCTIVITY[12]

Production in the modern economy is usually planned and carried on in advance of buying actions; in fact, frequently in advance of any expressed intention to buy the output of a particular producer. Today, production is carried on in the faith that within the necessary time limits, production can be sold to bring the necessary income required for survival and profit. Businessmen who are responsible for disposing of the products of producing enterprise make large expenditures for selling effort, which they would certainly not sanction if they did not hold such effort to be necessary and effective. Any thoughtful businessman must and does count upon the effectiveness of the selling effort put forth on behalf of his product.

---

[12] The influence of selling effort through buying actions upon production and productivity has been discussed at some length in Chapters VI and VII.

The fact that selling causes people to buy more goods in total than they would otherwise permits and encourages greater production. It provides the basis for large-scale operation, which enables the producer to employ to a greater extent the machinery, equipment, and know-how required for economic production. Next, selling effort causes people to buy new or improved products in amounts that permit economical production sooner than they would have done otherwise. Thus selling enables enterprises and innovators to recover more rapidly expenditures and outlays for plant, equipment, and services. More projects can be undertaken and more enterprises started if income can be secured within shorter time periods. The opportunity for survival and growth is increased. Risks of failure for lack of capital are reduced although not eliminated. Risks of failure because offered products are not intrinsically acceptable or too high in price will continue. New products may not fill a sufficient need or may be offered prematurely.

Selling may also cause buyers to prefer certain types of products to other types, thus shifting purchases from one industry to another and possibly shifting allocation of economic resources. The effect of aggressive selling of electric refrigerators, for instance, and the comparative lack of selling effort for ice refrigerators in earlier days hastened acceptance of electric refrigerators and the consequent allocation of resources to the new industry.

In the competition among firms, successful selling tends to expand the production of particular firms, and a decline of competitors' sales or a decline in competitors' position in the industry may take place, but not necessarily so. Firms that find themselves at a disadvantage in the particular field, either because of lack of successful research or high costs, may shift to other fields or go out of business. It is the shift of sales from one firm to another without increase of total production that gives rise to the charge that productive advertising and selling are largely waste, a charge which is examined elsewhere.[13]

Selling does not only support and permit increased production and more economical scales of production. It contributes

---

[13] Cf. Chapter IX, p. 201.

to increased productivity, innovation, technological advance, competition, and selling.[14] Improved management and the wider application of available machinery procedures and processes are influenced both directly by selling and indirectly by the competition of those who have already been convinced that they should adopt such procedures and processes so as to give them an advantage in competition or profits. Improvement of equipment, machinery, and processes does not come automatically as the result of the operation of the profit motive on producers of "end" items. Machine makers also know that their own survival depends on convincing owners and managers of enterprises to adopt the latest processes and to purchase and utilize machinery and other improved production equipment. The speed with which American industry has adopted modern methods of production is as much a tribute to the effectiveness of selling effort as to the inventiveness of those who have produced the machines. As has been pointed out in some detail earlier, the very production of new processes and new machines and the research necessary to devise them can be undertaken on the scale that characterizes our economy only because of the assurance that successful results can be marketed with such speed as to enable enterprise and projects to "pay out" within reasonable time periods.

Producers are human and fallible. They, like consumers, have many general and vague desires for improvement, which will not result in action without leadership. Their knowledge is necessarily limited in view of the great quantity and wide range of technological research and technological change. What a particular executive knows is limited by environment, training, experience, and multiplicity of duties. Consequently, even the most intelligent producers require help. If the metalworking manufacturer uses machine tools, the specific processes for cutting metals such as drills, lathes, broaches, milling machines, and grinders overlap in performance characteristics, so that even technicians sometimes diagree as to the best machines for specific jobs. Ultrasonic, electronic, chemical, and biological processes may all be involved in particular executive decisions.

---

[14] Cf. Chapter VII, p. 153.

The highly specialized single-purpose machine, which can be used only for a limited portion of a complex process, becomes economical only if the quantities to be produced are large. The quantities depend upon the extent of the existing market and the extent to which the market can be expanded by selling effort within a given length of time. Machine makers cannot, any more than producers of consumer goods, wait for the slow processes of buyer initiative, reputation, or influence of social environment to create demand sufficient to warrant low-cost production. Long before such demand would develop, bankruptcy and failure would take place. History furnishes little precedent for the innovator to expect that the world will beat a path to his door in the industrial field any more than in any other field. For instance, the insurance firms with a great deal of clerical work and much record keeping may desire to reduce costs, but the application of a large electronic computor involves far-reaching changes, high expenditure, and great risks. For these as well, the computor manufacturer must provide selling assistance, which is in part informational but in part, also, persuasive.

To repeat, it should finally be understood that it is not only the immediate buying actions of ultimate, intermediate, and industrial consumers but the possibility of influencing the amount, direction, and timing of future buying actions which are important. These factors enter into the decisions of business and industry involving the types and quantity of production, nature of production, methods, processes, and equipment utilized.

SELLING AND PRICES

Precisely because selling effort causes consumers to want goods more intensely, it affects prices. But that statement does not imply that the consumer pays more for what he purchases than he would without selling. The influence of selling upon price is not simple. Selling causes the buyer to increase his valuation, both of the goods he is considering buying and of the attendant services and other parts of the sales offer. Increased purchases and increased sales result, even making allowance for some of the alleged "canceling" effects of competition in selling.

The effect for the individual firms and in general for industries is to increase the volume of production that can be disposed of. Therefore, a more economical scale of operation can be developed—and lower costs. While in some cases the lowering of costs is not sufficient to offset the costs of creating demand, evidence indicates that on the whole the balance is decidedly in favor of large-scale production and the necessary high selling costs.

Prices, insofar as in the long run they are based on costs, are lower than they would be without selling, if we look squarely at the facts. Theoretically, if we assume that demand and purchasing power would rise, or at least remain constant, then prices might be lowered. But the assumption is contrary to observed characteristics of human behavior, whether in the economic sphere, or elsewhere.

The pricing decisions made by the business administrator concern a variety of policies and practices with some of which economists are not concerned. The level of prices at which goods are to be sold must be determined by reference to market conditions and the characteristics, attitudes, and desires of buyers, because the buyer is interested not only in the actual level of payment but also in the terms of sale, the credit arrangements, and the dependability, disposition, and attitudes of the vendor.

The existence of competition is a major factor in prices and pricing decisions. Competition is more or less agressive depending upon the selling effort put forth as well as upon prices and products offered. The seller seeks competitive advantage in various ways. For instance, in his effort to sell products which are similar to those of competitors, he may:

1. Seek to influence buyers to buy on a scale which will cover costs and yield a profit, at market price.
2. Offer prompter or more dependable deliveries, or in other ways differentiate ancillary services without changing price.
3. Actually or apparently differentiate product itself without lowering price, hoping to make more sales with a more desirable product. He may alternatively raise price.
4. By making products available at convenient points, by convenient packaging and devices for greater convenience in use, seek to increase sales.

The business executive need not be content with these measures. He may seek to secure competitive advantage in other ways:

5. By lowering prices below the prevailing market in the expectation that greater volume may enable him to lower costs and obtain a satisfactory profit.
6. By developing superior products and selling them aggressively.
7. By developing new products to fill potential needs and selling them aggressively.

Many of these measures, which have been considered as normal and beneficial practices, have been characterized by economic writers as phenomena of "imperfect" or "monopolistic" competition because they depart from the highly theoretical concept of "perfect" competition.

In our present-day economy, the average seller seeks to dispose of goods and services that he has produced or purchased or has prepared himself to produce or purchase. He must sell in order to survive. So must his competitor. Consequently, as seller encounters competitive seller in the market, each seeks to make initial sales; but more important in most situations is his effort to establish the basis for repeat purchases by the buyer. The seller would ordinarily like to be in a position to sell a product clearly much more desirable than competitors' products at a substantially lower price; but where competition is effective and aggressive and working to achieve similar advantage, great differences in offers tend to disappear.

The application of the term "monopolistic" to the sellers who differentiate or improve their offers and thus make them more attractive to prospective buyers is misleading because of the popular and evil connotations of the word "monopoly." Economists declare they use the words "monopoly" and "monopolistic" without such connotations, but popular usage implies something detrimental to public welfare. Consequently the effort to secure so-called monopolistic advantage is regarded as bad, even though efforts of these types may lead to large social benefits rather than the reverse. Even in extreme cases, where the differentiation is minor or appears to be meaningless, the public may benefit because, as has been pointed out earlier, major improvements in product are often the result of an accumulation of smaller variations. The automobile of 1956 is the cumulative result of thousands of changes extending over half a century.

SELLING, COMPETITION AND MONOPOLY

The relationship of selling to monopoly and the possibility of creating or developing monopoly by selling effort must, however, be considered from other points of view than divergence from some concept of "perfect" competition. Can selling effort create monopolistic control over a market for an individual seller? Has it done so? Is the public interest injured thereby or endangered?

Selling has been presented as a form of leadership. Leadership in other areas of human activity has sometimes led to greater or lesser injury to the welfare of the people. Why shouldn't this happen in selling? What checks are there to prevent selling from creating monopoly?

These are questions that need to be answered.

Selling and advertising can certainly create preferences and even insistence of consumers for the specific products of a particular producer. Generally, selling effort can develop recognition of product and maker. Sometimes, it develops preference, but usually only if the product fulfills the expectations of buyers. Rarely does a product achieve that degree of preference which causes the consumer to insist that he get that particular brand.

It is common observation in many fields that the bulk of the industry business is done by a few firms. While this is regarded in some quarters as undesirable, little has been done to show that such situations have had their origins in the superior service to the public—or that they have achieved position by practices contrary to public interest.

On the whole the small and medium-sized business has available to it the same means of selling as the larger concern. Each hires salesmen, and in competition the salesmen of small companies have the opportunity to excel. The large enterprise may hire more salesmen, make more frequent calls. More formal training may be provided; but the motivation of the small-company salesman and his relationship with executives may be superior.

Newspaper, direct-mail, and other forms of advertising may be adapted to local and regional plans. There are available arrangements whereby smaller regional companies can sponsor radio or television programs at reasonable costs. Only in the case of magazines of national circulation is the medium-sized or small enterprise at some disadvantage. Full-page insertions are expensive, and only by infrequent insertions or small-space advertisement can costs be brought within feasible limits.

It will be obvious, however, that the large company possesses advantages in selling as it may in scale of production, research and development, and financing. The large, well-financed company may by increased selling and advertising hasten the development of a market for new products, because it can hire more salesmen, do more advertising and secure both greater exposure to sale and more aggressive selling than the smaller competitor. But when that is said, it must be kept in mind that the large company as well as the small company must get results in terms of buying action. Neither can wait indefinitely, although the large company may be able to wait longer than the smaller enterprise.

The buying action that measures success in selling is not a foregone conclusion in large-scale selling effort. Many large companies could if so disposed furnish ample evidence. Widely advertised and aggressively promoted products have failed, because buyers' decisions and desires cannot generally be dictated by advertising or selling effort. So long as consumer freedom of choice is a reality and competition remains free, we can expect that firms that become large will have done so because of the consumers' free choice. So long as firms fail because of incompetence of management and lack of service to the public, the results of competitive selling are good. Only when some competitive sellers engage in practices that enable inferior goods and inferior services to displace sellers who can better serve the public must we have recourse to legislative and other controls to curb practices of the unethical and to maintain the realities of workable competition. As a matter of general economic policy, we have in the United States consistently striven to maintain competitive selling effort and have taken the point of view that with all its wastes, competitive selling furnishes dynamic forces that energize and create vastly more than might appear to constitute "waste" or "duplication." Our Sherman, Clayton, and Federal Trade Commission acts and their amendments, and the state antitrust statutes, are useful and on the whole effective influences toward the maintenance of competitive selling.

However, the limitations imposed by legislation, by types of competition or the limitations of the extent of competition by government decree may lead to undesirable forms of competition. For instance, the enforcement of the so-called fair-trade laws to promote resale price maintenance by contract with a single merchant in the state, now on the statute books of more than forty of the United States and supported by federal statute in the McGuire Act, tends to limit competition in "fair-traded" products to competition in the amount of selling effort. Manufacturers, retailers, and wholesalers who wish to compete actively cannot cut prices on fair-traded products without violating the law. They must compete, using more personal selling, more advertising—in short, more selling effort in its various forms. Such limitation of price cutting is undoubtedly more "comfortable" for many retailers who do not care to compete actively for customers or to prove that the margins which they ask and secure for operations are warranted by the services they perform for their customers and prospective buyers.

Inevitably such laws restricting competition tend to create pressures among retailers, wholesalers, and salesmen to serve that portion of the public which prefers lower prices to additional selling effort or prefers less service by retailers, less elaborate establishments, etc., and lower prices to more elaborate services and higher prices. Thus, various tactics are resorted to in order to cut prices even at the risk of violating statutes. The present growth of discount houses in major household appliances and other fields is clear evidence of the strength of this tendency. Furthermore, the changes in policies of department stores during recent years and the changes of policies of distributors and manufacturers, all reflect the deep need of maintaining competition in price as well as in excellence of product and in selling effort. That these are having an effect upon legislators and the courts is evident in several recent decisions and in the pressures to repeal the fair-trade laws.

To repeat, selling and advertising as effective forms of economic leadership can exert influence toward market control. There are, however, few cases where selling effort alone can do more than create and maintain a definite preference so that the final task of getting buying action is greatly facilitated. However, the costs of securing market control have, in the experience of many companies, proved so high as to limit monopolistic operations severely. One specialty food manufacturer who sold 20 per cent of the total market decided he would try for 25 per cent. He increased selling effort to do so and learned to his sorrow that while sales increased, competitors' efforts soon reduced his sales to the earlier level; but meanwhile his higher costs had absorbed all profits and his company showed a loss.

There is clearly a very potent check in the fact that efforts to gain a larger proportion of any market are likely to involve higher costs. Those costs may be more than in proportion to additional sales and profits. Our abilities to forecast the results of selling effort are subject to such wide margins of error that risks are inevitable in any effort to achieve dominating position— risks that both the costs of achieving position and the costs of maintaining it may be excessive.

Finally, the businessman who would like to impose his control of the market may be dissuaded from doing so by fear of adverse publicity or prosecution under law. On the positive side he may, in his desire to attain good corporate citizenship, seek expansion in other fields or other activities.

Competition in selling can exist only if in the endeavor to secure buying action, certain sellers are successful in some cases and competitors are successful in other cases. If the first sellers are successful in selling more than competitors, the competitors may feel hurt and may fail to recover their outlays, with the result that a few may eventually go out of business. In competition, as in any other human rivalry, not everyone can win.

Competition without "hurting" competitors does not exist. But if the losers in a competitive struggle have potentially and actually been able to serve the public better than the winners, then competition has failed. For that we must find remedies. But if losers lose because they have not served, because they have failed to earn sufficient public approval in terms of buying action, then we have the beneficent working of competition and a powerful incentive to improve performance.

SELLING AND THE BUSINESS CYCLE

A high standard of living makes any economy more vulnerable to influences that affect buying and selling, for the characteristic of a high standard of living is the large amount of discretionary spending. When the consumer's living goes beyond subsistence levels, he must exercise choice—make selections—more or less limited by availability of goods, social environment, and other factors. But when standards are high and freedom of choice to buy or not to buy persists, consumer buying action will indicate and even determine basic health of the economy. If consumers in large number refrain from buying, business suffers, employment goes down, incomes therefore decrease, costs go up and business losses mount—effects that in turn lead to further cessation of buying and a downward spiral.

Consumers as a whole in a high-level economy can postpone a large proportion of their buying for months, even years, if they are so inclined. Since disastrous declines in business profits require only a substantial, but far from complete, cessation of buying to start the downward spiral with increasing unemployment, it is evident, therefore, that any such evidence of downward spiral of buying activity and resultant business activity must be stopped as early as possible in the interests of the people.

The attitudes that cause consumers in significant numbers to exercise their right not to buy more than the minimum required for maintenance usually are based upon fear of the future, or anticipation of lower prices, which will enable them to secure added satisfactions when they do buy. Fear of unemployment and fear of loss of income may, of course, spread rapidly over an area of the country. Larger groups may govern their actions accordingly, change their purchase intentions, postpone purchases, and thereby contribute to bring about the result they fear. In a recent minor recession, one large rubber-goods manufacturer gave blanket orders to stop all negotiations on new plants and branches and to undertake no new construction.

How can this fear be allayed so that buying actions continue and so that our economy continues to function in producing and distributing a high standard of living? Obviously there are various types of actions and propaganda that government and business may undertake in order to bring about a change in public sentiment. However, the most pervasive form directed toward restoring confidence is actually selling effort as performed by tens of thousands of persons, each endeavoring to influence others to buy. Selling effort is directed squarely at correcting the maladjustment by securing the buying actions necessary to the restoration of confidence.

It must, of course, be granted that selling effort in times past has not demonstrated that it can eliminate or offset depressions, although it has undoubtedly eased them and has tended to speed up recovery once the turn had taken place. An analysis of the policies and actions of sellers discloses some of the reasons. It is clear that uncertainty as to the resultfulness of the selling effort of a particular firm has led many executives to question the wisdom of increasing the expense involved in increasing selling effort. They have hesitated to add salesmen or to increase advertising when the downward spiral started. They have reasoned on occasion that the effort of a few firms will have little effect in stemming the disastrous decline and that there can be no assurance that enough firms will undertake to intensify selling effort to bring about a change in ideas sufficient to give a better tone to the buying-selling situation. It is not always clear to the businessman that the better policy is in "bucking" a downward movement rather than adjusting to it by cutting down its own expenditures and refraining from new capital expenditure. They would admit that this is a policy that tends to contribute to the severity of the decline, but would say that in the specific instance, it is necessary to look to the preservation of the firm.

The risks of increasing capital expenditure at such a time in order to be ready for later demand may well appear greater to the executive than the price differentials or the preparation for future demand seemed to warrant.

Here again, the influence of sellers may be effective in changing some policies; but it must be recognized that the greatest incentive to purchase new machinery, equipment, and processes comes from a feeling of confidence that the ultimate demand is stable and increasing and that further lengthy declines are not reasonably to be expected.

If fear of unemployment is a major deterrent to buying action, the fact that "sales make jobs" means that selling is, and should be, a major corrective. The salesman who, in this respect, also realizes his potential responsibility, can find both pride and moral justification for doing as good a job of selling leadership as he can. He can take it as demonstrated that, except for brief periods of inventory accumulation and of inventory reduction, the rate of consumer buying tends to determine the employment rate. Employment alone does not determine buying but only employment coupled with the several influences, the most important of which is selling effort. Both actual current selling and the projected results of future selling enter into the producer's calculations as he produces in advance of sale.

The greater difficulty of selling when confronted with unusually adverse attitudes of fear and reluctance to spend, provides a challenge that in past depression periods has been met only inadequately. Here and there, firms have demonstrated what could be done by intelligent and industrious selling. But too often in past practice, the desire to conserve assets has led to a reduction of selling effort at a time when tasks were more difficult and more work was to be done. In the extended sellers' markets of the postwar era, there is much reason to be skeptical as to the probabilities of personal selling at the retail level contributing as much as it should to the stabilization of the economy in the case of a serious recession or depression. A large proportion of salespersons and their superiors have had no personal contact with severe buyers' markets. As a consequence of that fact and of the further fact that in some consumer fields an increasing part of selling has been done by advertising, a lag in meeting the challenge of a depression is to be expected. But a lag of any considerable length would expose the economy, possibly disastrously, to the force of a reduction in buying action that our high standard of living makes possible.

CONCLUSION

Basically, economic theory and business theory have diverged in their attitudes toward selling, not merely because the former tends to be abstract and general while business theory is limited, practical, and often narrow. The assumed characteristics of the behavior of buyers, whether industrial or ultimate consumer, have introduced hypothetical and unreal behavior into study; the businessman has had to learn the basic realities of demand and adapt to them in order to survive.

More and more economists are perceiving this. The modification of demand and price theory introduced by Chamberlin,[15] Joan Robinson,[16] and others, is recognition that earlier assumptions were inadequate as a basis upon which to build sound theory. The increased emphasis upon the study of consumer demand should eventually furnish economists with more concrete data upon which to base theoretical structures. But no theoretical structure will be adequate unless it recognizes that buyer behavior is often neither rational nor logical. To assume that buyers, whether ultimate consumers, or commercial or industrial purchasers, always act to maximize satisfactions might be sound if we assume full knowledge on the part of buyers and if in measuring the satisfactions we take account of the great complexity of human motivation.

Finally, the economic importance of the *intensity* of desire should be stressed. In a high-level economy, unlike a subsistence economy, many people have a choice between more or less

---

[15] Edward Chamberlin, *The Theory of Monopolistic Competition* (Cambridge: Harvard University Press, 1938).

[16] Joan Robinson, *Economics of Imperfect Competition* (London: Macmillan & Co., Ltd., 1933).

leisure, or between more or less work. Many persons could exist without as much work as they actually do, even though what they do in their vocations may involve shorter hours than in earlier periods of their careers. At a given level of technological progress, there is a minimum degree of employment and work needed to produce the goods and services required for high and rising standards of living. If the work input is reduced the rate of rise is slowed down. People need to be motivated to work beyond the minimum required for such minimum standards of living as they insist upon. That motivation comes from various sources, but certainly selling is one of the most potent and most flexible. Custom exerts pressure but can be built up only slowly. Selling must initiate future sales and lower the costs of obtaining buying action.

Chapter XIII

THE PEOPLE WHO SELL

IN PREVIOUS CHAPTERS selling work and the selling function in our economy have been examined. Selling has been viewed as an economic function, as an economic and social force, and, of course, as an essential part of business operation. What about the people engaged in the work of selling? What about those who thrive or fail, about those who serve society and those who suffer from lack of understanding? What about the bad actors, those who fail to serve society and frequently fail to serve even themselves?

Several central facts must be recognized if we are to arrive at some understanding of the people who sell and obtain some comprehension of selling occupations and careers. First, we must realize that there is a very wide range of selling work in terms of the types of work to be done and in terms of the man-power requirements. For selling work as the effort of persons to bring about buying action is performed by men who may range from the house-to-house peddler to the president of a very large corporation who takes part in the negotiations to sell a large contract to the president and members of the board of directors of a large public utility firm. The engineering specialist who works with engineering and production managers of large manufacturers to sell a new process is to be contrasted with the indifferent clerk in the "Five-and-Ten."

The average person tends to obtain only restricted contact with those who sell. He meets retail clerks in stores and in

wayside stations. He may be annoyed by house-to-house salesmen and peddlers. He encounters various forms of advertising,
some good, some bad. He rarely comes in contact with negotiations of corporation officials, of professional purchasing officers whose transactions involve thousands, sometimes even
millions, of dollars. He does not come into contact with the
work of specialized engineers or of physicians who sell for
pharmaceutical firms; of lawyers and teachers who engage in
the sale of specialized products. In fact, he usually does not
come into contact with those who sell to retailers or to wholesalers or to manufacturers. And what is called institutional selling
is unknown to him.

Careers in the advertising part of selling are varied, although
not quite as numerous or varied as in personal selling. Nevertheless, they add to the wide range of types of work involved
in selling effort and to the wide range of careers available to
those wishing to sell.

The easy access to some types of selling work tends to
create a one-sided impression. Almost any person can get into
some type of selling work. But there are types of selling that
require college or even graduate degrees, plus years of experience
and further training in industry, before aspirants are allowed to
approach a prospective buyer alone.

The result of the ease of access is that while rigid selection
prevails in some parts of the selling field, little or no selection
is the rule in others. It is significant that the areas of selling
work with which the average person comes into contact include
most of those to which access is easy and in which standards
of selection are relatively low.

TYPES OF SALESMEN

Careers in Personal Selling

The term personal selling suggests immediately those who
are called salesmen and saleswomen; but titles and jobs are so
varied that many persons not called salesmen are engaged essentially in selling work. In fact, the tendency of some persons

to look down upon selling has led both companies and individuals in many cases to use terms and titles such as service representative, company representative, merchandising counsel, and many others in the endeavor to avoid the simple term salesman. Furthermore, when persons of high corporate rank participate in buying decisions, it sometimes becomes necessary to give titles such as district manager, branch manager, regional manager, or vice-president in order to place the selling representative title-wise on a par with the representatives of the buyer. Many a vice-president is responsible for personal selling to important customers and prospective buyers, and this may constitute his major and perhaps only responsibility. The importance of the work cannot be denied, and vice-presidential status is thus in part recognition of the fact. Since the work of the salesman constitutes the bulk of personal selling work, we shall deal primarily with them, recognizing that some official title in addition to sales representative may be given to many of them.

Those who work as personal salesmen fall into two main groups according to certain government classifications, namely: "Inside" salesmen are those who are stationed at the seller's place of business and wait for prospective buyers to come to them; "outside" salesmen are those who generally solicit custom at the prospective buyer's place of business or home or office. In the first group are included primarily salespersons in retail and types of service establishments to be found in every quarter of our land. Whether proprietors, executives, salesclerks, or other employees, these are the most commonly observed. They range from the fill-in clerk, possibly a young clerk whose interest is only lightly in her work, to the able and mature person who sells products, whether furniture, jewelry, shoes, or garments, knowingly to intelligent customers. Examples of such retail selling, good, bad, and indifferent, are to be found in the millions of retail enterprises in our land. The low average quality of that selling has often been remarked upon. There is much good retail selling, but there is so much that is indifferent and inept that we tend to apply disparaging terms not only to retail selling but to all selling work.

Outside Salesmen: Their Work and Responsibilities

In general, the group of salesmen who approach the prospective buyers at their places of business or elsewhere comprise the most highly trained and the ablest groups engaged in personal selling work outside of executives who are not classed as salesmen. Here are to be found the men who sell consumer goods in quantities to retailers and wholesalers. Here are the sales engineers, the pharmaceutical "detail" men, the specialty salesmen, the manufacturers, the men who introduce new products and many, many others. A more detailed consideration of the salesman's task will be helpful in understanding not only the work of salesmen but the whole selling task for the performance of which our society pays.

THE SALESMAN'S JOB

That the salesman's task is merely one of pleasant conversation accompanied by unlimited expense accounts, a task for which he is paid while other people have to work for a living, is humorous and extreme but not an uncommon misconception. On the contrary, the tasks that the salesman is paid to perform are more numerous and more exacting than is ordinarily comprehended. The basic task of the salesman is one of informing and persuading prospective buyers, of establishing in buyers' minds those attitudes which lead to buying action, either immediately or subsequently. Such work must be in accord with the policies and limitations of the seller and must be done under the general supervision of superiors who are working for the success of the enterprise. In a free-enterprise economy the salesman must usually deal with persons who are subject to the persuasion of other salesmen, whether those salesmen are selling competing products or trying to sell goods to satisfy other needs, the purchase of which consumes a share of the buyers' limited income.

There are, therefore, several sets of intangibles of human behavior with which the salesman must be continuously concerned. First, he must deal with his superiors under whose administration and direction he is expected to sell the employer's products or services. Again and most important, he must study and adjust his actions to the behavior of prospective buyers, both those with whom he has previously had buying and selling relationships and therefore classes as customers, and those to whom he expects to sell for the first time. Buyer behavior is obviously to a considerable extent influenced and may even be governed by factors outside the company's and the salesman's control. In the third place, the salesman is compelled to take account of the behavior of competitors. Competing sellers may make statements intended to influence buyers to buy or not to buy. Furthermore, competitors may have changed prices or products, or taken other actions that affect the salesman in the market in which he operates. Finally, the behavior of his own selling colleagues must at times influence the actions of a salesman. While these colleagues may not be selling to the same prospective buyer, their actions in sales conferences and in field contacts and through supervision of superiors will influence the way in which he performs his selling task. It is clear, therefore, that the range of intangibles with which the salesman must deal is wider than that which represents the common experience of factory or office worker. The work of the salesman, therefore, resembles more the tasks of professional workers in fields of training or teaching, politics, or religion, in which persuasion plays an important part.

Analysis of the Salesman's Job

The tasks for which salesmen are responsible may be analyzed in various ways. One may distinguish among direct selling, indirect selling, and nonselling tasks, defining direct selling tasks as those which involve the solicitation and taking of orders, i.e., the making of sales in the ordinary meaning of the term. The principal form is that of direct solicitation of orders for the employer from those who buy or influence buying. The solicitation of orders, for instance, by a manufacturer's salesman, on behalf of wholesalers, retailers, or others, from those buyers whose orders are then turned over to the salesman's customer for handling—variously termed "missionary," "turnover," or "detail" selling—is another form of direct selling, although the orders are turned over to retailers or to wholesale middlemen to be filled and delivered.

A second group of indirect selling tasks of salesmen comprises a varied array ranging from so-called promotional work in which no taking of orders is involved, to giving management or technical advice, creating ideas and designs for a manufacturer to whom the salesman may be trying to sell a new material or process, putting up displays or posters, or arranging display materials, handling complaints, caring for customer's stock, and many more. Commonly they do not involve taking orders or making sales directly, although the ultimate purpose is to secure profitable sales at lower cost; all involve direct contact with buyers at their places of business.

Nonselling duties are mainly concerned with communication between salesmen and supervisors, with records and the reporting of activities, and with continuous preparation for selling work. The problem of maintaining two-way communication between the salesman in the field and his superiors is a peculiarly difficult one. Many techniques and procedures have been proposed and used to overcome the handicaps to free and easy interchange of information and opinion. All these methods require time and effort on the part of the salesmen. Similarly, reporting and record keeping may vary from an irreducible minimum to an almost intolerable burden of several hours per day added to a full day's selling activity.

In the milk, beverage, tobacco, food, paper, and a few other trades, delivery of goods and collection of accounts usually become a part of the duties of the driver-salesman. And in the field, salesmen may become responsible for gathering credit information and making collections.

And, finally, the salesman's task of keeping informed both in market contacts, through the employer, and in other ways, with regard to the product, prices, new uses or applications, and many other aspects is only a part of the work which the salesman must do to maintain and improve his preparation for the selling task. To the ambitious salesman, no small amount of the task lies in the daily continuous preparation for the job.

The study of customers, the acquisition of knowledge and familiarity with new products, the development of selling techniques to meet new conditions, all reflect the fact that the outside salesman's responsibilities remain stable only in general terms but may vary greatly in their detailed content from year to year and even from day to day. The salesman must further take time to plan his work carefully to get the best results, and since he usually visits the buyer at his place of business, the responsibility of providing transportation, whether by plane, rail, or automobile, consumes some part, often a sizeable portion, of his working day. While some sales managers declare that the only reports they desire are orders, even these expect some oral report as to conditions at the end of each trip. More frequently, reports and correspondence are required of salesmen as a means of keeping in touch with changing market conditions.

The variety of assignments and the conditions under which salesmen operate compel them to work long hours, although it appears that a surprisingly small percentage of the working day is spent in the selling interview itself. Time studies that have been made have revealed that less than half the working day, and often less than one fourth of the salesman's working time, is devoted to actual solicitation of orders in the presence of prospective buyers.

Selling Duties

The most common and in fact the basic selling task of the outside salesman is that of approaching the prospective buyer at his place of business or elsewhere, and presenting his sales proposition in the effort to secure an order.[1] The salesman's selling duties therefore involve essentially the task of securing favorable buying decisions. The decisions involved range in importance from those which involve only pennies to those whose

---

[1] The term "sales proposition" is used because it is intended to cover (1) the product or service offered for sale; (2) the prices, terms of sale, and other conditions of the sales offer; (3) the seller as a source of supply; (4) competitive situations and a comparison of the sales proposition with those of competing companies; and (5) the nature and development of the industry of which the seller is a part.

size is measured in millions of dollars, from quick impulse purchases to negotiations that may extend over a period of years. If the company and its policies are sound, the decision of the buyer to buy is one that is believed to be and actually is favorable to both, so that there will be an inclination to repeat the experience if further need for similar products arises.

The need for facilitating repeat purchases and sales may easily be established in many companies by quick comparison between the cost of initial sales to prospective customers and the cost of subsequent sales to those same customers. The costs of initial sales are often very high. Where it is expected that the first purchase of orders may induce repeat purchasing, the cost of the initial sale has sometimes consumed not only the profit margin but the entire cost of the article sold. If the difficulty of selling could not be lessened by converting one-time buyers into customers or repeat buyers, the cost of distribution would be enormously increased. Product value, product differentiation, technical service, advertising, careful and accurate order filling, tactful correspondence, all play a greater or lesser role in developing goodwill; but the persuasive contact of the salesman as the direct personal representative of the seller is of major importance in most company's programs for development and maintenance of goodwill.

The selling process has been subjected to many different analyses. The task of the salesman has been described as that of creating a series of mental states involving the securing of attention, the development of desire, and the securing of conviction followed by buying action—an analysis that merely indicates a theory of successive mental states preceding buying action. Other psychologists have likewise analyzed the selling process of supplying wants, viewing the salesman's task as that of creating the consciousness of the wants, demonstrating to the buyer the nature of those wants and the relationship of those goods to the satisfaction of that want and expanding that want so as to result in buying action.

In all selling in which the seller takes the initiative, a more prosaic analysis would start with the assertion that the salesman must acquire information about prospective buyers, as members of a group and as individuals, in order that he may know whom to solicit and how to adjust his solicitation to the requirements of prospective buyers. Such knowledge as the salesman possesses regarding the location of buyers must be supplemented by more specific information often made available to him by his superiors. It is hoped that buyers will come to know him favorably and be disposed to purchase from him when he offers his selling proposition.

To be most effective, the salesman must plan his work. In salesmen's training programs, much stress is laid on the various phases of planning and preparation so as to increase the effectiveness of selling, particularly in the selling interview. For the interview is the point at which the salesman with an acceptable sales proposition succeeds or fails in his selling task. Securing access to the buyer for the purpose of interview is obviously essential and may on occasion present hurdles in making initial sales or in regaining lost customers; but obviously access to buyers is enormously facilitated once the seller is favorably known and once purchases have been made satisfactorily from the seller. The interview itself furnishes the salesman with the opportunity to present his offer, directly and personally, to the buyer and to make the sale. If presentation is made at a time when the buyer is in a position to purchase, successful representation means that the sale has been made.

The range of ease or difficulty of bringing about the successful conclusion of selling effort is so wide that only with considerable experience can one appreciate the problems to which this variation gives rise. In periods of shortages or active demand, the task of the salesman may cease to be that of inducing buyers to purchase; it may become rather that of allotting an inadequate amount of product to insistent customers. Persuasion under such circumstances may become the task of the buyer who wants goods. The seller's work may be that of persuading the buyer to accept with goodwill the limited amounts that can be allotted. In order to build for the future and to deal fairly with customers and prospective buyers, the salesman under such circumstances has to exercise judgment and convince customers that he is treating them fairly and avoiding favoritism.

The normal situation in the American economy has been that of a buyers' market in which substantial competition existed among sellers in attracting the favor of buyers. Following a decade of buyers' markets, the war brought sellers' markets to the fore. In the postwar period, we have had a recurrence of sellers' markets in various industries, even after it appeared that the sellers' market era was drawing to a close.[2]

Indirect Selling and Nonselling Tasks of Salemen

The indirect selling tasks that salesman are expected to perform are intended to increase the effectiveness of direct selling work, decrease its costs, and increase the stability or persistence of sales volume. Assisting a purchaser to make the best use of a purchase, inspection of complex purchases, sometimes with installation of equipment and assistance in planning resale of the salesman's product, making displays, and many other types of work, tend to create favorable attitudes and facilitate future sales. Such tasks may be made a definite part of the salesman's assigned task because, in the experience of the employer, it has been demonstrated that they possess distinct value as a part of the promotional plan. In other situations, salesmen may perform them on their own initiative because they have found them to be effective. The sales engineer selling equipment may find that a part of his task, in order to keep the product sold and in order to furnish a basis for additional sales, is to serve

---

[2] The businessman of experience will realize that in any discussion of buyers' and sellers' markets, it cannot be said that every market is a buyers' market or that every market is a sellers' market. The terms really mean that for a large number of products, the condition is either that of high demand and short or no more than adequate supply, or the reverse, a condition of low demand and high supply, so that the tone is given by either the predominant position of the sellers or the position of the buyers. Nevertheless, in a buyers' market, there are likely to be some products which enjoy a sellers' market; and in a sellers' market, some products in which the buyers enjoy the preferred position. Thus, at any time there are some markets in which sellers are compelled to exercise their ingenuity where, for instance, allotment is not the order of the day; and other markets in which buyers do not call the tune for the sellers.

as "trouble shooter," or to train operatives or advise as to changes in product to make the fullest use of equipment. The "detail" man in the pharmaceutical trade calls upon physicians who, if convinced, prescribe the new pharmaceuticals. To catalogue the variety of such tasks would be impossible, but various case studies cited below furnish further illustration.

Patterns of Salesmen's Duties

No salesman performs all the duties that have been mentioned. In various industries, patterns or combinations of duties tend to develop so that it is possible to distinguish a limited number of marketing patterns, which cover a substantial portion of our selling organizations. In the recent survey, the more common patterns were outlined as follows, particularly in their relationship to the place of salesmen's work with reference to those patterns:

House-to-house canvassing.

Selling consumer products of high unit value like automobiles, major appliances, etc., direct to final users.

Selling various products like milk, laundry, etc., on retail truck or wagon routes.

Selling life insurance.

Selling securities or liability, fire, and other forms of insurance.

Selling consumer goods on wagon route to retailers for resale, combining delivery, order taking, and other selling functions.

Selling grocery or drug products, etc., etc., to retailers and wholesalers for resale on established routes, including in duties routine merchandising service like display help, etc.

Selling to retailers or dealers, combined with missionary or detailing work to induce use, specification, prescription, etc.

Primarily missionary work to obtain use, specification, display, etc.

Specialized selling of consumer products to retailers and wholesalers or distributors for resale, with responsibility for narrow line of products, and emphasis on retail sales program development.

General line selling of consumer products to wholesalers and retailers for resale, with responsibility for wide product lines.

Selling advertising service, space, printing, employment service, and other business services.

Selling office equipment, supplies, and similar products requiring technical training for design of systems and installations.

Selling equipment, supplies, and materials to hotels, hospitals, restaurants, public institutions, schools, etc.

"Sales engineer"—selling machinery and equipment of high unit value to manufacturers or processors, where chemical, electrical, engineering, etc., knowledge is required for design, installation, and "trouble shooting."

"Sales engineer"—selling supplies and materials where similar technical knowledge is required to give adequate service.

Selling industrial equipment, supplies, and materials where less technical education is required, but great familiarity with trade customs, markets, and personalities is essential.

Selling industrial equipment, supplies, and materials to dealers and distributors for resale.

These patterns frequently overlap. Companies selling many products or to varied groups or markets may display several of these patterns, sometimes within the same line but more frequently varying according to the lines for which the salesman is responsible. A company manufacturing both industrial and consumer goods may have different sales forces, each of which shows a different pattern of selling duties for its salesmen. To make these patterns of duties more concrete, several more detailed examples are given.

The Westcott Company, a large petroleum organization, analyzed the activities of a small group of salesmen to ascertain the apportionment of time to products and customers. The products which Westcott sold were primarily in the automotive trade, consisting of premium, standard, and third grade gasoline, various grades of motor oils and greases, a wide line of accessories sold to service station, garages, and similar outlets. Gasoline, kerosene, and oil were sold to farmers and a number of commercial users, among whom were department stores, contractors, and transportation systems. In addition to selling, the company's general salesmen were each in charge of one or more bulk plants and spent considerable time checking stocks and records and supervising plant operation. General salesmen were further classified as "country" or "city" depending upon the area in which they worked. Industrial products, such as lubricating oils, selling to dry cleaners, manufacturers, and others, were sold by a separate group of salesmen. The results of this study point out the types of duties for which the salesman is held responsible and give one a general idea of the apportionment of time to those duties.

Time Analysis for Typical Week
General Country Salesmen
Average working time per salesman........................47.8 hours

Distribution of Working Time

Clerical and supervisory	15 hours	31.4%
Travel time	14	28.9
Time with customer	19	39.7
	48 hours	100.0%

Clerical	%	*Travel Time*	%
Clerical time*	13.7	On customer calls	20.9
Bulk plant supervision	7.1	On other business	8.0
Other office time†	6.5		28.9
Meetings	2.4		
General	1.7		
	31.4		

Time with Customer	%	*Other Time with Customer*	%
Commodity selling‡	14.4	Collections	1.4
Other time	25.3	Lease arrangements§	1.9
	39.7	Service station appearance	2.1
		Advertising	2.2
		Equipment	4.2
		Waiting	4.5
		General time	9.0
			25.3

Type of Customer

	% of Time	
100% Westcott dealer	83.5	
Service station leased to dealer	7.5	
Competitive dealer	6.8	
Commercial account	1.8	
Farmer	0.4	100.0%

* Clerical time indicated that time which the salesman spent in making out daily reports and other routine work.

† Other office time was really a catch-all including time in the office rather than that actually spent in dealing with routine clerical matters.

‡ Of the total time spent with customer, only 36.4% was concerned with commodity selling.

§ Under this heading was included time with dealers in contracting new leases, renewing leases, etc. Salesmen were expected to take care of signing of leases as well as details connected with their execution.

A manufacturer of toilet preparations in his effort to improve the effectiveness of his field men carried the study of the salesman's job into greater detail and conducted a time and duty analysis of the work of several salesmen with the help of representatives of Ohio State University. Here are the results of a breakdown of selling functions together with average times secured on time and duty analysis.

Breakdown of Selling Routine		Average Time in Minutes
Selling time total..................................		10.13
Printed matter................................	3.37	
Samples.......................................	2.62	
Printed matter and samples.........................	.62	
Without material (or stock checking)..............	3.52	
Nonselling time total..............................		54.83
Display installation.............................	.53	
Instructing clerks...............................	.31	
Awaiting interviews.............................	6.07	
Broken interviews...............................	7.08	
General conversation............................	7.93	
Miscellaneous*................................	8.93	
Travel..	23.93	
Total interview minutes†.........................		64.96
Idle time‡......................................	7.36	

* Writing orders, phone calls, waiting for wholesale salesmen to make sales, gassing car, etc.
† Total interview time consisted of the time elapsed between the salesman's arrival at one store and his arrival at the next.
‡ Meals and personal time.

The interest in the chart is not the precise timing or the amount of time taken by interviews but rather the list of things the salesman did within the interview as an example of the task performed by the salesman.

A well-known producer of several widely advertised proprietary drug products, selling through wholesale druggists to 53,-000 retail drug outlets, employed 85 salesmen responsible for soliciting wholesalers as well as selected retail drugstores. Recognizing the impact of this advertising on the salesman's job, sales executives asserted:

Where producers were advertised to the consumer as heavily as their major brands, the salesmen's influence on sales was largely limited to two functions: first, they obtained intensive distribution in channels appropriate to reach the consumer; and second, they obtained coordination with consumer advertising by obtaining point-of-sale display cooperation from the retailers, considered of special importance by the executives. However, obtaining good retail display cooperation was very difficult inasmuch as competition for display space in the retail drugstores was intense. Satisfactory results required continuous attention and effort on the part of the salesmen. It was relatively easy for supervisors to check on the adequacy of distribution in retail stores, but the quality and quantity of the display job in those stores was much harder to determine. A salesman might successfully persuade a retail druggist to place a good display in favorable location, but three days later it might well be emptied and moved into the back room, filled with competing products, or moved to less favorable location in favor of a competitor salesman's more recent persuasive efforts. Consequently, suitable display was a matter that required continuous effort by each salesman whenever he entered a drugstore.

But, by way of contrast, here is the description of a salesman's duties of a competing drug product manufacturer:

Salesmen have three specific functions: (1) selling to wholesale druggists; (2) selling to chain and department stores; and (3) writing orders for retailers which were turned over to the company's distributors (turnover business). The bulk of the man's time is taken up by the promotion of "special deals" which were offered by the company successively for periods of three or four months. Whenever the sales department planned a new deal, the sales manager called a meeting at the home office which was attended by the entire sales force. The deal was explained, men were given promotional material and literature and were briefed on sales approaches and selling points which might be used in announcing the offer to the trade. The salesmen then returned to their territories and solicited all wholesale customers, explaining the new deal and making arrangements to hold similar meetings with the wholesaler's salesmen. After the men had organized schedules of appointments with wholesalers, they concentrated on selling to chains, department, and retail drugstores. In the latter case, the job was to convince buyers of the value of the deal so as to pave the way for the wholesaler's representatives. The company sold direct to chains and department stores.

Salesmen sold these deals to the wholesaler first, covering in detail with the latter's salesmen the methods of promoting the deals to the retailer and his clerks. He next stocked the wholesaler with sufficient goods to start the drive, then proceeded to show the wholesale salesmen, demonstrating with two or three of the accounts in each man's territory, how to sell the offer. After the drive was under way and all wholesalers and their representatives had been thoroughly instructed, the company's salesmen devoted their time to direct (chain and department store) and turnover business.

A prominent producer of sterling silver flatware and hollow ware, traveling forty salesmen, emphasized that the problem which the company encountered in compensation related to the nature of the salesmen's duties and to the results it desired.

The sales manager had found that sterling flatware was the easiest for salesmen to sell and that the salesmen tended to neglect the hollow ware line because it required different techniques and was likely to encounter more sales resistance from retailers because of the problem of financing and of giving space to the large number of types and styles of bulky pieces. The salesman could carry and easily present a sample case showing the flatware to a prospective purchaser, show leaflets illustrating patterns and table settings, and discuss the effectiveness of the company's national advertising to the consumer. In contrast, to present the hollow ware line the salesman had to travel with trunks of carefully packed samples and was required to rent a display room in a hotel and spend some days arranging to have buyers for his retail accounts view the line away from their own places of business. Furthermore, the hollow ware did not readily lend itself to presentation or promotion through printed leaflets or through advertising. Although some salesmen seemed to show greater interest and skill in selling one or the other of these product lines, and specialization of salesmen had been considered, the executives continued to have each salesman handle both product lines in his exclusive territory.

A prominent fountain pen manufacturer declares that the salesman's job does not consist merely in selling fountain pens to dealers:

It consists primarily of selling a program to the dealers with whom he works. From that point of view, it is to the salesman's benefit in the long run to avoid overstocking. Salesmen are responsible for keeping inventory control books for each dealer or supervising the stock and the balance of stock on hand. Returned goods if any are charged back to the salesman, with commissions figured at the same rate at which the salesman was credited. The company accepts no returns; although formerly there was a very liberal policy, the abuses of that policy impelled the adoption of the rigid reverse policy.

Turning to industrial products, the Williston Textile Machinery Company illustrates in more detail the responsibilities of an industrial equipment salesman:

The Williston company, located in Lowell, Massachusetts, employed about 2,000 people. Machinery and supplies were sold direct to textile weaving mills. Its potential customers were a readily definable group of companies, well known to the executives and salesmen of the company, and concentrated regionally in the New

England area and certain Middle Atlantic, South Atlantic, and southwestern states. The company maintained three branch offices with warehouse facilities for supplies in Philadelphia, Pennsylvania, and Charlotte, North Carolina. The sales force consisted of about 15 salesmen. Several were assigned to work out of each of the branch offices. In the home office were four general supplies salesmen and four senior men who had developed specialties in some of the more complex technical areas, such as machinery for weaving silks, narrow fabrics, ducks, worsteds, and carpets. The executives tried to develop salesmen with as general technical background and ability as possible, so that any salesman would be able to discuss the problems of any customer. However, the technical problems involved in the fields mentioned above were unique so that a certain degree of specialization was absolutely necessary. The general salesmen in the branch offices could call on the home office specialists for assistance in particular cases. By keeping the specialists in the home office, the salesmen who were most likely to be asking for special designs and modifications on the company's machinery to meet particular customers' needs were kept in close contact with the executives and the engineering department. The West Coast was covered by one salesman, a commission agent who had worked for the company in the East for some time before the war but desired to settle on the West Coast.

The more complex pieces of equipment manufactured by the company were largely built to the specifications of each customer. Although the engineering and research of the company might develop ideal specifications and dimensions for the various parts of a loom for most economical run of a particular type of cloth, these new models would not necessarily be the most efficient for the particular conditions existing in the mill of a customer. This mill was probably equipped with machines at an earlier date with sizes and specifications that had been superseded by more recent improvements. Even though it was proved that this mill would have lower costs if it replaced all its machinery with the latest models, nevertheless for replacement purposes or for minor expansion, machines corresponding in size and specifications to the older ones in the mill had to be supplied. In addition, the mill practice was determined to a great extent by prejudice and habit rather than laboratory research. Each mill superintendent had his own deeply rooted ideas of what type of equipment was suitable for running particular cloths. Therefore, the Williston company was frequently required to produce a machine which would meet some of the specifications of the oldest machines in a particular mill.

The sales force was closely integrated into the organization of the company, both in the manner in which the men performed

their jobs and in administration. An important part of the salesman's job was to understand the conditions existing in the mills of
the company's customers. The salesman was the liaison between the
company's engineering and production and his customers' needs
and plans for replacement and expansion. The salesman had to make
his recommendations to customers for new and replacement equipment in the light of the particular conditions set by the existing
machinery of a customer rather than pressing aggressively to sell
the latest developments in efficient sizes or cost-saving equipment.
The salesman had to have a very wide technical background, a
thorough knowledge of the traditions and practices of the industry
and the jargon of the trade. He had to have a real understanding
of the customers' special requirements and their reasons for them.
Furthermore, he had to have an attitude combining pride and loyalty in his company with the desire to be of real service to the mill
operators. Working as a salesman in this field had to be a lifelong
occupation in order to develop the background of experience required for the solution of the sometimes baffling technical problems.
An extremely important part of the salesman's job was to get to
know the men owning and operating the mills. Except for supplies,
a salesman might go for a long period of time without completing
any sales to a particular customer. When sales of machinery were
consummated at irregular intervals, they were likely to involve very
high dollar figures.

Although also requiring highly trained men, many of them
engineers, the Hillsdale Company, selling a diversified line of
cutting tools through distributors and dealers, and special tools
direct to manufacturing concerns, describes salesmen's tasks in
somewhat different terms:

Their work required them to have a theoretical knowledge of
the stresses developed in various types of cutting tools and a working knowledge of shop practice, strength and properties of materials, and speeds and feeds for cutting all types of materials under
many conditions. Such information was needed as a service to the
company's customers and as a protection for Hillsdale's good reputation. The salesman was frequently called upon to represent the
company as a trouble shooter in situations where Hillsdale's products seemed to fail to give proper performance. Frequently the
well-informed salesmen ascertained that the tools were being improperly used, that the wrong type of tool was being applied to
the material at hand, or that speeds or feeds were incorrect.

In addition to his job as a technician the company's executives
regarded each salesman as the sales manager in his own territory

charged with obtaining the maximum effective sales efforts for
Hillsdale products. Approximately 80% of the company's sales was
through distributors and dealers. During the decade preceding
World War II the company had transacted business with many exclusive distributors and had followed the practice of selling direct
to manufacturing companies rather extensively. In 1940 the sales
policy was directed toward supporting and building up the company's distributors. By 1947 the company had built up a group
of 200 selective distributorships, very few on an exclusive basis.
Where possible, orders from manufacturing companies were referred to Hillsdale distributors. Direct sales to manufacturers were
declining, and by 1950 the bulk of sales was made to and through
mill supply firms. Each salesman devoted a considerable amount
of time to the distributors in his territory, helping their salesmen to
become well versed in the technical problems to make them realize
the profit opportunities in selling Hillsdale tools. The salesmen conducted sales meetings for the distributors, traveled with their salesmen, and occasionally helped solve technical problems for their
customers. The Hillsdale salesmen found that their products had to
compete with many other types of products for the mill supply
salesmen's time and attention.

Finally, we have the illustration of the Moffat Feed Company,
producing feeds for farm use, which were sold throughout the
United States to farm supply dealers through a sales force of
350 men:

The salesmen, paid salaries plus bonuses for quota achievement,
were expected to function as managers of their sales territories and
were held responsible for maintaining and stimulating the tonnage
flow of feeds in every active market. The company followed a policy of direct sale to selected farm supply dealers who in turn sold
feeds to farmers and livestock feeders in their areas. The company's
salesmen paid particular attention to developing the sales volume
of the dealers in their territories by maintaining personal contact
with the leading farmers with substantial amounts of livestock,
cattle feeders, and poultry farms.

Much of the Moffat salesman's work was educational, providing
his dealers with information about best feeding techniques and data
showing the results expected from Moffat products. He worked to
eliminate misconceptions about feeds and animal feeding, such as
effect of variations in color and texture on nutritive quality. He tried,
by personal solicitation, to have selected key feeders in each area
follow feeding programs developed by Moffat research.

Although Moffat salesmen did not require extensive background in formal education, they had to know farming and in particular had to become experts in animal feeding. An important factor in the success of the company's leading sales territories was the ability and willingness on the part of the salesmen to understand and serve farmers and rural dealers. The salesmen had to show good judgment in the selection of suitably located dealers with the facilities and personal ability to handle volume feed business. They assisted the dealers by advising in store management and training of their sales personnel in addition to providing information on products and feeding and the wide range of promotional materials and direct mail advertising pieces developed by the company to help dealers tie their selling efforts in with the radio, farm journal, and outdoor advertising of the company.

Salesmen's contracts, specifying the details of legal relationships between employer and salesmen range from simple oral arrangements to elaborate written contracts. It might be expected that since compensation and other arrangements are spelled out carefully tasks which salesmen were to perform would be similarly described. Examination of pertinent clauses of a number of such contracts is disappointing in that respect; for both employers and legal counsel, recognizing the difficulty of describing and specifying duties in detail, have taken refuge in general statements, including specific restrictions only as to territory to be covered, products to be sold, the treatment of credits, trade-ins, and prices, and the like. Union contracts are even less illuminating although the informed reader of such contracts can draw some inferences as to the salesmen's task. The main provisions are those which relate to wages and hours, vacation, holidays, notice of leaving or discharge. What the salesman must do in his selling work is not described.

CAREERS IN SELLING:
FACTORS TO BE CONSIDERED

Even the inadequate descriptions of the work of those who sell, coupled with the analyses which have been the subject of preceding chapters, indicate that selling careers offer the possibility and even probability of social contribution. Those who sell can take satisfaction in knowing that they do necessary work and that in the absence of fraud or misdirection they contribute to the welfare of the people. Sometimes that satisfaction will be much more concrete and definite in the very obvious improvement and increased welfare of specific customers. Unfortunately, sales work has not been attractive to many young men and women because it appeared to lack status. Public opinion and the opinion of friends seemed to class it as a second-rate occupation in terms of its contribution to society. Because of that opinion men and women who would have derived great satisfaction and been able to make great contributions have been dissuaded from considering it.

It follows from the descriptions of types of selling that the training required for selling careers runs the gamut from no training, even of a general sort, to the highest professional training. For some selling jobs, a common school education suffices. For others a high school diploma is needed. But for more and more selling jobs at least a college degree is required and often specialized training in preparation for an advanced degree. Some firms require fullfledged pharmacists or physicians. Others make it a point to hire only engineers, those with advanced degrees. Still others require legal training.

In addition to the general preparatory training, which aspirants to sales careers must usually provide on their own, firms provide more or less elaborate training programs for which they spend each year great sums of money and long periods of time. It is not uncommon to hear the statement from businessmen that it costs them $5,000 to $10,000, or even $20,000, to get a salesman ready to deal with customers. The extent of training given by particular firms varies from the very brief orientation on an informal basis given to the experienced salesman when he joins a new firm, to an elaborate system of training courses for trainees and apprentices, who work in various portions of the organization and then are assigned for further training.

The conditions under which salesmen work vary from those of considerable luxury to hardship and privation. The well-paid successful salesman of a large company may on his work live in fine hotels, eat good food, and return to his headquarters frequently. One outstanding characteristic, however, is that for many types of outside salesmen's positions, it is necessary to be away from home or headquarters' points for considerable periods of time. Some outside salesmen can reach their homes every evening. Others are compelled to be away for several days at a time. Still others must be away for weeks or months on selling trips. It is particularly true in seasonal industries that the extent of absences from home base becomes greater and the pressure more intense to complete selling trips while seasonal buying is continuing. Nevertheless, with the increasing density of markets, the territories and customers to be covered by the individual salesman have been reduced so that long absences have today become the exception rather than the rule of an earlier day. The speed of air travel and the flexibility of the automobile have changed salesmen's routes and plans. To some men the hardship of being away from home for longer periods is a compelling one, and at times refusal to travel may bar certain men from interesting and remunerative careers. The salesman's attitudes are influenced by family conditions and attitudes of the salesman himself, as well as by his general social environment. The importance of right attitudes to successful selling can hardly be overestimated.

The opportunity to travel and to meet many different people is considered by many salesmen to be one of the most alluring aspects of selling work. The constant and repeated contacts with prospective buyers have led not only to fuller knowledge of territories and markets but also to widened acquaintanceship and even strong friendships. Many a salesman begins to look upon his old customers as old friends, although if he is wise, he realizes that such friendships cannot be maintained on a reciprocally advantageous basis unless the salesman continues to sell products that are mutually beneficial to the buyer and the seller.

No prospective career can be properly described without reference to hardships and dangers, which may be a part of the work. The hardships of selling and particularly in outside selling are likely to be those that relate to irregular hours of work and to the discouragements that come from failure to make sales, whether those failures are the result of the salesman's own deficiency or are caused by factors not under the control of the salesman himself. As pointed out before, selling is leadership, and leaders are not uniformly successful in inducing everyone to follow.

From the standpoint of compensation, selling occupations again cover the range from very low paid to the highest paid in the country. Many salesmen earn as much as leading executives in principal companies, but at the other extreme are those salespersons who get no more than minimum wage rates; and more than that, there are some so-called salesmen on a commission basis who fail to make even that minimum wage because they are in unprotected areas, possibly as independent contractors. A study made some years ago of the average compensation of outside salesmen places the figure at $5,400 with industrial and wholesale salesmen securing several hundred dollars more, and less demanding types of salesmanship earning about $5,000.[3] It is generally agreed that these figures have been advanced on the average by 15 per cent to 20 per cent in the five years following the study so that the average of the high-paid groups, excluding specific industries in which the averages are very high indeed and excluding those salesmen who receive little or nothing, we arrive at a figure approaching $7,000 with over $6,000 as the general average for outside salesmen.

Many salesmen are paid on a straight salary basis. This is particularly true of inside salesmen, as well as some groups of outside salesmen; but more outside salesmen and some inside salesmen are paid on an incentive basis, which includes some fixed income with a commission or bonus based upon performance. In some companies there is no upper limit on compensation, and able salesmen have advanced their own earnings to a point exceeding that of top executives of the company. In other cases there is a range within which compensation tends to fall.

---

[3] H. R. Tosdal and W. W. Carson, *Salesmen's Compensation* (Boston: Division of Research, Harvard Graduate School of Business Administration, 1953), Vols I and II.

In addition to monetary compensation, which in selling compares favorably with any other field requiring comparable training and experience, there are nonfinancial rewards, such as satisfaction that comes from selling good products which benefit the prospective buyers, and friendships developed in the accomplishment of a difficult task. Within companies the status of the successful salesman is frequently an enviable one; and since selling is even more necessary in periods of poor business than in periods of easy buying, the security offered by selling positions is much greater than is commonly believed.

Selling careers, particularly those in line selling, tend to furnish a type of experience in dealing with people and in getting things done by and through people that is very useful in management as well as in selling itself. As a consequence, salesmen are frequently promoted to become branch managers, district managers, or sales managers. It is necessary, however, clearly to recognize the fact that management ability and ability to make specific sales of specific products are not identical. The salesman who has management ability is helped by his sales ability; but the salesman who does not possess management ability will still find room for growth in meeting the challenge of selling work because of the range of difficulty of selling tasks and the range of compensation. Selling careers, therefore, do not depend purely on promotion to managerial rank. Expanding income does not require executive status. For, as has been pointed out earlier, the incomes of many salesmen are no smaller than the incomes of those in high managerial ranks.

It is significant that in some of the recent studies of the origins of top executives of companies, more come up through selling than through production or any other part of the business enterprise.[4] This is not surprising if we remember that as men rise from echelon to echelon of business command, they have less and less need of highly technical knowledge and more need for those skills that have to do with the management of men, with administration, often defined as "getting tasks

---

[4] See *Fortune*, November, 1952, for a study of the origins of 900 top executives from 250 largest industrial companies, 25 of the largest railroads, and 25 of the largest public utilities.

done through human beings." The transferability of selling experience in its broadest aspects of influencing people to action is without question one of the great arguments for entering selling careers, even on an experimental basis. For careers in management in the selling field itself, field sales experience is essential, because neither through books nor through formal educational processes can one get that command and "feel" of what is required in order to make selling leadership effective. Only actual responsible contact of the salesman with actual buyers can be reasonably expected to furnish that background.

EXECUTIVE POSITIONS IN SELLING

The direction of selling operations and the supervision of selling personnel require administrators who not only understand selling in personal contact but who are competent to make decisions covering the whole range of problems that must be solved in order to achieve satisfactory business results.

Problems in sales management vary from broad problems to detailed ones, from unusual nonrecurring problems to those which are perennial, those which constantly harass the sales executive. For purposes of study, however, these problems may be grouped into a few broad divisions, although any grouping is bound to encounter objections from some point of view. At the best, such classification is artificial and serves only as a convenience in organizing work.

While companies vary widely in their organization and practices, sales and marketing executives are continuously confronted with more or fewer problems involving the following:

1. What to sell; merchandising policy and merchandising organizations.
2. To whom shall products be sold? Market channels; market research and analysis.
3. At what prices and terms shall products be sold? Prices and credit terms.
4. Market and sales planning. Total sales task, its determination and breakdown. Sales estimates, territories, quotas.
5. How shall the product be sold? Sales methods; sales promotion; sales campaigns.

6. By whom is the work to be done? Sales organization; management of sales force.
7. Planning and control of sales operations.

Sales departments vary widely because among sales and general executives there is a lack of any common conception of the functions of such a department. In some firms the sales department is given control of advertising; in others not. Some firms give the sales executive control of credits; others accord him advisory control; still others permit no control whatsoever. In some firms the sales department takes what the production department chooses to turn out; in others the production department makes what the sales department orders. In relatively few firms is definite and effective provision made for co-operation between production and sales interests in order to produce wanted goods with maximum manufacturing efficiency. Sales organizations vary, likewise, with respect to their interest in the handling of orders and shipments of goods, both as to policy and as to method. The function of delivery seems to have been neglected as compared with the pure selling functions.

However, these differences in conception of the functions of the sales department on the part of executives do not explain the wide differences in sales departments. In the variations between sales departments, much is to be attributed to the necessity of adjusting organizations to the capacities, prejudices, and desires of individuals in positions of authority. Such adjustment is apparently much more easily effected where there is no clear-cut conception of the extent or limitations of the proper grouping of activities. Under such conditions, titles may be loosely given and, accordingly, will not indicate the same offices or same responsibilities in different organizations.

Nevertheless, selling and the direction of selling, require the broadest abilities and command generally higher rewards than staff functions. To direct and inspire sales leaders so that in widely scattered, possibly country-wide or even world-wide, areas they work successfully to persuade buyers to take buying action, requires an increasingly higher type of ability because with supervisory functions are combined responsibility for planning and research and for all the elements of the marketing task.

The chief marketing executive must plan and delegate and in general perform functions similar to those of other departmental executives. But he, together with the sales manager, the advertising manager, and all those who are concerned directly with getting buying action, have to work with more intangibles and more unknowns than their colleagues in production or financial positions.

CONCLUSION

Even a limited recital of the types of work involved in selling and advertising would be beyond the scope of this volume. Standard works in the field of retailing,[5] wholesaling,[6] and sales management[7] and advertising[8] can be consulted by anyone who has special interest. The United States Department of Commerce has also published a thin volume, *Opportunities in Selling.*[9]

The study of demand has enlisted the services of market researchers, psychologists, and statisticians. The planning of products for the market uses these plus technically trained chemists, physicists, engineers. Sales planning may call for the employment of the talents of economists, accountants, and statistical experts. Actual selling may use all of these plus many others. Thus, in those services which come under the authority

---

[5] D. J. Duncan and C. F. Phillips, *Retailing*, 4th edition. Homewood, Illinois, Richard D. Irwin, Inc., 1955. Paul Nystrom, *Marketing Handbook*, New York, Ronald Press, 1948. C. W. Barker, I. D. Anderson, and J. D. Butterworth, *Principles of Retailing*, 3rd edition. New York, McGraw-Hill Book Company, Inc., 1956.

[6] T. N. Beckman and N. H. Engle, *Wholesaling, Principles and Practice.* Revised edition. New York, Ronald Press, 1949.

[7] D. M. Phelps, *Sales Management*, Homewood, Illinois, Richard D. Irwin, Inc., 1951. H. H. Maynard and H. C. Nolen, *Sales Management*, N. Y. Ronald Press, 1950.

[8] Otto Kleppner, *Advertising Procedure*, 4th edition. New York, Prentice-Hall, Inc., 1950. C. H. Sandage, *Advertising, Theory and Practice.* 4th edition. Homewood, Illinois, Richard D. Irwin, Inc., 1953.

[9] U.S. Department of Commerce, *Opportunities in Selling.* Washington, Government Printing Office, 1948.

of chief marketing and sales executives are many kinds of work and many kinds of specialized positions where volume of work warrants. Clearly, the crucial responsibility of such chief executives is getting sound buying action. To lose sight of that is to run the risk of decline and eventual failure.

The impending need for selling talent and ability is being emphasized in many quarters. Projections of possible rates of production of goods and services, as we develop ways and means of using electronic and other control devices and apply atomic energy to peacetime purposes, only a short time ago would have appeared fantastically large. But they will add to our levels of living only if buying actions keep up with development. Only then can production be continued and expanded in a democratic economy. The essential buying actions will require more and better selling. And to the young man who possesses the spirit and the ability to tackle selling as a career, is offered a great challenge and corresponding reward, not only materially but also in the consciousness of doing a valuable work for society and of having contributed to the preservation of economic freedom.

Chapter XIV

SUMMARY AND CONCLUSION

I

IN THE preceding chapters, selling efforts including personal salesmanship, advertising, and other forms of effort directed toward securing buying action have been described and analyzed as a form of economic leadership. They constitute leadership because each seller seeks to persuade some or many people to take action. The leadership effort is huge in total and widespread in application. It is exercised by millions of selling "leaders" who influence tens of millions of people. Selling is directed to rich and poor alike, to the masses mainly but not exclusively.

The immediate objective is buying action; the ultimate objective high levels of living. A high level of living is desirable from the social standpoint. In this respect the professed aims of various types of social organization have all been pretty much in agreement. The promises made to the public in Soviet Russia and in fascist countries, in the Western world, that higher standards of living would come eventually, have been a strong incentive although there has been wide difference in the ability of the various societies to achieve this objective. In a philosophy of life that attempts to reduce the desires and importance of material things and that in extreme form would declare that the mode of living with a loincloth for clothing, with a bit of bread, goat's milk, and cheese for sustenance, and a tent for shelter are all that man *should* desire, obviously the work of business in developing

319

new products and trying to secure wider and greater use of existing products would be considered superfluous or undesirable. Fortunately that belief is not widely shared.

The aggregate objectives of those who sell are economically and socially desirable because in their totality the achievement constitutes high and rising living standards for all the people. The aggregate objective in a high-level economy characterized by consumer freedom of choice is attained only by billions of consumer buying actions. These are based upon individual decisions, individual choices. In short, to rephrase Thomas Nixon Carver's statement about prices when he said, "There are no such things as general prices, only millions of individual prices in individual transactions,"[1] so there are no such things as general sales or general buying action, only billions of individual sales or individual purchases. If the results of these buying actions lead to higher standards of living and the methods of leadership to bring about these purchases are consistent with social welfare, we can conclude that the objectives, both in aggregate and individually, are socially desirable.

The economic and social desirability of high and rising standards of living for the whole population of a country has been asserted and defended above. Some have objected that the success of our economy in raising levels of living will in the not far distant future bring us to the point of "saturation." One must disagree for a variety of reasons. Professor George Katona of the University of Michigan, a penetrating student of consumer demand, writes to this point in a recent editorial:[2]

The notion of "saturation" of the market is based on old-fashioned psychological assumptions which in turn rest on the analogy of biological drives; for example, if an animal is hungry, it is motivated to search for food; after it has eaten, the motive disappears or becomes weak. The saturation concept has resulted in dire predictions about the future of the U.S. economy. Some people point to the large pro-

[1] Thomas Nixon Carver, *Distribution of Wealth* (New York: Macmillan Co., 1904).

[2] *The Wall Street Journal*, October 14, 1954. See also George Katona, *Psychology* (New York: McGraw-Hill Book Co., Inc., 1951), pp. 92, 106, 147; and H. G. Moulton, *Controlling Factors in Economic Development* (Washington, D.C.: Brookings Institution, 1949), p. 123.

portion of U.S. families that already possess major goods, such as refrigerators (over 80%) or automobiles (about 70%), and they argue that in the future sales will be limited largely to replacement needs.

But social motives are different from biological ones. Levels of aspiration—in sports, for school grades, for position, for income and for goods—most commonly rise with achievement. A beginner in golf, for instance, may strive hard to achieve a score of 100. When he has achieved his goal, he invariably raises his sights. We give up aspirations when we have failed, not when we have succeeded.

In the economic field a family that has saved enough to buy a home usually sets out on a new objective, such as college education for the children; fulfillment of one aim leads to striving for another. Indeed, in a recent survey it was found that this applied to goods already owned; families with a refrigerator in good operating condition often were preparing to buy a larger one or one with shelves on the door and a better freezing compartment.

We translate our needs into demand when we are optimistic, confident and secure. We are saturated, on the other hand, when we are pessimistic, insecure, and especially when our past endeavors have been unsuccessful.

It is conceivable that we may arrive at the point where having achieved generally the quantitative and qualitative standards of consumptive desire, we shall choose more leisure to attain greater progress in areas other than material advancement and thus eventually reach a plateau of production of goods and services. But the world generally is far from any such point so that we may accept the need for high and rising standards of living as a working hypothesis that will serve for an unforeseeably long period.

There are those who, of course, take the aristocratic point of view that high and rising standards of living are for the "classes"—not for the "masses"—a viewpoint implicit in Ortega y Gasset's *Revolt of the Masses*. It reflects the attitude of those who believe that culture should be and must be the possession of the few, a philosophy that is being disproved.[3] There are others who assert that the good life can best be attained by limiting desire and consumption to subsistence, and few comforts. Emphasis is to be placed on nonmaterial activities, on education,

---

[3] Cf. Chapter VIII, p. 172.

literature and the arts, religion, avocation, recreation. But all of these hold exceptional views, and throughout the world there is a desire for higher standards of living, which constitutes a powerful social and political force for good or evil. For that desire may lead to political and social upheavals of types that can bring only disaster unless conditions are basically favorable to increasing production and productivity of the population.

The objectives of selling and the methods used to intensify desire are consistent with public welfare despite the fact that the motives of most sellers are concerned with the sellers' welfare. The buying action that results is usually an element in the complex of buying activities that bring high and rising levels of living into being.

II

The results of selling in terms of high and rapidly rising standards of living mean that whatever the factors involved, multitudes of purchases have been made. The influences of education, habit, example have all been operative, and the bulk of sales has probably been helped by one or several of these. Consumption habits, even though not grouped into stratified patterns, require effort to change. As research has shown, many consumers cling to a standard of living once attained and change with reluctance. Social pressures and the desire to emulate friends and neighbors play an important part. Education brings children and youth into contact with aspects of better living standards and affect later desires for housing, furnishings, food, and dress.

Powerful as all these influences are, it must be remembered that some of them owe their origin and characteristics to previous selling effort. The neighbors may have bought the refrigerator or the television set when influenced to buy by a salesman or advertisement. If satisfied, the buyer began to tell others about it. As several in a group had purchased a television set, the pressure on nontelevision owners to buy increased. Meanwhile, regularly, persistently, selling effort continued, so that later buyers were induced to purchase both by social pressure and selling effort, past and current alike.

Education is likely to follow rather than to lead the procession of those who seek to influence the consumer to buy. Education may develop levels of aspiration for standards of living. It may or may not furnish help to attain those standards. It tends not to push specific products, at least not until products are established and much selling has been done.

The persuasive effort of sellers appears to be enormously more potent than the efforts of consumer groups, government consumer advisory services, or educational institutions in the development of buying action for those goods and services which fall in the classification of postponable,[4] caprice,[5] or discretionary.[6] More people are engaged in influencing purchase, more effort is expended and the motivation to sell is greater and more direct. While no statistical records are available for measure, it appears that selling effort is so important a form of economic leadership in terms of employment, cost, and achievement that neither laymen nor economist should be indifferent to it.

III

The results that have been achieved and for which selling should receive its full share of credit have been attained because through selling a chain reaction is started that energizes the whole economic system. In brief, selling:

In making a sale and obtaining immediate buying action, plus establishing a better basis for making future sales:

Justifies and permits production, usually in advance of sale;

Enables improvements in production methods to be adopted and processes improved so as to increase productivity of labor and capital investment;

Enables research to be carried on to find new end products and better methods of making them;

Enables enterprise to introduce new products and recover

---

[4] H. R. Tosdal, "Sales Management: Retrospect and Prospect," *Harvard Business Review*, Autumn, 1942, p. 71.

[5] W. H. Lough, *High Level Consumption* (New York: McGraw-Hill Book Co., Inc., 1935).

[6] J. Walter Thompson Company, *Population and its Distribution* (7th ed., New York: McGraw-Hill Book Co., Inc., 1952).

costs and obtain profit within time intervals necessary for existence and growth;

Reduces the time required for production so that buyers have more time to enjoy results of labor;

Enables new enterprise to start and secure income needed to survive and prosper.

It is obvious that a high and rising standard of living means high and increasing production of goods and services. For Santa Claus politics to the contrary notwithstanding, standards of living for all the people depend upon the production of goods and services and not upon political promises or redistribution of the earned production of the few. Unless there is an increasing production of goods and services, there can be redistribution only of what has been produced. Generally higher standards of living cannot thus be developed or sustained. To bring about that high production of goods and services requires large-scale production on the supply side and the application of pertinent technology.

Since it is evident that a higher standard of living for the people requires that goods be distributed to them, we must recognise that in a money economy with consumer freedom of choice, in a society in which allotment by government is not the rule, those who aspire to consume must purchase and must have purchasing power with which to acquire those goods in exchange. By and large, therefore, beyond the necessities of life provided under relief, pensions, and limited plans for social care, those purchasers who desire to participate in the high standard of living must acquire purchasing power with which to make that desire effective.

In our society, men ordinarily must work for what they get in the way of income. Although fraud, luck, inheritance, and stealing may furnish purchasing power to some people, most of us expect to have to work for a living. Our effectiveness and usefulness in that work is at least a rough measure of the kind of living standards that we enjoy individually. Both the amount of work we do, the character of that work, and the intelligence with which we apply ourselves to work will depend upon whether the incentive is sufficient to induce us to put forth our best efforts.

For a large proportion of our people, the principal incentive is the paycheck, because that represents the means of acquiring the things that are considered desirable.

People work to get the things they want. If they do not want things that require money, they will not work to get money. The general truth of this statement and its limitations are attested by many types of war and postwar experience; further proof has been developed by psychological, sociological, and anthropological investigation. At any rate, there are many facts in all these fields which warrant the hypothesis that human beings will not work for those things that make up a high standard of living unless they want those things enough to overcome whatever disutility work possesses for them. Historical evidence supports the statement that standards of living in many parts of the world have remained at the same low levels for centuries. Innovation was frowned upon and social stratification apparently froze living standards. One could point out that even during World War II, the production of essential war materials in the Philippines, for instance of oils and fats, as well as production of other types of products elsewhere, proceeded very slowly whenever the workers found they could not buy things with the money they were given in return for the work. Again, it has been asserted that absenteeism in England was prevalent because under the austerity regime workers could not buy the things they wanted for the pay they received. These are little more than straws in the wind; but I think we must recognize the importance of the factor of wants and demands, not only in determining the types of goods to be produced, but also in motivation to produce. The intensity of desire has a direct bearing on the amounts and types of work that will be done in order to secure such goods and therefore, in part, in order to produce the goods necessary for a high living standard.

IV

In our existing economy, goods must be produced in large quantities, distributed over larger or smaller areas to eventual retail buyers. Consumers' knowledge, both of the goods which are or might be available and of their own future desires at the time that the goods are manufactured, is extremely limited. The producer must, therefore, produce in advance of his detailed knowledge of consumer desires and consumer wants. He often produces for a market of which he knows nothing directly, selling his goods to those middlemen who have come into existence in order to help with the function of distributing goods in small quantities to fit the consumer needs.

It has been shown that established producers must dispose of their goods at remunerative prices if goods are to continue to be made. Prospective buyers must be induced to buy in quantities that permit eventual profitable operation of the enterprise. Such inducement to buy, such persuasion as may be utilized to get prospective buyers to purchase, may be subject to abuse. But by and large, such persuasion is consistent with public interest and is, in fact, essential to the maintenance of free enterprise, to the development of new and better products and services, and indirectly, therefore, to the growth of employment. Eventually, even technological progress depends upon successful sale of industry's production.

A new business in order to survive under our free-enterprise system must sell a sufficient volume of goods year by year to cover its costs and make a profit. Otherwise it ceases to be a producer and sooner or later goes out of existence. During the formative period, enterprises often encounter such difficulty and costs in getting started as to involve losses for a longer or shorter period of time, although it is expected that those losses will be recouped later. Similarly, temporary adverse conditions, whether from general economic conditions, incompetent management, or the like, may have to be endured. Business records show that many firms do not survive these initial periods or these temporary adverse conditions. In fact, the majority of business enterprises cannot survive any sustained period of failure to cover costs and yield a profit.

The experience of businessmen and the observation of others will support the assertion that not enough goods would be disposed of to keep most of our business enterprises alive and growing without the initiative on the part of either aggressive sellers or aggressive buyers. The role of those aggressive buyers who propose new products and induce their development is confined to a minority of professional industrial and merchandise buyers. The average buyer, the average retailer, the average manufacturer, rarely adopts more than a passive role with respect to his suppliers. Consequently, the seller must ordinarily take the initiative.

Similarly, consumer demand, the demand of ultimate consumers, while powerful, is exercised primarily by selecting from what has already been developed and offered for public approval. Businessmen, actuated by motives of service and the hope of profit, must take the initiative not only in the development of products but in getting them in full-scale production before the consumer begins to exercise his prerogative of accepting or rejecting the product.

The initiative of sellers in offering new products to the public would be slowed up, if not entirely stopped, if in the absence of selling effort firms were compelled to wait for that public acceptance for new products. The great majority of firms introducing important new products or the great majority of firms newly entering private enterprise, could not survive the period of waiting for public taste to develop to the point which would give them adequate volume of business. One of the prime functions of selling effort is to shorten the period from initial production to sufficient acceptance of the product by the public so that the venture becomes self-supporting.

There is much evidence that improved economic conditions or higher standards of political and social conduct, or in fact improvements in any sphere of human activity, have come about primarily as the result of continued leadership and persuasion. Where such leadership is lacking, they do not take place; where such leadership is present, changes occur. In the development of those desires which cause people to work to get the goods and services required for a high standard of living, similar leadership and persuasion appear to be necessary. This form of leadership and persuasion involved in guiding the mass of people to better living standards has been furnished primarily by the various forms of salesmanship and the corollary management functions.

In short, selling effort is the energizer of our economic machine. Its power may be misapplied, but its necessity in influencing our people to want higher and rising standards of living cannot be denied. Selling effort is necessary to make people both desire and achieve a higher level of living. Selling is necessary that firms which introduce unfamiliar products may live and old firms may continue to exist and perform their services for the public. The development and functioning of the production structure necessary for a high standard of living has depended and will continue to depend upon the energizing influence of selling effort, whether that effort be in the form of advertising or personal selling, or in the manifold minor aspects of marketing persuasion.

The need for improved effectiveness in all phases of marketing effort is admitted; and the challenge to business to bring about improvement is furnished by free competition. The alternative of detailed government planning and allotment assumes a degree of understanding and wisdom, a managerial and administrative capacity of a magnitude that mankind has not produced. And no society has yet matched the free-enterprise system of the United States in its provision of higher standards of living for all the people. But we must not forget that while free enterprise connotes freedom to fail as well as freedom to succeed, the urge to succeed furnishes the motive power for producing and distributing the commodities and services required for the standards and planes of living to which we aspire. And only with the contribution of adequate selling leadership can the people in a free enterprise economy achieve both high material levels of living and an unparalleled opportunity for the development of the other areas of the good life.

INDEX

This book has been set on the Linotype in 11 and 10 point Janson, leaded 2 points. Chapter numbers are in 14 point Janson italics and chapter titles in 18 point Janson caps. The size of the type page is 25 by 43 picas.